Flexible Childhood?
Exploring Children's Welfare in Time and Space

Volume 2 of COST A19: *Children's Welfare*

*Helga Zeiher, Dympna Devine, Anne Trine Kjørholt
and Harriet Strandell (eds)*

Flexible Childhood?
Exploring Children's Welfare
in Time And Space

Volume 2 of COST A19: *Children's Welfare*

2007

Flexible Childhood?
Exploring Children's Welfare in Time and Space
Volume 2 of COST A19: *Children's Welfare*

Price: 62.25 Euro per set of two volumes.

© Helga Zeiher, Dympna Devine, Anne Trine Kjørholt, Hariet Strandell and the contributors

This book has been financially supported by
COST, European Cooperation in the field of Scientific and Technical Research
The Research Council of Norway

COST is an intergovernmental European framework for international cooperation between nationally funded reserch activities. COST creates scientific networks and enables scientists to collaborate in a wide spectrum af activities in research and technology. COST activities are administered by the COST Office.
Website: www.cost.esf.org

Neither the COST Office nor any person acting on its behalf is responsible for the use of which might be made of the information contained in the present publication.

Published by
University Press of Southern Denmark
Campusvej 55
5230 Odense M
Denmark

University of Southern Denmark Studies in History and Social Sciences vol. 338

Set and printed by Narayana Press

ISBN13 97-887-7674-202-7
ISBN13 97-887-7674-208-9 (vol. 1 and vol. 2)

Table of Contents

Helga Zeiher, Dympna Devine, Anne Trine Kjørholt, Harriet Strandell
Introduction   9

Conceptualising Time and Space

Helga Zeiher
Valuing Children's Temporal Quality of Life   27

Harriet Strandell
New Childhood Space and the Question of Difference   49

Anna-Liisa Närvänen and Elisabet Näsman
Time, Identity, and Agency   69

Enlargement of Space

Heinz Hengst
Metamorphoses of the World within Reach   95

An-Magritt Jensen
Mobile and Uprooted? Children and the Changing Family   121

Dympna Devine
Immigration and the Enlargement of Children's Social Space in School   143

FLEXIBILISATION OF TIME AND SPACE

Anne Trine Kjørholt and Vebjørg Tingstad
Flexible Places for Flexible Children?
Discourses on New Kindergarten Architecture   169

Hanne Warming Nielsen and Jan Kampmann
Children in Command of Time and Space?   191

Karin Jurczyk and Andreas Lange
Blurring Boundaries of Family and Work – Challenges for Children   215

Contributors to this volume   239

Foreword

The two volumes *Childhood, Generational Order and the Welfare State* (volume 1) and *Flexible Childhood?* (volume 2) are the last publications from COST A19 – Children's Welfare. The background of the Action, which began in 2001, was the all-European experience of population ageing which currently is causing concern in practically all countries of Europe and the insufficient attention – both scientific and political – paid to one highly significant part of the population, namely children. They are logically becoming much fewer in this process of ageing, but in a number of other ways children and childhood have been impacted by processes taking place simultaneously and intertwined with population ageing and its consequences.

These processes are identified, described and analysed in the Country Reports – Children's Welfare in Ageing Societies – and in the two volumes that are now published. It is important however to underline that the Action has hosted also a huge number of meetings with a lot of interventions from both external lecturers and members from the Action itself. While creating space and time for creative deliberations among participants from more than 20 countries, the Action has in the truest sense of the word constituted a network for both more and less experienced researchers. This is, in fact, one of the rationales of the COST framework. It has been a network that has conveyed and been conveyed with blood and flesh in terms of conceptual, substantial and methodological contents, which – so it is hoped – will be of value and inspiration also to practitioners and politicians in their effort to improve the welfare of children as well as of adults and the elderly.

The Action has been made possible first of all by the COST framework. A number of its officers have been very helpful in guiding us through this system. We are grateful for all the help and compliance we have received. The Action has also been met with generosity from The Norwegian Research Council which has been helpful with financial assistance. We wish to express our gratefulness also to Karin Ekberg, senior executive officer at the Norwegian Centre for Child Research. She has used her efforts and long standing experience to smooth the process and keep the wheel running.

In the very last moment we were lucky enough to have Petra Essebier, University of Halle, with us in Trondheim. She kindly offered her expertise for the proof reading and provided assistance in an efficient and professional manner, for which we thank her very much.

Last but not least, we wish to convey warm thanks and gratitude to all our colleagues who have ventured to embark on this long journey and who have shown confidence in and been supportive of this endeavour.

We do hope that the Action will leave quite a few positive imprints in its wake – not least in terms of carrying forth the plenty of unanswered not to say unaddressed problems that have come up during the Action.

An-Magritt Jensen, Chair of Action
Jens Qvortrup, Co-ordinating Editor

Introduction

Helga Zeiher, Dympna Devine, Anne Trine Kjørholt and Harriet Strandell

The aim of the book

One of the characteristic features of modernity has been to create clear boundaries between categories of people, forms of living, and activities. Among those are the boundaries between children and the adult generation. The great and successful childhood project of modernity was to confine children in a separated social space in order to prepare them for their future contribution to the adults' economic world by protecting them, rearing them into good physical and mental health and by teaching, educating and socialising them into the dominant norms of adult society. However, in recent decades profound changes in the structure and culture of modern societies have become increasingly obvious. Within some sociological analyses this is referred to as an epochal shift from industrial modernity to 'post-modernity' and 'post-structural modernity', while others interpret it as changes within modernity, called 'late', 'liquid' or 'reflexive' modernity. These changes are linked to the revolution of information and communication technology and processes, which foster globalisation in the economy, and alter the organisation of work as well as people's times and spaces for social relations within families and friendships. The boundaries within the established figuration of clearly separated societal institutions seem to blur in some respects, as do the dualistic orders of social categories of people. The question is to what extent the boundaries between childhood and adulthood, characteristic of modernity, are also changing and 'blurring'. The aim of this book is to address recent social change and its consequences for the position of childhood in the generational order of European societies, and, in so doing, to evaluate the changes with regard to children's welfare. How are children's ways of living their everyday lives, as well as the structural position of children and childhood in society, alongside representations of childhood, influenced by these broader processes of recent radical societal change?

A separation between childhood and adulthood also took place on the scientific plane. In modernity, childhood had become a concern of child specialised sciences including pedagogy, developmental psychology and pediatry which focused at ameliorating and extending the positive upbringing of children within the specialised childhood institutions of the family and the education system. From the beginning of the 1980s, evidence of blurring boundaries between private and public, family and work, childhood and adulthood ensured that sociologists began to look at children and childhood in a new way. Since then, the concept of children being excluded from society in a separated childhood space has been examined within a wider societal and historic perspective revealing it as bound to modernity, and in some regards only to a particular period of it. The greater the impact of recent societal upheavals upon people's lives, the more questions are raised within the sociology of childhood with regard to *changes in childhood*, that is in childhood structures, in discourses and representations of childhood, and in the lives of children. This book, as a joint endeavour between researchers from several countries in the field of childhood studies, seeks to contribute to that effort.

The specific focus of the book is upon *time and space*. However no author writes neither on children's time and space as such, nor are the chapters restricted to a description of how children spend their time and where they spend it. Rather, all authors examine temporal and spatial phenomena in order to reveal characteristics of societal childhood and question its recent changes. Key themes include temporal and spatial phenomena in which separation processes of modernity, as well as recent processes of blurring boundaries, occur. The authors explore aspects of childhood which are materialised in features of places or time structures, occur in children's active construction of their social places and times through interaction with others, or are verbalised in adults' discourses on childhood; most chapters relate phenomena on different levels to each other.

Time and space are everywhere. They are cultural and social phenomena, which are central to individual lives and activities, in social organisation and in all systems of representation. Features of time and space which are characteristic for the society at large impact on individuals' lives in so far as they shape the concrete temporal and spatial possibilities and constraints for activities and social relations. These include temporal and spatial positions for particular acts, distances, rhythms, speed, and sequences, as well as modes of temporal and spatial agency and thinking. Spatial and temporal devices can thus be viewed as key elements in the exercise of power generally in society, but also between generations, i.e adults and children. Since every act needs a place and a position in the flow of time, space and time occur in all areas of life, nobody can withdraw from them, and everybody must engage with the societal power which is transmitted by these temporal and spatial possibilities and constraints.

Both time and space form and are formed in and by social relations, they are fixed in particular structures, modes and representations, but they are also flexible and changing.

It is in the performance of individual agency that societal and individual processes meet each other, where they are intertwined, and in which one side impacts on the other. Time and space related agency, as well as representations of time and space, are driving forces in social change, and social change occurs in temporal and spatial phenomena. As to society at large, it is not by accident that the spatial dimension became manifest in many of the terms used to describe features of societal trends in the develoment of modernity, including 'separation', 'exclusion', 'border', 'erosion', 'liquidisation', 'flexibilisation' and 'globalisation'.

These ongoing changes in society are connected to the explosion of the amount of information in society, the speeding up of information transfer and enlarged mobility leading to a compression of time and space and to less rigid time and space regimes. New tendencies point towards more flexible time conditions and time use and towards a shrinking of future oriented time perspectives, and point from enduring time towards more momental time, time with less duration. Changes in working life, family life, and leisure dissolve standard times and places, providing increased choice to individuals, yet also pressing them by the need for more complex coordination and by economic forces for speeding up time.

Childhood is embedded in and thus transformed by these changes. The chapters of this book each present particular aspects of change in childhood that occur in temporal and spatial phenomena. They point to structures, definitions and representations of childhood which emerged in modernity and that are now changing in a social world which is becoming more de-structured and diverse, more spatially enlarged and temporally flexible. Evidently the childhood construct is not being replaced by a new one. What happens is not a shift from one childhood to another, but rather a multiplying of structured and de-structured times and spaces, of different modes of time and space, in sum, a tendency toward a more ambiguous and contradictory world which requires flexible responses and activities also from children. As a tendency, *the childhood construct is becoming more flexible*.

It is important to keep in mind that a tendency or trend is an abstraction from actual social life. When we in this book single out one dimension of reality by exploring children's exposure to increasingly flexible structures in society and childhood as part of it, the outcome cannot be taken as a complete representation of contemporary childhood. As is discussed in *Anna-Liisa Närvänen's and Elisabet Näsman's* as well as in *Harriet Strandell's* and in *Heinz Hengst's* chapters, social reality is multifaceted and contradictionary, and elements which are rooted in the past are mixed with others that are produced by recent developments. Each single situation, structure, event, activity or argument in social reality can be seen as a concrete realisation of many different trends and – as already stated by Karl Mannheim (1952/1928) – »the contemporariness of the incontemporary«; it is a kind of crossing point of all these. To deny the emergence of a new trend by referring to persistences of the old, would negate consideration of such emerging tendencies as one of the many dimensions of social reality. It is rather a question of both-and than either-or.

Last but not least: this book goes further than just identifying evidence of changes in childhood. We also want to evaluate such trends in terms of challenges to and opportunities for improving the quality of children's lives. Today the question of *welfare in time and space* becomes a new challenging task. Since former boundaries between generations begin to blur and neo-liberal forces enter all realms of people's lives, it can no longer be taken for granted – as it was in former periods of modernity – that continued efforts to realise the childhood project of modernity will automatically guarantee the 'best interest of the child'. Today, when children are required to deal with flexibility in a changing modernity, we have to re-think the consequences for children's welfare.

Changing Childhood and Changing Concepts of Time and Space

In its focus on the social dynamics of time and space in childhood the book reflects a broader interest in issues of time and space in contemporary sociology's theorizing about modernity (e.g. Bauman 2000; Beck 1992; Castells 1996; Giddens 1984; 1991; Sennett 1998), and is part of a growing consciousness of the temporal and spatial features of childhood in childhood sociology and anthropology (James and Prout 1997; Olwig and Gulløv 2003; Zeiher 2001) and in human geography (Holloway and Valentine 2000; Matthews and Limb 1999). Within the social sciences consideration is given to how the concept of time and space changes historically, both mirroring and governing the construction of society and people's experience of their everyday lives within it. The three chapters in the first section of the book address this relatedness between recent changes in childhood alongside changes in the concepts of social time and space.

In her chapter, *Helga Zeiher* starts from the *temporal* aspects of the construction of modern childhood and shows the relation of these to the concept of objective linear time which prevailed in industrial modernity. The long-term progress orientation of this concept is mirrored in the understanding of childhood as development, which led to a temporally long distance between the generations, and which became ideologically reified by a particularly strong emphasis on the image of the child being outside society, deviant and different by nature. Through applying the rationalising and economising temporal means of the objective linear time concept, the age category became strictly time structured, and the course of childhood thereby institutionalised. In particular school times made childhood a detailed temporal corset for children's lives. In the working world today, future oriented perspectives are shrinking, time requirements become de-structured and flexibilised, and individuals have to integrate a growing diversity of time options and modes of time in their own lives instead of just adapting to externally fixed and inflexible schedules. Now theories about social time which challenge the objective time concept are more appropriate. The author points firstly to Norbert Elias' (1984/1992) concept of time as socially constituted knowledge by which societal processes of individualisation of time use can be grasped, and secondly to concepts of the multiplicity of times (e.g. Adam 1995), as used by the time-ecological critics of modern time rationalisation and economicalisation.

Also *Anna-Liisa Närvänen* and *Elisabet Näsman* emphasise the concept of multiplicity of times, referring to scholars who criticise the one-sidedness of analyses based on linear clock time alone. They highlight oppositional features of time, including cyclical/linear, repetition/change, and reversible/irreversible. Within the realm of these critics, the authors' contest the relevance to reality of two time related aspects of social change which are discussed in post-structuralist theory: the moving from long-term future orientation toward living in the 'present present', and from biography-based stable identities toward an erosion of identities. According to the authors, the embeddedness of these phenomena in the multiplicity of time in real life is often overlooked. The authors discuss the claimed impact of a shrinking of the past-present-future extension on the manner in which people conceive their life course and their identity. Relating the debate to childhood, they point to the enduring importance of age in the social construction of children's identity as children, and of their representations of the life course. They base their argument on a thoroughly elaborated analysis of the importance of age in external social age categorisations and in processes of identity formation, as well as on the importance of temporal representations and age norms within processes of agency performance.

When looking at *spatial* phenomena and recent ways of theorising space, developments toward more mixed, diverse, heterogeneous and individually constituted social worlds can be identified. *Harriet Strandell's* analysis draws parallels between childhood sociology and post-colonial theorising in cultural anthropology. Both study socially and physically separated and marginalized groups in modernity, and both try to deal with late modern blurring of separating boundaries. Such parallels are found on the level of representations, a term which refers to particular ways of conceiving of space and time that arise from social practices and then become a form of regulation of these practices (Harvey 1996). The chapter discusses parallels in representational change between 'culture' and 'childhood', including changes in the concepts of otherness, under-developedness, and inferiority. It concludes by pointing to the need for overcoming dualistic thinking, not by homogenising generational experiences, but rather by becoming aware that greater diversity and the expansion of dialogical space increases sensitivity to differences (Featherstone 1995) in post-colonial as well as in childhood related thinking. There are new clashes and mixtures of culture as well as of age identities, and 'old' and 'new' ideas and practices add and combine in various ways. Childhood sociology can therefore no longer treat childhood and adulthood as fixed categories, and there is a need to move beyond dualistic thinking when discussing generational difference. These arguments are underlined by the thorough critique of dualistic thinking related to generational relations given in *Heinz Hengst's* chapter.

Children's Changing Times and Spaces

In the course of the 20th century, children have become increasingly spatially and temporally confined to child specialised places and strict time structures of schools, care and leisure institutions, as well as to the privacy of the family home. Through both spatial confinement and temporal structuring, a powerful control on children's lives is exerted. However contradictory tendencies towards de-structuring and individual determination of time are increasing as well, and both tendencies are interdependent. Institutionalised facilities for children's leisure time activities have multiplied in recent decades. They are often scattered in space, 'insularised', and have to be accessed through the children's own mobility or parental help. This requires children to organise and synchronise their individual time schedules – a shift to a more individualised way of shaping life.

The late modern tendency toward blurring of boundaries, de-structuring and flexibilisation only in some minor aspects leads to a diminishment of such physical separation of activities, while at the same time blurs social and cultural borderlines. The material space in reach is enlarged by increasing mobility and speed of movement. Social and cultural spaces are increasingly decoupled from local material space, and new virtual spaces emerge. Different kinds of spaces have to be integrated in daily life by individuals. Three chapters of the book each pick up particular phenomena of such *enlargement* of children' spaces.

New societal features arising from technological advances and rapid communication through virtual space enlarge experienced space through people's increased contact with seemingly unlimited diverse others. *Heinz Hengst* elaborates in his chapter how, in a mediatised and globalised society, children's social and cultural space, their »world within reach«, is extended and changed. He particularly discusses the interconnectedness between physical and virtual spaces and shows how new media expand children's space and allow them to create new and less age-specific experiential and existential spaces. He refers to current debates on 'de-territorialisation'. This includes e.g. debates on 'translating' Mead's concept of the 'generalised other' in the process of identity constitution of the 'self' to a spatial equivalent 'generalised elsewhere', meaning that people we experience as 'significant others' are no longer confined to those we know from direct unmediated interaction. The generalised other becomes – according to Meyrowitz (1985) – mediatised and extended towards a 'generalised elsewhere'. The chapter shows that today cultural and social space becomes highly complex, and individuals are required to create simultaneity and co-presence between real and virtual, local and global spaces.

An-Magritt Jensen points to a particular phenomenon of enlarged material space related to changes in family structure. When their parents live separately, many Norwegian children travel between parents' remote homes by railway or airplane without being accompanied by a parent. She argues that this mobility is due to the high priority given to the 'needed father ideology' by parents and also by Norwegian family policy, while concerns over children at risk when moving alone in public space are suppressed. These children are no longer anchored to just one family home, but rather to two remote homes. According to the author, the resulting demand for the children's spatial and social flexibility mirrors the flexibilised life style which is required from adults.

Another phenomenon of enlarged social and cultural space is the increasing migration in a globalising world, both from former socialist countries in Eastern Europe and from non-European countries. People from distant places and cultures find themselves together with people who feel themselves to be the original inhabitants of the place. In schools children are confronted in a very direct way with cultural diversity in their everyday life – maybe even more direct and inescapably than in the case of many adults –, as *Dympna Devine* reports from an empirical study on Irish primary school children. When meeting immigrant class comrades in school, children are challenged to integrate the otherness of these children into their cultural representations and social lives, and social difficulties of the children are revealed when traversing the ensuing cultural and social boundaries. While the classroom environment is enriched through exposure to diverse cultural experiences and norms, underlying dynamics of inclusion and exclusion in children's friendships on the basis of ethnic difference are also displayed.

These three chapters, by exploring change in children's use of space, each reveal the tendency toward a more individualised and multiple 'texture' of space that interrelates material, virtual, social and cultural spaces. As to children's use of time, similar changes towards individualisation as well as multiplicity are the themes taken up in the further three chapters highlighting particular changes in the domains of institutionalised child care and learning, as well as in family life. Contradictions in pedagogical discourse are evident with on the one hand an emphasis on preparation of children for the adult working world through adaptation to the time regimes of adult society while on the other an increasing awareness of children's human rights to autonomy and individualised agency. By implication the organisation of time in institutions such as schools, is closely intertwined with developments in the economic sphere. Demands on 'productive' time use also influence children's lives out of school, as their 'playtime' becomes increasingly curricularised into activities that are not only fun, but also important in providing the required social and cultural capital essential to success in the adult labour market. However, the recent social changes in time impact also upon the area of education. Scholarisation, a core process in the development of modern childhood, once created a strict and detailed time regime for all children, thus mirroring the time regimes of industrialised work and bureaucracy. In the last decades of the 20th century these time structures on the one hand have been supplemented by time regimes of institutionalised day care and structured leisure activities. On the other hand, with the temporal shifts in the adult working world as mentioned above, schools and care institutions are today exposed to a drive toward greater flexibility in the organisation of time and space, and a desire to equip children with necessary skills enabling them to work in flexible, changing environments, where they also learn the discipline of self-regulation and control. Children are thus involved in the tendency to replace rigid time structures by a more individualised and active 'doing time' in learning and structuring daily life.

Changes in the way time and space is organised and structured in children's formal institutions are dealt with in two chapters. *Anne Trine Kjørholt and Vebjørg Tingstad* pick up a particular political reform activity related to daily life organisation in Norwegian kindergartens. They report on a project aimed at changing the physical design of kindergarten buildings in order to realise new pedagogical aims inscribed in discourses on flexibility, individual choice and user-adjustment. This has resulted in kindergarten buildings which are designed in a functionally less specialised way, allowing the children to decide where to 'play and stay' during the day, and also when to engage in different kinds of activities. The authors discuss the changing aims and their realisation in response to the requirements of a growing market orientation and neo-liberalism.

The new flexible time and space regimes represent a new form of governing, including disciplining the individual child to be responsible for her or his own choices, a theme which constitutes the focus of *Hanne Warming Nielsen's and Jan Kampmann's* chapter. They begin with a description of a (fictional) day course of a Danish family consisting of two children (one in day care and one in school), mother and father, which they analyse in relation to societal changes in social integration and control. This day course picture is used as a means of illustrating the splitting up of life arenas and activities in time and space and the communication and temporal organisation which is required to co-ordinate the individuals' lives as well as the togetherness of the family members. They also highlight the pedagogisation of family life which creates opportunities as well as risks for the children, all within a context of the powerful educational norm of self-government.

Through the impact of parents' changing working time regimes on family time at home and on the time children are cared for outside home, children experience the shift to de-structured, flexible times occuring in the working world. While standardised time in earlier industrial societies represented the main principle for the organisation of working hours, increased temporal flexibility is required by the new form of production in a post-fordist society. In their day course picture, the authors demonstrate in fairly positive terms the possibilities which parents' flexible, unpredictable working times create for children's use of time.

Karin Jurczyk's and Andreas Lange's chapter captures the consequences of flexibilisation and intensification of working life on parents' time management in family life with children in a more comprehensive way. The authors give an outline of the kind and amount of recent changes in Germany from standardised to de-structured, flexible working times, and refer to changes in the organisation of family time as a consequence of these changes as well as of increasing participation of mothers in the labour force and the blurring of boundaries between former gender specific spheres of family and work. They discuss the impact of flexible working times on the togetherness of the family and on children's time schedules and their well-being drawing on interview data with children on these matters.

Since childhood cannot be defined other than by relating it to adulthood, reference to changes in childhood implies reference to changes in *generational relations*. In modernity, when childhood emerged through constructing boundaries between child and adult specific activities and institutions, distance and difference between childhood and adulthood became the basis of a social concept of childhood. In this book the *generational perspective* primarily reveals phenomena of the blurring of spatial and temporal separations between childhood and adulthood.

Challenges posed by a globalising society to representing childhood in terms of physical and social distance and spatial separation from adulthood is the central issue of *Harriet Strandell's* chapter on the »question of difference« between the generations. Spaces and related activities emerge in contemporary society which do not have a clear reference to a specific age group, and which consequently blur generational difference. Such tendencies can be identified inside the traditional childhood institutions as well as outside. *Heinz Hengst's* reflections on the »metamorphosis of the world within reach« which focuses mainly on media related changes identifies how children and adults may be considered as contemporaries in dealing with the complexity of space in a highly mediatised and globalised society, leading to the consequent blurring of more traditional generational boundaries. Temporal aspects of the erosion of the construction of childhood as generational difference are discussed, by *Helga Zeiher*, as a shrinking future orientation in society, manifesting itself as a diminishing competence gap between children and adults. All these phenomena of a decreasing rigidity in the separation between the generations demand for a conceptualisation of childhood which moves beyond dualistic thinking.

How profound the changes are, and how they mix with existing structures and practices requires further investigation. Some theorists of late modernity, like Bauman, point to the demand for and the possibility of creating the individual's social identity in a society which tends to break down the former progress orientation and time ascriptions to people's lives into short term time options and multiple times. One might argue against an overestimation of that tendency and highlight the fact that within the multiplicity of times strict social time ascriptions are still important, as *Anna-Liisa Närvänen and Elisabeth Näsman* do in their chapter. They exemplify their theories on time, age, social identity and agency by a description of time and age related features of the processes in family and school, highlighting in their analyses continuities of practices and institutional resistance to change, and thus pointing to persistent features of childhood. They do not develop a perspective on the changes in temporal and spatial phenomena. However, this analysis is counterbalanced by differing analysis in other chapters. Undoubtedly, the new tendencies increase the multiplicity as well as the need for individualised temporal agency which emerges from that multiplicity. Today's children are required to act flexibly in a highly complex multiple time-space world.

Looking at children's access to and use of time and space, ambivalent and contradictory phenomena of the ongoing developments in childhood are reveiled in this book. Children's lives are becoming increasingly culturally and socially extended: the global virtual world of information penetrates children's everyday lives, alongside the transnational cultures of mobile people from remote parts of the globalising world. At the same time the vision of the childhood project of modernity of a protective and preparatory childhood space separated from adult society is still very much alive, and the project is still progressing by the continuous adult focus on educating, protecting, providing and controlling children. However, in spite of increasing pedagogical effort invested in institutionalised childhood, the boundaries of this particular childhood space are becoming more permeable, and the family and the care and learning institutions are showing signs of change in how they structure children's time and space. While requirements and time pressures from working life have always influenced childhood through their impact on these institutions, now demands of globalised neo-liberalism and the resultant changes in the societal pattern of the use of time and space are becoming evident in child institutions, themes which are addressed in this book.

Flexibilisation and Children's Welfare

The aim of the book involves more than pointing to temporal and spatial opportunities for and restrictions to children's agency, revealing these as phenomena of recent social changes in childhood. Deriving from the COST action on children's welfare, the book focuses ultimately upon the evaluation of such changes with respect to children's welfare. Where recent changes in childhood require for more flexible use of time and space, do these changes ameliorate or deteriorate children's quality of life?

This aim requires the interrelation of three social areas and their respective conceptualisations: childhood, welfare, and time and space. While adult-centred notions of social and economic welfare are well elaborated, it is only recently that children's welfare has been placed on the agenda of social policy and theory by relating welfare to thinking within the 'new' childhood sociology (Alanen 2006; Kränzl-Nagl et al. 2003). In contrast, valuing temporal and spatial resources and opportunities in regard to children's welfare is still an unusual undertaking. The concept 'space welfare' is not yet adequately conceptualised, and 'time welfare' is a new concept which only now is beginning to be elaborated to coincide with the recent changes in social time and conceptulisation of social time (see Helga Zeiher's chapter). This book marks an advance in the area, being the first which is entirely devoted to a consideration of children's time and space welfare.

The chapters of this book each start by analysing a particular aspect of recent social change in children's times and spaces and then query how the respective new phenomena support or undermine children's welfare, well-being or quality of life. Questions arise in relation to the criteria drawn upon in valuing children's times and spaces – with respect both to the judgement of temporal and spatial welfare implied in political and pedagocical discourses and the structures of childhood institutions as well as the criteria the authors themselves use when they discuss the impact of investigated conditions on children's lives. Undoubtedly societal discourses on childhood which focus on human rights to autonomy, equality and participation, have implications for the quality of children's experience of time and space e.g. the degree of self-determined use of time and space, or equality in the access to times and spaces between the generations and between groups of children to times and places. However the level and rate of recent changes in social times and spaces which are documented throughout this book require a detailed analysis that connects broader social goals with specific welfare criteria.

An outline of the interrelatedness between recent social changes in the use as well as in the conceptualisation of time, recent social changes in childhood, and time welfare criteria is presented in *Helga Zeiher*'s chapter. Throughout history, as reflected in dominant discourses on childhood as well as in adults' constructions of childhood, criteria for evaluating the temporal features of children's lives have always mirrored the time use prevailing in working life, and changed according to that (see also the chapter of Anne-Trine Kjørholt and Vebjørg Tingstad). Predominant values have been justified by appeals to 'the best interest of the child', and the 'nature of the child'. Since in childhood, like in all realms of contemporary society, objective time loses its predominance in individuals' lives, individuals are confronted with and have to integrate multiple modes of time. Not only do they have to individually synchronise and coordinate their own time schedules, but even to reflect on their personal time values. Therefore criteria for evaluating temporal quality of children's (like adults') lives – 'time welfare' and 'temporal well-being' – can no longer relate only to the impact of external social time structures to the demands on self-determination, but rather to the impact on children's agency from multiple times and time options, and to the impact of individualisation processes on social relationships. An important welfare criteria which should be considered in relation to children is the impact of on-going processes of social change on the time and space available to them in the performance of social relations.

Social changes in space and thus space related aspects of welfare in childhood show similar features. As described in all space-related chapters, the blurring of spatial boundaries, the increasing multiplicity of spaces, and the interpenetration between the local and the global lead to more demands on people to combine, interconnect and switch between nearby and remote places, and between physical and virtual spaces. In this way, cultural identities as well as social relations become more detached from physical places. Cultural and social spaces have to be constituted individually and become more enlarged and complex. Here too, the welfare question must be addressed as to the impact of features such as the multiplicity and the individualised constitution of children's spaces, to the emergence of 'new spaces' and related changes, on children's possibilities for the performance of social relations.

Changes in children's welfare are discussed in smaller or greater detail in all chapters. The authors' reflections point to ambiguous developments. The positive impact of increasing opportunities for temporal and spatial self-determination in the arenas of the family, care institutions and school is highlighted, and the enrichment of children's cultural and social world by the enlargement of space is emphasised. However, all authors also point to possible risks related to the demands for more individualised agency and to the implications for children's experience of personal social relationships. In the following we want to highlight four questions on new risks in children's time and space welfare which are posed in this book.

Firstly, particular risks are related to *new forms of inequality* in children's positions in school life and the peer group. In her examination of Irish pupils' attitudes towards their immigrant peers, *Dympna Devine* points to the significance of an enriched cultural and social space for the children's capacity to reflect upon their understanding of and dealing with sameness and otherness However a further aspect of children's well-being, namely the 'experience of belonging and adaptation to school' may be influenced by the differing cultural, social and economic resources children bring with them to school, giving rise to inequalities between the 'old' inhabitants and the immigrant children in blending in to the requirements of school life. . The fact that a great deal of children's positioning of themselves and others in the enlarged cultural space takes place out of sight of adults, in the back stage regions of school life, according to Devine, raises the need to create a discursive space in the front region of classroom life in which issues of recognition of and respect for difference are brought to the fore. *Hanne Warming Nielsen and Jan Kampmann* also highlight the inequality of chances to participate in the new 'normal' way of school life deriving from children's differing personal competencies and capacities to deal with the new demands on their agency. They refer to »new types of exclusion mechanisms« linked to the socio-cultural, geographical and ethnic background of »children – and families – who do not on their own initiative act in accordance with the expectations of responsibility, participation and commitment in learning processes«.

The increasing *priority given to autonomy, flexibility and individual choice* in late modernity is a second crucial issue to be analysed in relation to children's welfare. In recent decades, discourses of autonomy in relation to children have gained prominence alongside the advent of the children's rights movement, as well as by developments in childhood sociology in the social sciences. Temporal structures in childhood which are still based on the strict external control mechanisms characteristic of industrial modernity have been increasingly criticised, and amelioration of the opportunities for children's agency and self-determination have been emphasised. Broader patterns of social change, both in terms of the economy and information technology are now giving rise to more individualised societal control mechanisms, coinciding in institutions such as schools with educational discourses which stress pedagogic autonomy. However power deriving from economic demands continues to govern what children do – what has changed is how such power is expressed – exercised now in the form of self-regulation and self surveillance in line with economic norms of flexibility and self-determination. This includes children being held individually responsible for their own learning and achievement and for their use of time and space. In this sense we can say that discourses of autonomy for children and childhood have become colonised by neo-liberal perspectives asserting the right to choice, self-determination and self-responsibility in many areas of children's lives. Such developments raise a key question about children's welfare resonating throughout all chapters in the book: In the recent development of modernity, does the degree of movement toward individualised rational control of time and space represent new forms of power and control?

Such new forms of power and control are discussed explicitly in two chapters which highlight the shift to late modern individualisation through transforming pedagogical discourses. *Hanne Warming Nielsen and Jan Kampmann* discuss risks deriving from demands on children to be autonomous agents and responsible for their own life, which is becoming a new norm in Danish society. They point to a paradox: greater self-governance is imposed as a goal by the ever stricter power of a 'new normality' for children's behaviour in school, day care institutions and family. They question whether children's well-being is actually increased when they are required to behave as competent and responsible beings, feeling the risk of failing to comply with the 'expected standard'. *Anne Trine Kjørholt's and Vebjørg Tingstad's* study of Norwegian kindergarten discourses show how the new 'normality' has been incorporated in the spatial patterns of the architecture. Their study raises questions about possible positive outcomes of changed pedagogical goals, and ask what is more in the interest of a child: the former emphasis on more clearly delineated space, belonging and a stable caring environment, or today's emphasis on individual choice, flexibility, competence and autonomy. Kjørholt and Tingstad point to collective responsibility and belonging to communities as values which should not be neglected. They plead for solidarity and care as a basis for welfare, to be supported by the spatial and temporal organisation of childhood institutions like kindergarten and school.

This argument leads to the third question on changes in welfare risks arising from late modern changes in children's times and spaces: the question of the possibilities of maintaining *close personal social relations and social belonging*. *Karin Jurczyk and Andreas Lange* raise this question about the impact of flexible and individualised working hours for children's embeddedness in family life. 'Doing family' under conditions of blurring boundaries between work and home, self-employed and contractual labour and – in Germany – an absence of sufficient state support for childcare, creates undeniable tensions for children and their parents as they struggle to negotiate an appropriate work-life time equilibrium. According to the authors, a gain in flexibility which allows for greater parental time is often accompanied by a lack of predictability of parents' family time – interviewed children value temporal predictablity to be an important aspect of their well-being. *An-Magritt Jensen's* concern is about children whose parents are separated and who are required to travel between their parents' homes. She problematises the detachment of social belonging to the family as well as to peers when children travel between two homes – two spaces. In such families children are required to carve out a social family space in their relations with both parents and in both homes. By commuting between two homes they learn to navigate between a family network of relations. This situation challenges the traditional rootedness of family relations in one home and in one neighbourhood. In both chapters, the ambiguity of the impact on children's welfare is discussed: a gain in children's autonomy on the one hand and a lack of 'rootedness' on the other. Like the changes in the area of peer relations and school achievement mentioned above, such spatial and temporal flexibilisation of social family life can influence children's welfare in different ways. Here, too, welfare depends on both the possibilities in the outer world and the children's competences to live in and sustain their belonging to people.

The fourth question of changes in children's welfare posed in this book is on the extent to which *'children's interests'* are taken into account when their everyday situation is changed by adults' measures. Key decisions about where to live and about basic time schedules have always been adult decisions. *An-Magritt Jensen* argues that this includes also the decisions on children's commuting between separated parents's homes when parents tend to give more weight to the 'needed father ideology' than to concerns about possible risks for the child travelling alone. When many time structures now become more flexibilised and space becomes more enlarged and multiple we should ask if these changes provide increasing opportunities to take account of children's interests and views. However as with other questions we have raised in relation to time and space welfare, the answer to this question is not straightforward.

A direct influence on children's flexible use of time and space is imposed by their parents' working time. Advantages and disadvantages of parents' flexible and extended working hours derive, according to *Karin Jurczyk and Andreas Lange*, from the possibility for children and their parents to spend time together. However, this depends on the particular working time policy of the employer which in today's neo-liberal economy often tends to be more determined by economic needs than by the employees' private wishes. Parents may wish to accommodate to their children's wishes for more time at home, including more predictable time schedules. However, they are themselves under ecomomic pressures, and children's own voice can rarely influence such decisions. Economic power on children's flexible use of time and space applies also to children in care institutions and schools. Here, according to *Anne Trine Kjørholt and Vebjørg Tingstad*, not only are the changing goals mirroring the changes in the use of time and space in the working world, but also financial ratio influences the decisions: the new 'flexible places for flexible children' in Norwegian kindergartens are cheaper and therefore satisfy dominant economic interests in contemporary society.

Enhancing children's welfare, be it by creating temporal and spatial opportunities through specific policies or through enabling children to develop time and space related competencies by pedagogical means, is a complex and challenging task. This book explores some of that complexity in a period of rapid social change and argues for greater sensitivity to the tensions that arise for children's welfare in both time and space. In particular, we should be aware of the tensions between demands from the market economy, dynamics of rationalisation and technology and childhood ideologies, on the one hand, and visions of a 'good childhood' and a 'good' human life within a 'good' society, on the other.

References

Adam, B. (1995): *Timewatch. The Social Analysis of Time*. Cambridge: Polity Press.
Alanen, L. (2006): »Theorizing children's welfare«. H. Wintersberger, L. Alanen, T. Olk and J. Qvortrup (eds): *Children's Economic and Social Welfare*. Vol. 1 of COST A19: Children's Welfare. Odense: University Press of Southern Denmark.
Bauman, Z. (2000): *Liquid Modernity*. Cambridge: Polity Press.
Beck, U. (1992): *Risk Society. Towards a New Modernity*. London: Sage. (First published 1986).
Castells, M. (1996): *The Rise of the Network Society*. Oxford: Blackwell Publishing.

Elias, N. (1992): *Time: an Essay*. Oxford and Cambridge (USA): Blackwell. (Orig. in German 1984).

Featherstone, M. (1995): *Undoing Culture: Globalization, Postmodernism and Identity*. London: Sage.

Giddens, A. (1984): *The Constitution of Society. Outline of the Theory of Structuration*. Cambridge: Polity Press.

Giddens, A. (1991): *Modernity and Self-Identity. Self and Society in the Late Modern Age*. Cambridge: Polity Press.

Harvey, D. (1996): *Justice, Nature & the Geography of Difference*. Oxford: Blackwell.

Holloway, S.L. and G. Valentine (2000): *Children' Geographies: Playing, Living, Learning*. London: Routledge.

James, A. and A. Prout (1997): »Re-presenting childhood: time and transition in the study of childhood«. James A. and A. Prout (eds): *Constructing and Reconstructing Childhood: Contemporary Issues in the Sociological Study of Childhood*. London: Falmer Press: 230-250.

Kränzl-Nagl, R., J. Mierendorff and T. Olk (eds) (2003): *Kindheit im Wohlfahrtsstaat. Gesellschaftliche und politische Herausforderungen*. Frankfurt and New York: Campus.

Mannheim, K. (1952): 'The problem of generations'. K. Mannheim: Essays in the Sociology of Knowledge. London: Routledge and Kegan Paul. (First published 1928).

Matthews, H. and M. Limb (1999): »Defining an agenda for the geography of children: review and prospect«. *Progress in Human Geography*, Vol. 23: 61-90.

Meyrowitz, J. (1985): *No Sense of Place*. New York: Oxford University Press.

Olwig, K.F. and Gulløv, E. (eds) (2003): *Children's Places. Cross-Cultural Perspectives*. London: Routledge: 23-38.

Sennett, R. (1998): *The Corrosion of Character: the Personal Consequences of Work in the New Capitalism*. New York: Norton.

Zeiher, H. (2001): »Children's islands in space and time: The impact of spatial differentiation on children's ways of shaping social life«. M. du Bois-Reymond, Sünker, H. and Krüger, H.-H. (eds): *Childhood in Europe. Approaches – Trends – Findings.* New York: Peter Lang: 139-159.

Conceptualising Time and Space

Valuing Children's Temporal Quality of Life

Helga Zeiher

Introduction

It seems paradoxical: in the rich societies of the northern world, people live longer than before, they work less time than before, and they are gaining more autonomy over their own lives due to increasing temporal de-standardisation and flexibilisation in many arenas of life. However, at the same time, people seem to be suffering more and more from time; many complain about lack of time and time pressure. In the last two decades, as a result, 'time welfare' has become an explicit desire, and an issue in social sciences as well as a policy goal. Do today's children also suffer from time? What are the consequences of the societal time crisis on children's time welfare?

The way in which adults perceive and control children's time, and which use of time they value as good for children, is part of the prevailing vision of childhood within a society. In modernity, this vision equates to the societal project of drawing a dividing line between childhood, as a protective and preparatory space, and the adult working world, and of strengthening this division ever further. Time plays a role in this project to the extent to which it serves the relevant purpose. One main concern is the amount of time spent on caring for children in families and child-specific institutions. Another is that children learn to deal with time in the way the working world will later demand of them. It is tempting to write the history of childhood as a history of time for children and children's time. The present transformation of time in the working world is reflected in the development of educational goals in the course of the 20th century, from strict time discipline to the aim of letting children regulate their own time, and in the temporal conditions for children within the two protective and preparatory institutions, the family and the school. That the family is no longer able to provide sufficient care time, and the school is still operated (at least in Germany) in forms of time organisation that have become obsolete in the working world, are manifestations, besides others, of a current crisis of the childhood project of modernity.

In the early 1980s, these and other crisis phenomena led to the development of a sociology of childhood, which enquires into the societal construction of childhood and societal changes in children's lives within the context of the society at large. Similarly to the new sociology of childhood, the new concept of time welfare is also a product of the crisis in which modern society has found itself in many respects since the late twentieth century. Time policy and time welfare, towards which it is oriented, have been increasingly subject to public debate, since problems for people's quality of life caused by the continuing rationalisation and economisation of time started becoming recognised in the 1990s[1]. In this chapter, I want to link these two directions of enquiry that have arisen for dealing with crisis phenomena of modern societies: the sociology of childhood and the analysis of time welfare. How can the recently developed concepts for studying time welfare be used to enquire into the temporal consequences of the crisis of modern society on children's lives?

I will use the term 'temporal quality of life' instead of 'time welfare'. Several authors (e.g. Mückenberger 2004: 268) rightly doubt the suitability of the latter, as 'welfare' implies an analogy to goods and money, and thus is restricted to an objectivistic and economics-related understanding of time, and because the term is limited to a specific concept of time, albeit to the dominant concept in modern societies. In contrast, the term 'temporal quality of life' appears more open; it enables the use of the paradigm of objective, linear time, but is also open for different concepts of social time.

How can Temporal Quality of Life be Valued?

Temporal conditions, temporal agency, and temporal quality of life

Quality of life is a subject oriented term. Positive or negative temporal quality of life comes about in the processes of individual dealings with all relevant conditions for acting and experiencing time. But processes as such cannot be observed. All that we can observe is, on the one hand, the conditions, and on the other hand, the results of processes: input and output. The output of a process attains certain characteristics through the specific time of a process of action, for example speed. Effects on the actor also become recognisable, for example happiness or stress. On the side of the 'output', doubtlessly a useful starting point for studying how societal conditions of life affect children's time would be children's agency in their temporal organisation of life. This approach is not chosen here[2].

Nor does this chapter deal with the way in which children themselves experience and valuate the temporal conditions of their actions, whether positively as good quality of life or negatively as causes of a lack or pressure of time. A recent tendency to interview children on their temporal needs (e.g. Galinsky 1999) corresponds with the desire to take children seriously by allowing their voice to be heard. This apparently simple research procedure does, however, entail the problem of taking the interplay into account, formed by society in a complex way, of particular experiences, patterns of explanation and evaluation that children take on from their environment, and of specific psychological processing of experiences (see Karin Jurczyk's and Andreas Lange's chapter). The reflections presented in this chapter may be regarded as highlighting some of these preconditions for studying children's temporal agency as well as children's experiences of time.

This chapter focuses on the 'input' side regarding the ways children's temporal quality of life is valued on the level of society. It concentrates on particular kinds of temporal conditions set by adults with which children are confronted in their actions: societal discourses and time structures by which children are expected and forced to deal with time in our society. Of interest are the ways of valuing which are fixed in societal childhood structures and predominant in discourses on the well-being of children.

Looked at from the individual's life, conditions arise on one hand from the temporal, spatial and social situation in existence at the moment of the decision on action and the beginning of action, and on the other hand from the individual himself or herself, from his or her cognitive, emotional and physical prerequisites relevant for the action. Competence for dealing with time is also one of these individual conditions. Conditions on both sides, in the external world and within the individual, are connected to the past, as outcomes of previous actions, and to the future as anticipations of future external and internal conditions and consequences of action.

Every process of action takes place within the individual's active dealings with many different conditions, whereby no one condition takes effect on its own; different modes of time, external and self-imposed constraints, conflicting demands on time are conveyed together in the individual action. The conditions broaden and limit options for action; what is then done and how it is done, however, are up to the individual. Every process of action comes about by a multitude of conditions which the person interconnects actively. In that process, no action impacts on its own, but rather adopts a certain character in the context of the whole, taking effect within this context. This means that the effect that a particular temporal possibility actually has at a particular moment on the action of a child is not independent of the child's entire current life situation and biography. The latter includes all temporal possibilities and limitations that have taken effect so far throughout the child's life.

This understanding is not only relevant for studies on the individual level, but also for studies on the societal conditions of childhood, as in this chapter. The significance of conditions for action in one arena of everyday life can only be estimated if these conditions are set in relation to the conditions a child experiences in other arenas. For example, the Taylorist time regime in schools has a different significance now than a few decades ago, as other modes of time bear a greater weight in children's lives outside of school to those Taylorist modes that dominate school life.

There are diverse theories of social time. Each one of these focuses on different temporal phenomena and suggests different valuations of time welfare. I will work on the basis of three time concepts, using these to analyse what kind of time prescriptions for children and valuations of children's time are inherent in the structures and discourses of childhood.

Objective time: having and controlling time

In modern times, the idea of time as an external reality, an objective, constantly flowing entity, has become extremely dominant. This determines the everyday understanding of time to this day, not least because mechanical measurement of time and the enormous proliferation of times fixed by society confirm this idea. The time of day is machine time, it progresses without end and can be randomly fragmented and expressed in numerical terms. We perceive time like a thing in relation to people's life processes, as something that we have or do not have, that can be dealt with on a rational basis by precisely planning and networking processes. These characteristics of objective time are the basis of the capitalist economisation of time. In economic thinking, time is a resource, which is divided up, shared out, allocated and exchanged for money, and its efficient use can be controlled and enhanced by means of rationalisation and acceleration. Certain requirements of people's way of dealing with time were characteristic of modern industrial societies: calculability of time used, methodical organisation of life, far-sighted planning and postponing present benefits in the expectation of future benefit, along with external and self-discipline to punctuality, regularity, steadiness and speed of working. In the course of the 20th century, people's everyday lives and biographies were increasingly fitted into institutionalised time structures. At present, however, in the context of increased options and the immense accelerations enabled by information technology, these time structures are eroding, on all levels of social life. The time regimes of the economy are changing from long-term to short-term planning, from externally determined, rigid standard working hours to flexible, individually determined working hours. Standardisations of the welfare state are breaking down; they are becoming more differentiated and offering more options. Everyday and life timing is now less easy to plan in the long term, its determination is increasingly left to individuals, who have to weave the complex temporal patterns of their lives themselves.

As far as the discourses on time welfare and temporal quality of life are confined to these phenomena within the paradigm of objective, linear time, they focus on two aspects: having time and controlling one's own time. In both aspects, time appears to be an asset that can be owned and manipulated by individuals. Not only having and controlling, but also the criteria for good quality of life that are dependent on these ways of using time are basic concepts of modern societies. The imperative of fair distribution is used for the valuation of 'having time' (Rinderspacher 2002), and 'controlling time' is founded on the 'right to one's own time', i.e. on the tradition of the rights of the individual (Mückenberger 2004). However these criteria raise the question of how to deal with the fact that individuals use the abstract rights for very diverse purposes (ibid.: 268).

Corresponding to modern societies' orientation towards work, *having time* has usually been discussed regarding time free from paid work, particularly as welfare policy takes this as a direct starting point; until recently, the successes of trade unions brought workers successively more free time. Since the famous study on the unemployed population of Marienthal (Jahoda et. al. 1971/1933), we have been well aware of the subjectively experienced devaluation of time when unemployment makes all time into free time. For those in employment, the value of free time has also become subject to doubt as its availability has increased. Staffan H. Linder (1970) pointed out a paradox in the relation of working time and free time: the more leisure time people have, the more their time free of paid work becomes an intensive time of working on leisure goods, necessary for the economy. Arlie R. Hochschild (1997) described how the 'free' time many parents have for family life is taken up by so many child-related tasks that they experience temporal quality of life more at work than at home – »work becomes home and home becomes work«. These examples show that the mutual influences and the increasing blurring of boundaries between working and free time make it appear relatively pointless to define 'having' time in a purely quantitative sense in contrast to working time. Free time, that is time not already occupied by something else, does not imply quality of life per se. In discourses on time welfare, 'having time' is therefore defined on a content basis, as having time for something: having common time in families and with friends, of time for private care, for civil involvement in society, for culture (Deutsche Gesellschaft für Zeitpolitik 2003).

Controlling one's own time is an other qualitative definition of 'having time', which can be valued as a source of quality of life. Objective time, rationing time by the use of clock and calendar, is a medium of control, that is of power over one's own life time or that of other people. The painful effect of external control over time has been the subject of much critique, from Marx's analysis of the alienation of labour through the sale of time on the labour market, to Foucault's (1976) analyses of disciplining to Chaplin hanging impotently on the wheel of time. In the course of the current transformation of the working world, tendencies towards devolving time determination to individuals are becoming increasingly dominant. Where strict time standards once forced people to adapt, the multiplication of options has led to flexibilisation and deregulation, and individuals are expected to link their times of their own accord within increasingly complex structures of conditions, not just at work but also in many respects in their private lives. This development represents an increase in self-determination, which can, however, when the expectations become very complex, cause lack of time that has no external cause. Such self-created time pressures are almost impossible to meet with a repulse on the basis of the human rights of the individual.

Due to the individualisation of time determination and the increasing amount of temporal constraints and time conflicts in many people's lives, non scheduled time, »one's own proper time situated in a momentous present« (Novotny 1992: 444; 1989) has become increasingly valued in recent times. This is evident by the many courses and books on time use and relaxation strategies that are now available.

External social compulsion and self-imposed constraints

The concept of time as an objective, linear directed entity separate from the processes taking place 'in' it corresponds with Newton's mechanical physics. Although this reificated idea of time remains the dominant everyday concept to the present day, a paradigm shift has long since taken place in physics, since Einstein, and more recently also in sociology (s. Elchardus 1988; Novotny 1992). Time is now understood as constituted in processes and as irreversibly connected with the processes that generate and perceive it.

In his essay on time (1992/1984), Norbert Elias works out such a notion of time from the focal point of his sociology of knowledge. In his view, time is knowledge that is produced by »the stream of many generations of people« in social processes as an abstraction of movements and changes, and became a social institution. Elias defines time as a symbol, which »refers to the relating together of positions or segments within two or more continuously moving sequences of events. The relation between them results from the elaboration of perceptions by human beings possessing knowledge« (ibid.: 10). »The uniqueness of time lies in the fact that symbols – at the present stage predominantly numerical symbols – are used for orientation in the incessant flow of events; events taking place on all levels of integration, physical, biological, social and individual« (ibid.: 14-15). Every individual from childhood on learns »to recognise 'time' as a symbol of a social institution, the external compulsion of which the child feels soon at first hand« (ibid.: 11). »The conversion of the external compulsion coming from the social institution of time into a pattern of self-constraint embracing the whole life of an individual, is a graphic example of how a civilizing process contributes to forming the social habitus which is an integral part of each individual personality structure.« (ibid.: 11) »All this becomes second nature; it appears, and is accepted, as the fate of all human beings« (ibid.: 7).

In the historical process of civilization, the relation between external and self-imposed constraints changed, »and especially the pattern of self-restraint and the way it is incorporated« (ibid.: 27). In modernity, »in conjunction with a shift towards increased differentiation and integration, ... a particularly complex system of self-regulation has developed within individual people as regards time, with a correspondingly acute individual sensibility towards time. The external social compulsion of time, represented by clocks, calendars or timetables, possesses to a high degree, in these societies, the characteristics of individual self-constraints« (ibid.: 22). Elias points to the possibility of individuals in contemporary societies to develop a certain amount of autonomy by learning social patterns of self-regulation, »but, on the whole, social control resists excessive variations in self-control« (ibid.: 27). In the end, it is a problem of balance: »Peoples' scope for decision, their freedom, rests finally on the possibility that they have to control in a variety of ways the more or less flexible balance between various compelling authorities, which, moreover, are constantly in a state of flux«(ibid.: 33).

Conflicts between 'living time' and objective, mechanical time

Due to the increasingly widespread recognition of the destructive consequences of scientific and technological progress from the 1960s on, awareness of the consequences of continuing rationalisation and economisation of time for people's quality of life has risen since the early 1990s. The »Dialectic of Enlightenment« (Horkheimer and Adorno 1947), the turn from the subjugation of the world under human rationality to the rule of products of rationality over humans, is also evident in the »detachment of time from its cyclic interrelations and its indifference to biological and cosmic cycles, ignorance of which can create risks« (Vinz 2005: 26). Since the late 1990s, a time ecological movement has been issuing warnings against the increasing compulsions for rationalisation and economisation of time, exhorting that the other temporal prerequisites for action that stem from nature-related growth processes and the rhythms of human life, »all that is processive«, should not be neglected (Adam 1999; 1998; Adam et al. 1998; Hofmeister and Spitzner 1999; Vinz 2005). Representatives of this movement demonstrate how the high societal value of ease of planning, speed and efficient use of time, the mechanical character of time arising from technology and rationalised organisation and the quantification of time and its monetary value conflict, in many areas of everyday life with life processes. They point to qualities of living processes, quality of life, which suffer hereby. Such studied conflicts are between time needed for care work, relationships, health and nutrition and the rationalisation and economisation of such activities.

Ecological critique expressly takes as its starting point contradictions, fractures and conflicts between 'time artefacts', 'industrial time', 'cultural time' on the one hand, and 'natural time', the 'temporal world of all living' (Adam 1999), 'sui generis time' (Elchardus 1988; Novotny 1992; 1989) on the other. To show that the transformation of life processes by societal processes has reached a critical phase, an 'other', marginalised and destroyed by the negative development, is held up against it. This 'other' is seen in 'nature', in 'living things'. It is referred to as 'Urzeiten' or primitive time (Adam 1999). However, the parallels to the ecology movement, which opposes geological and biological destruction of nature, suggest an opposition that risks implying a dualism of society and nature – a problem recognised and discussed by the representatives of time ecological approaches (Vinz 2005: 59-64).

The fact that nature-related conditions of social actions are more or less transformed by societal processes into 'second nature' is an accepted truth within the social sciences. Argumentations on the relation between natural time and social time focusing on the genesis of social time can refer to various sociological time theorists. For instance, Norbert Elias (1992) emphasises that the social construction of time is an abstraction of social processes, which are integrated into cosmic time (e.g. seasons, times of the day) and biological time (e.g. life development from birth to death) and relate to these; nature, society and individuals »are embedded in each other and are interdependent« (ibid.:16). Mark Elchardus (1988) goes much further, writing ironically that »some 'kinds of time' are seen as more natural than others« and »usually 'clock time' is regarded as artificial, compared to the more 'natural' subjective perception of time or the temporality that results from certain kinds of adaptation to seasonal rhythms and other environmental or biological constraints«, is »a beautiful illustration of how past contingent arrangements and selections can come to be considered as natural.« »In general this proposition devalues the temporality of formal organisations and of a great many social systems, which depend on clock time for their coordination and functioning, in favour of temporalities that can be discovered in the organism and the psychological system and that are supposed to have been realised in the agrarian communities of before.« (ibid.: 1988: 43).

Another argumentation against a dualism of nature and society is specifically ecological. This argument is based on the highly complex, dynamic and self-contradictory network of temporalities of societal life and simultaneousness and contradictoriness of a variety of different logics of time in which every human lives. Barbara Adam has coined the term 'timescape' for this concept: »This timescape consists on all levels of existence of its rhythmicity and timescales, pace and intensities, pauses and regenerative rest periods, its unavoidable irreversibility, its immanent and latent processes, sui generis time and system time, its symphony of timings and synchronisation, lengths and sequences, the permeability of past, present and future« (ibid.: 1999: 53; see also 1998). Natural and cultural time, according to Adam, are inescapably connected within the timescape. This is firstly, she explains, because landscape is a »chronic« or »record« of everything »that has an active effect upon it«, and secondly because every person lives in a complex web of all these things. Therefore, »the view underlying the concept of landscape is fundamentally different from the dualistic conception, which sees nature and culture as mutually exclusive – even opposite – spheres. Culture has never existed without nature, but now nature is also no longer thinkable without the influence of culture« (1999: 52-53). From her perspective, there is thus »no choice« between nature and culture. She sees it as a necessity »to theoretically reflect the shares of one in the other«, and thus recognise and overcome the superior position of economical concepts of time (ibid.: 48). The image of timescapes enables scholars to study the relationships between different temporalities that collide in the course of certain activities. The criterion for quality of life is then a successful balance, the achievement of the highest possible level of freedom from conflict. Elias also takes the concept of balance as his criterion for describing historical developments – albeit a different balance, that between external compulsion and self-constraint of social time. Whereas the ecological perspectives of time focus on seeking options for a better future, and thereby enquire into criteria for valuing quality of life, Elias expressly has no intention to value, but concentrates on working out lines of historical development.

Conditions for Temporal Quality of Life in Structures and Discourses of Childhood

Times that children need »by nature«

There have been sociocritical considerations on the relation of natural time and cultural time in relation to children ever since the Enlightenment. For anthropological reasons, children are in a state of growth, formation and thus only become 'mature' people in the future. The long process of development makes it necessary in many respects to pay particular attention to children's nature-related temporal needs and possibilities of dealing with time. The fact of development is the natural basis for the fact that childhood is constructed in a particular way by society. This construction includes the way in which children are introduced to the dominant modes of time and temporal forms of life in their respective societies, and in which their respective state of development in dealing with time is perceived and taken into account. Society thus processes 'natural time' in childhood from two temporal perspectives. In relation to the future, it becomes lengths, paces, rhythms and levels of the process of growth and development, which (with the aid of developmental psychology) is pictured within objective temporal structures and fixed as developmental norms (James 2005). Related to the present, it becomes time guidelines that adults believe to be appropriate for the respective age of a child.

The construction of childhood in modern societies places children at a distance to society: childhood is separated from adults' working world, and therefore appears to be located outside of society. Childhood is constructed in such a way that children are prepared for their later life as productively working adults in special institutions:

the family and the school. Children thus occupy a different position within society to adults, are treated differently and perceived as different. This 'otherness' is generally explained on the basis of their different nature, and the very pronounced institutional separation of children has led to a particularly strong emphasis on the other nature of the child in discourses of childhood. Jean-Jacques Rousseau's »Emile« (1762) contains one of the first emphases on the nature of the child and its counterposition to society, and it was the educational progressivists of the early 20th century who purported the moral superiority of the child's nature and established the perception of the child as a victim of society. Michael-Sebastian Honig (1999) points out the utopian aspect of the positive moral valuation of the nature of the child in Rousseau's theory, in contrast to the previously emphasised evil nature of the child due to original sin: »The pedagogical discovery of the child as discovery of its 'nature' is founded on the anthropological reforming of the theological distinction between good and evil into a 'good' nature and an 'evil' society« (ibid.: 34). Due to this moral difference, pedagogy must not simply aim to adapt the »growing human« to society, as »after all, the nature of the child symbolises a utopia of human development: it is that universal good towards which education in the name of reason orientates« (ibid.: 35). »The motif of a nature of the child to be realised through education is… a vision of non-alienated life. The child becomes a hope for salvation from the contradictions of modernity« (ibid.: 41). In the educational progressivist movement, the child's own, natural development is then taken as the yardstick of education, founding the child's autonomy towards adults; »the nature of the child is the measure of what is 'suitable for children', 'appropriate for children'« (ibid.: 52). The 'myth of the child' romanticised (Baader 2004) the nature of the child, »which precedes all historical and social reality and at the same time suffers under the adult and his or her demand to educate« (Honig 1999: 57). Until now, the image of the child as innocent and vulnerable to societal evils, as well as the image of the child in need of love have proven to be very influential in public debates, policy and marketing (Bühler-Niederberger 2005).

In modernity, the counterpositioning of the nature of the child and the treatment of the child by society is institutionally consolidated in the construction of childhood, namely in the division of tasks between the two institutions of modern childhood, the family and the school. Whereas the school deliberately confronts children with societal organisation of time (see below), the bourgeois core family is the institutional home to the image of the child as a being by nature alien to society and separate from the working world. The task of the private family, separated from working society, is care for physical and emotional growth and all aspects of the body, i.e. 'nature'. Here, the child is allowed its own time for playing, dawdling and dreaming. It is thus not surprising that the ideas of which time and which modes of time children need by nature are linked to the respective historical character of the institution of the family. The 'nature of the child' is taken to justify and maintain the respectively represented family model, and alters along with the institution of the family. In particular, discourses on how much care in a family setting children need, and how much institutional care children can cope with, refer to differing 'natural needs' of the child according to the respective image of the family in the social policy in a country at a time.

Let me quote some examples. Franz-Xaver Kaufmann (1980) portrayed a picture of children who by nature, as they are still in a state of development, are necessarily in an outsider position in modern society. A quarter of a century ago, he regarded children as reliant on »consistency of their life world«, on socially integrative, not excessively heterogeneous situations and on »clear sensual worlds«. However, he was of the opinion that they could only be granted these conditions in the modern society differentiated according to functions »at the price of isolation within society«. The family, which he saw as specialised in meeting these needs, was, however, becoming under strain as a result of working mothers. Kaufmann maintained that it needed increasing support in formally organised care institutions, but that these exposed children to the principles of modern society, particularly rationalisation, which was not appropriate for their needs. Thus, according to Kaufmann, children represent »a complication that runs counter to the dominant pattern of rationalisation« (ibid.: 771) in modern society. In the meantime it has become normal for both parents to work and to outsource care, and the arguments have changed: children are regarded as rather robust, resistant and adaptable by nature, and are considered to cope well with different and alternating time modes (Dencik 1989; Hungerland 1999). Today, as new forms of time constraints, pressure for flexibility and de-standardisation extend from the working world into family life, yet another aspect of children's nature is emphasised: children are thought to need forms of time that are reliable and calculable (see Karin Jurczyk's and Andreas Lange's chapter).

In the 1980s, when rationalisation and planning of time penetrated the previously less affected private sphere of children through institutional leasure time activities and children's lives organised around appointment diaries, a popular discourse on the 'hurried child' (Elkind 1981) and the 'over-planned child' also made recourse to the nature of the child. Adults' resistance against the temporal constraints imposed on children's leisure time activities arose from the now nostalgic idea of children who could meet up spontaneously to play at home and in the neighbourhood.

In relation to external control and self-determination over time, views of what children need by nature and what they are capable of have also changed. Up until the 1960s, children had experienced the rigid time regime of industrial society also at home. As at school, the idea that children need a strict time regime was dominant in the family, and this was imposed upon them from birth onwards by means of fixed mealtimes and bedtimes. In the late 1960s, in a period of transition to the service economy and increased democracy, people began to believe the opposite: children could and should regulate their own time. From this point on, mothers breastfed their children when they were hungry, and no longer timed by the clock.

Specific time needs have repeatedly been purported as universally nature-related prerequisites for children's quality of life. The above examples of historical change illustrate how temporal needs are embedded in specific social contexts, disproving the claim to universality. Both reservations described above towards the determination of temporal quality of life on the basis of a supposedly natural time requirement apply to both children and adults: the sociological argument that time does not exist from the beginning, neither in an objective sense nor as a subjective characteristic, but is created in the process of social life, and the ecological argument that 'natural time' can never be separated at any point in an individual life from the complex web of nature's and societies temporalities and modes of time, from 'timescapes'.

With reference to children, as I have mentioned above, there is a particular tendency to contrast 'natural time' and societal time, since young children are in the process of learning the meaning and importance of social times in their society and their own lives. In the course of their individual development they learn what has developed historically. As long as a child – to use Elias's terms – has not yet transformed external compulsion into self-constraint, serious conflicts often arise between the forms of time in his or her own current life process and external temporal demands. An obvious example is adults' frequent demands on children to do something faster or not now, or to interrupt doing something. Such conflicts may well be painful for the child. However, valuations of quality of life would be naïve if they were to simply take one side of the conflict over the other. In terms of the two approaches outlined above, Elias's and the time ecological approach, valuations have to focus on the type of balances between the individual and society and between the child's states as 'being' and 'becoming'.

Between future and present quality of life

I will now go into further detail on an other example of that which is considered the 'nature of the child' as variable and formed by society. Children grow, get taller, gain more and more knowledge – in short, they are an embodiment of progress. In progress-oriented modern societies, children's anthropological 'becoming' has become the basis of society's vision of childhood, and this aspect is extremely emphasised. Everything children do and experience in the present is measured against and determined by the future. Children are perceived, valued and guided in their actions according to aspects of development, socialisation and learning for their later contribution in the working world. The strong emphasis on the future means that the image of the child is dominated by the child's unfinished status, deficiency, weakness and need for care. Due to this minorisation, the distance from adulthood appears particularly great, as does adults' superiority over children. On the sociostructural level, childhood has also been defined by the subjugation of the present to the future. Children are excluded from paid work and separated off in a specific space in society – in the family and in the educational and care system – they grow up cared for and protected by parents and professionals, and are prepared for their future lives. Society's efforts on behalf of growing children are regarded as an investment in future human capital and as a prerequisite for further economic growth. As individuals who have not yet fully entered society, children are not viewed as a group of the population on its own, but rather as dependent family members and dependent clients of the educational system.

The progress related concept of childhood increased its influence over children's life time up to the end of the 20th century, not at least because the development of the economy required ever more education for all children. This requirement is not only met by extending and intensifying learning time at school, but also by placing more weight on implicit learning in other areas of everyday life. Everything children do, from birth onwards, is valued in terms of importance for learning and socialisation. Learning is specifically promoted at an increasingly young age, and diverse structured leisure time arrangements offer opportunities for learning-based activities. Most parents see themselves as responsible for a 'successful' child equipped for the future, regard play and social contact between children as important for learning and development, and support educational activities for their child outside of school. Through the increasing weight of learning, children's use of time has become ever more influenced by expectations for the future.

Although it dominates childhood more radically than ever before, the future focus has recently entered into a crisis. In no area of life can one now continue to adhere to modern society's confidence of progress, including its application to children's futures. The future is less calculable than it has at least appeared in earlier times. We are less able than ever to predict how the working world will be when today's children are adults. The short-term nature of planning possibilities and knowledge are shrinking the future and placing greater weight on the present. As knowledge is replaced by new knowledge at an accelerating pace, adults' head start in terms of knowledge is also shrinking. This is particularly obvious with respect to the way children deal with the new information media. In consequence, adults' superiority is decreasing in some regards. Children are now regarded less as deficient, but rather their ability for agency and self-determination is recognised and taken seriously from a very early age.

In this context, the sociostructural position of childhood is also in transformation. One important initial step is the fact that the future focus has been reflected as such since the 1980s. From its inception the sociology of childhood pointed to the one-sided character of the socialisation perspective and analysed the positioning of childhood in society's generational order alongside the changes which have occurred. In the current discourses on children's economic situation, new arguments related to children's present lives are appearing. One example is the call to base transfer payments for children on civil rights rather than regarding them solely as an investment in future human capital, and thus to accept children as members of society in the here and now (Olk 2004).

Alongside childhood's subjugation to the future, however, the modern vision of childhood is also characterised by a tendency to emphasise the present from the outset. This tendency also has very far-reaching significance in children's lives, and also gained importance in the late 20th century. It is concerned with the emotional value that children hold for adults' lives (Zelizer 1985). Most children are very much loved; it is expected and demanded that they are happy in the present and reciprocate this love. Expectations of motherly love and of the child's love for her or his parents play a significant role in the pattern of the bourgeois family. Such expectations have the character of norms that must be fulfilled, and are now more than ever supported by identity needs and fears for the future on the part of parents. The more partner relationships appear under threat of collapse, and the less other relationships, be they at the workplace or in leisure time, are upheld for life, the more the relationship with the child becomes the only stable, lasting relationship in the eyes of parents. Parental love combines current affectivity with hope for lifelong affection. Parents thus generally not only go to great efforts for their children's future opportunities, but also for their current well-being.

Demands made on children arising from anticipation of the future and the desire for children's present happiness are often conflicting, i.e. since children are supposed to both play and learn. During the last decades many attempts were made to combine the two and thereby blur the differences. Examples are the blurring of differences through entertaining learning toys and play-based forms of learning, and rewarding children in the present for future-oriented good behaviour such as success at school. On the one hand, the boundaries between play and learning are becoming increasingly blurred. On the other hand, there are indications that many parents' worries and fears for their child's future participation in working life are growing in view of the increasing unpredictability of the future, and they are therefore exerting intensified pressure to learn, at an earlier age. In this respect children's present lives are even more subjugated to the future, however to a more unpredictible, risky one.

Adaptation of children's time to the working world

The area of life in which the course of childhood and children's everyday lives are exclusively determined by the focus on the future is at school. The goal of qualifying children for the working world determines both the content of teaching and the temporal organisation of learning. As the temporal patterns of the school are organised according to the pattern of the working world, the school is the place where children are directly confronted by the time modes that dominate the working world. It has always been taken for granted that this is in the best interest of the children, because it is done for the sake of their future well-being.

As we are aware from historical studies, great efforts were made to impose the use of objective, rational time that was necessitated by industrialisation and state bureaucracy in the 19th century. The industrious use of time was extolled as a virtue in church sermons, and in factories steadiness, regularity and temporal precision were enforced by means of strict discipline. The younger generations had to learn this in childhood, compulsory schooling had a central role to play. Since then children have been forced into an institutionalised temporal corset characterised by successive grade levels, the yearly alternation of term time and holidays, and the daily alternation of lesson time and free time. The breaking down of lesson content into consecutive, linear steps means that students have to attend school regularly and punctually in order to keep up with the curriculum. Teacher-directed group instruction requires children to be present at the same place and the same time. Prolongation of the time of confinement by keeping children in was a much-used means of punishment in former time (see Anna-Liisa Närvänen's and Elisabet Näsman's chapter).

Legitimated by the need for future members of a time-economically organised working world, the spatial and temporal disciplining of children was an explicit educational goal. Students were given grades for their punctuality and steadiness. The family too was involved in drilling temporal discipline. From the 1930s to the 1950s, in several European countries very popular books advised parents to keep strictly to children's set mealtimes and bedtimes, and to implement these rigidly from birth. Mothers were taught that it was absolutely essential to acclimatise the body to rationalised time as early as possible – they were to ignore their baby's cries of hunger.

The time regime of Fordist industry, to which schools (in Germany) still adhere to a great extent today, began to become obsolete in the 1960s. At that time, the scales started tipping away from industrial manufacturing to service and knowledge production, and the democratisation tendencies of the post-war period started taking effect. Adults called for more authority over their own time at the workplace, and this was matched by demands to allow children to regulate their own time for learning, eating and sleeping. An intensive scholarly and public discourse developed against the previous authoritarian educational style and in favour of more autonomy for children, and developmental psychologists and educationalists developed concepts of the child as a subject and actor. Within the transformation of the working world at that time, these discourses became so influential that self-determination has been regarded by most parents and teachers as the key educational goal since the 1970s, and personal relationships between children and adults have since been characterised to a great degree by a lack of hierarchy where negotiation has taken the place of orders.

Self-control of time may well have taken priority over external control as an educational goal, but it has not done so in practice. Tendencies towards autonomy and individualisation have affected childhood with the same contradictions that are characteristic of the development of society as a whole (Beck 1986). Simultaneously with the decline in personal control, structural control over children's time multiplied. The educational system expanded in the early 1970s because the economy's demand for qualified labour increased. Learning was planned in greater temporal detail at schools, and more pre-school institutions and structured leisure time activities were established outside of schools. This multiplication of structures was accompanied by a multiplication of options. Children were presented with options through more opportunities for choice between in-school educational routes, but particularly in their free time through the new variety of structured leisure activities in courses, events and specialised sporting activities, from which they can put together their own free time programme outside of school. Options require children to inform themselves of activities in advance, coordinate appointments and make binding decisions for the future – self-determination and rational time administration of an everyday programme, which must be strictly adhered to. Peer relationships between children also exhibit this tendency. If children spend a great deal of time within institutions they have less time to play in the neighbourhood; children thus meet less frequently in the neighbourhood. The choice of possible playmates then takes place less in the neighbourhood, and meeting up requires that children arrange an appointment in advance, thus planning their time. Children were thereby included in the tendency towards individualisation of life organisation that is spreading across society since that time, and also in its contradictions between standardisation and self-determination (Zeiher 2001; 2003).

Now, at the beginning of the 21st century, the requirements for dealing with time are changing in a new way in all areas of society. Following the previous multiplication and frequent optionalisation of time structures, externally fixed time structures and constraints are now eroding and individual rational time management becomes more 'just in time'. At more and more adult workplaces, the time in which work has to be done is less strictly or not at all regulated. Time regimes are becoming even more individualised, and the balance of external temporal compulsions and self-constraint is tipping further towards the latter. Children experience this temporal transformation most clearly outside of school. Leisure time management is changing along with the transformation of information technology; the Internet and Playstations are available without any time restriction, and mobile telephones reduce the temporal horizon for making arrangements, enabling children to meet up spontaneously. Families no longer live within the rhythms of the traditional daily schedule, and children experience at home that times are changed and improvised at short notice. In the lives of many adults, the individualisation of time determination creates a new form of lack of time, which extends into family life and thus also affects children. In some situations, more self-determination is demanded of children; in others, appointments and schedules are no less externally determined than previously, however less regular and less predictable for the child. (Zeiher 2005a; see Karin Jurczyk's and Andreas Lange's chapter). Presumably, a tendency arises in many families to avoid and reduce time constraints wherever possible.

In schools, calls for individual learning speeds have been voiced for some time, however, it is only now that de-standardisation, flexibilisation and individualisation of time use are so widespread in the economy that working processes at schools are being adapted to them. Schools' time regimes are beginning (even in Germany) to break away from the time modes of industrial society, in order to qualify future workers for the self-determination of working time that has now become economically functional. The individual pupils' creation of learning and studying time is becoming more important. The self-imposed time constraint that is expected to be learned by today's children no longer affects only the old working virtues of modern societies such as punctuality, steadiness and fulfilment of plans and schedules but also efficiency in making of one's own times (see Hanne Warming Nielsen's and Jan Kampmann's chapter).

The new temporal conditions in the school and the family are formed on the basis of developments in the economy and information technology. The renewed rise of educational theory discourses on self-determined action – 'self-socialisation', 'self-learning' – merely accompanies these developments (see Anne-Trine Kjørholt's and Vebjørg Tingstad's chapter). Even more research is necessary into how the temporal quality of children's lives is affected by this latest change in dealing with time.

Valuing Children's Temporal Quality of Life – New Criteria?

This chapter has pointed to the historicity of valuations. It has be showm how temporal expectations to children and explanations why their lives should have particular temporal qualities change in line with society. If, however, the valuation criteria must be historically relativised and references to the nature of the child prove themselves not to be free from ideological elements, how can we then determine which conditions enable children's temporal quality of life? I want to summarize some answers to this question provided in this chapter.

In modernity, the value criteria changed in line with economic structures and conditions. Temporal requirements are becoming more heterogeneous and inconsistent. Each person is on its own exposed to the heterogeneous time demands of several everyday arenas developing according to their own dynamics, and neoliberal society leaves it to individuals to put these together. Challenges for individual temporal agency are based more on conflicts and ambiguities than on single external time prescriptions. Thus a valuation of people's temporal quality of life can no longer start with temporal conditions for single actions, but with conditions for the *possibility of creating balances* in the overall context of life. Bearing in mind the mutual permeations of nature-related, societal and individual time, the valuation cannot fix its criteria on one or other side alone – neither to a pre-societal natural time, nor to the necessity for external constraints, nor to the achieved self-constraint. The valuation of temporal quality of life – children's as well as adults' – is a question of how everything is placed in relation to everything else, how the weights are counterbalanced.

The fact that the temporal quality of many peoples' lives suffers today from lack of time and time pressure indicates how difficult it is to find balances entailing temporal quality of life. In a more varied and less certain world, the time welfare criterion 'the right to one's own time' can no longer be attached only to control of time through time management and time economy, as people have learned in modern society. Furthermore, quality of life must also be defended by means of resistance against temporal constraints, both external compulsions and internalised, self-imposed constraints, on the basis of which individual control over time takes place. Finding balances that entail quality of life therefore also requires rationality on the level of *reflecting upon one's own dealing with time*. It is becoming necessary to make oneself aware of what one's own temporal quality of life should be, and to control one's internalised constraints towards this objective. Possibilities of gaining the relevant skills to do so from childhood constitute one of the prerequisites for temporal quality of life.

Pointing out the need for reflection on time and individual balancing is not sufficient in itself since these criteria are free from social content. Values must be related to societal developments, to society's desired processes and respective times. In order to determine what constitutes good quality of life, one needs a vision of a good life on the one hand, and a vision of a 'good' society and a 'good' childhood within this, on the other. The way to search for such visions is on the basis of a critical analysis of tendencies of contemporary society.

During the last decades the vision of less dependency and more self-determination, of more participation, and of less minorisation and marginalisation has been highlighted by childhood sociologists, educationalists and those engaged in childhood policy. These aims correspond to human rights in modernity in general and particularly to the societal individualisation tendency. However, individualisation means not only shifting the power to make decisions to individuals, but also releasing individuals from social ties. The tendency towards multiplication and optionalisation, de-standardisation and flexibilisation of temporal structures of everyday life means that previously external temporal links between people's daily routines and interaction possibilities show a tendency of unravelling. The increasing freedom of individual determination of time is accompanied by a reduction in security and reliability of social times; the *individuals' social integration* is becoming precarious. This also applies to children. It is becoming more difficult for them to find joint time for social relations within the family and with their peers. Therefore, today's vision of a good childhood should include particular emphasis on possibilities for children to live in good balance between independence and social ties, individualised identity and social belonging.

References

Adam, B. (1998): *Timescapes in Modernity. The Environment and Invisible Hazards*. London and New York: Routledge.
Adam, B. (1999): »Naturzeiten, Kulturzeiten und Gender – Zum Konzept 'Timescape'«. Hofmeister, S. and M. Spitzner (eds): *Zeitlandschaften. Perspektiven öko-sozialer Zeitpolitik*. Stuttgart: Hirzel: 35-57.
Adam, B., Geißler, K.A., Held, M., Kümmerer, K. and M. Schneider (1998): *Tutzinger Projekt »Ökologie der Zeit«. Ökologie der Zeit – Vom Finden der rechten Zeitmaße*. München: ökom Verlag.
Baader, M. S. (2004): *Erziehung als Erlösung. Transformationen des Religiösen in der Reformpädagogik*. Weinheim und München: Juventa.
Beck, U. (1986): *Risikogesellschaft. Auf dem Weg in eine andere Moderne*. Frankfurt am Main: Suhrkamp.
Belloni, C.M. (1998): »Tempi della citta: the temporal organisation of red collar work«. *Time & Society*, Vol. 7: 249-263.
Bühler-Niederberger, D. (2005): *Kindheit und die Ordnung der Verhältnisse. Von der gesellschaftlichen Macht der Unschuld und dem kreativen Individuum*. Weinheim und München: Juventa.
Christensen, P. and A. James (2001): »What are schools for? The temporal experience of children's learning in Northern England«. L. Alanen and B. Mayall (eds): *Conceptualizing Child-Adult-Relations*. London and New York: Routledge Falmer: 70-85.
Christensen, P., A. James and C. Jenks (2000): »Home and movement: children constructing 'family time' «. Holloway, S.L. and G. Valentine (eds): *Children's Geographies. Playing, Living, Learning*. London and New York: Routledge: 139-155.
Dencik, L. (1989): »Growing up in the post-modern age: On the child's position in the modern family and on the position of the family in the modern welfare state«. *Acta Sociologica*, Vol. 32: 155-180.
Deutsche Gesellschaft für Zeitpolitik (2003): Zeit für Zeitpolitik. Bremen: Atlantik Verlag.
Elchardus, M. (1988): »The Rediscovery of Chronos: The New Role of Time in Sociological Theory«. *International Sociology*, Vol. 3: 35-59.
Elias, N. (1992): *Time: an Essay*. Oxford and Cambridge (USA): Blackwell. (orig. in German 1984).
Elkind, D. (1981): *The Hurried Child. Growing up too fast, too soon*. Reading, MA.: Addison-Wesley.
Foucault, M. (1976): *Überwachen und Strafen. Die Geburt des Gefängnisses*. Frankfurt am Main: Suhrkamp.

Henckel, D. and Eberling, M. (eds) (2002): *Raumzeitpolitik*. Opladen: Leske + Budrich.

Hofmeister, S. and M. Spitzner (eds) (1999): *Zeitlandschaften. Perspektiven öko-sozialer Zeitpolitik*. Stuttgart: Hirzel.

Hungerland, B. (1999): »Childhood as a product of parental time management«. *Journal of Social Sciences*, Vol. 3: 65-71.

Galinsky, E. (1999): *Ask the Children. What American Children really Think about Working Parents*. New York: Williams, Morrow and Company.

Hochschild, A.R. (1997): *The Time Bind. When Work Becomes Home and Home Becomes Work*. New York: Metropolitan Books Henry Holt and Company.

Honig, M.-S. (1999): *Entwurf einer Theorie der Kindheit*. Frankfurt am Main: Suhrkamp.

Horkheimer, M. and T.W. Adorno (1947): *Dialektik der Aufklärung. Philosophische Fragmente*. Amsterdam: Querido Verlag.

Jahoda, M., P.F. Lazarsfeld and H. Zeisel (1971): *Marienthal: The Sociography of an Unemployed Community*. Chicago: Aldine and Atherton. (orig. in German 1933).

James, A. (2005): »Life times. Children's perspectives on age, agency and memory across the life course«. Qvortrup, J. (ed): *Studies in modern childhood. Society, Agency, Culture*. Basingstoke, UK and New York: Palgrave macmillan: 248-266.

Jurczyk, K. and M.S. Rerrich (eds) (1993): *Die Arbeit des Alltags. Beiträge zu einer Soziologie der alltäglichen Lebensführung*. Freiburg: Lambertus.

Kaufmann, F.-X. (1980): »Kinder als Außenseiter der Gesellschaft«. *Merkur*, Vol. 34: 761-771.

Linder, S.B. (1970): *The Harried Leisure Class*. New York: Columbia University Press.

Mückenberger, U. (2004): *Metronome des Alltags. Betriebliche Zeitpolitiken, lokale Effekte, soziale Regulierung*. Berlin: edition sigma.

Novotny, H. (1989): *Eigenzeit. Entstehung und Strukturierung eines Zeitgefühls*. Frankfurt am Main: Suhrkamp. (second edition).

Novotny, H. (1992): »Time and Social Theory. Towards a Social Theorie of Time«. *Time & Society*, Vol. 1: 421-454.

Olk, T. (2004): »Kinder und Kindheit im Wohlfahrtsstaat – eine vernachlässigte Kategorie?« *Zeitschrift für Sozialreform*, Vol. 50: 81-101.

Rinderspacher, J. (1985): Gesellschaft ohne Zeit. Individuelle Zeitverwendung und soziale Organisation der Arbeit. Frankfurt am Main and New York: Campus.

Rinderspacher, J. (ed) (2002): *Zeitwohlstand. Ein Konzept für einen anderen Wohlstand der Nation*. Berlin: edition sigma.

Vinz, D. (2005): *Zeiten der Nachhaltigkeit: Perspektiven für eine ökologische und geschlechtergerechte Zeitpolitik*. Münster: Westfälisches Dampfboot.

Zeiher, H. (2001): »Children's islands in space and time«. M. du Bois-Reymond, H. Sünker and H.-H. Krüger (eds): *Childhood in Europe*. New York: Peter Lang: 139-159.

Zeiher, H. (2003): »Shaping daily life in urban environments«. P. Christensen and M. O'Brien (eds): *Children in the City*. London and New York: Routledge Falmer: 66-81.

Zeiher, H. (2005a): »Neue Zeiten – neue Kindheiten? Wandel gesellschaftlicher Zeitbedingungen und die Folgen für Kinder«. A. Mischau and M. Oechsle (eds): *Arbeitszeit – Familienzeit – Lebenszeit: Verlieren wir die Balance?* Wiesbaden: Verlag für Sozialwissenschaften: 74-91.

Zeiher, H. (2005b): »Der Machtgewinn der Arbeitswelt über die Zeit der Kinder«. Hengst, H. and H. Zeiher (eds): *Kindheit soziologisch*. Wiesbaden: Verlag für Sozialwissenschaften: 201-226.

Zeiher, H.J. and H. Zeiher (1994): *Orte und Zeiten der Kinder. Soziales Leben von Großstadtkindern*. Weinheim and München: Juventa.

Zelizer, V.A. (1985): *Pricing the Priceless Child: the Changing Social Value of Children*. New York: Basic Books.

Notes

1. Time policy means to exert political influence on the temporal conditions of people's everyday lives such as the impact of prosesses on economy and transport, in family life and care and education institutions, in order to enhance people's time welfare. Since the 1990s, the consciousness of a need for time policy emerges increasingly in several European contries, including Italy, France and Germany (e.g. Belloni 1998; Deutsche Gesellschaft für Zeitpolitik 2003; Henckel and Eberling 2002; Hofmeister and Spitzner 1999; Mückenberger 2004; Vinz 2005; Rinderspacher 1985; 2002)

2. I refer readers to my own earlier studies (Zeiher 2001; 2003; Zeiher and Zeiher 1994) and those of other scholars (e.g. Christensen and James 2001; Christensen et al. 2000; Jurczyk and Rerrich 1993) for such an approach.

New Childhood Space and the Question of Difference

Harriet Strandell

Introduction

Though there has been much controversy around Philippe Ariès' (1962) argument and the evidence he raised for the discovery of childhood as a specific sentiment, most childhood and family historians reasonably agree that childhood in pre-industrial society was socially and spatially integrated into the rest of society to a considerably larger extent than what is the case in modern society.

In contrast to pre-modern society, modern childhood, as we have learned to know it, rests on an explicit spatial segregation: children are located in families, day care centres, schools, and playgrounds – particular childhood places which are clearly delineated and separated from the rest of society, both in a physical and in a social sense. In terms of social space, children are sited, insulated and distanced, and the boundaries of childhood space are legitimised through ideologies of care, protection and privacy (James et al. 1998: 37-38; Zeiher 2001). A morally and ideologically loaded spatial separation, in combination with the separation of 'proper' activities for children (play and learning) from those of adults (work), forms the basis for the specific age order of modern society. Childhood identity becomes fixed to certain places and activities.

The more or less taken for granted identification between childhood and place(s) has, however, become questioned in late modern society. Economic and cultural globalisation and increased mobility inside and between nations and cultures blur the boundaries between activities, places and age groups, forming increased cultural contacts and interchange as well as dissolving old and creating new divisions and interdependencies.

Information and communication technology decreases the significance of physical presence and weakens the connection between social and physical place, blurring the traditional notion of childhood as a separate sphere. Electronic media, then, changes the situational geography of social life and reorganises the social settings for interaction (see Heinz Hengst's chapter in this book). Globalisation and ICT multiply the flow of people, technology, ideologies, media images and information across boundaries, and detach experiences and orientations from the physical locations in which we live and work (Featherstone 1995: 93, 102).

With decreasing predictability on the basis of age, the question of children's proper place in society and of the relation between childhood and adulthood is becoming less self-evident. As Nick Lee (2001a) has noted, not only has the stability of the category of childhood diminished, but also the stability of adulthood. A 'standard' childhood has ceased to exist, and so also has a 'standard' adulthood. The destabilization of adulthood as the standard model undermines the childhood position as opposite to adulthood, resulting in a disturbance or even a breakdown of the generational order. In Zygmunt Bauman's (2000: 61-62) terms, life is becoming more open-ended and identity a constant becoming, »the sweet taste of 'freedom to become anybody'«, in which at the same time everything is up to the individual.

Childhood Theory and Difference

How has childhood research managed to meet the challenges, which have been posed to social theory and childhood theory in particular? Alan Prout (2005: 61-62) locates the beginnings of the sociology of childhood in the crisis of modernist social theory, in the midst of which it found itself presented with a double task: on one hand to create a space for childhood in sociology overall and on the other hand to deal with post-modern challenges to modern social theory.

Childhood research has had a long tradition of separating theorising about childhood from other branches of social theory and of treating childhood and adulthood as opposites, where childhood is everything adulthood is not. The belief in the separateness of childhood from adulthood was both a condition of and an effect of constituting childhood as a special sphere of study (ibid: 2005:35).

The 'developmental paradigm' – in psychology represented by developmental psychology and in sociology by socialisation theory – is the theoretical construction which has long underpinned the understanding of modern childhood and is the clearest expression of theoretical separation. Conceiving of childhood as a range of developmental stages, as preparation for adulthood, and of children as uncivilized, as not-yets are central to these theoretical constructions (Alanen 1988: 57-59).

The new social studies of childhood have addressed the relation between childhood and adulthood by seeing children rather as 'beings', as already being part of society, instead of treating them as individuals on their way to membership in society. Theorising children as 'beings' thus represents a first step in overcoming the theoretical separation of children and childhood from social theory. However, by redefining the status of childhood from becoming to being, the theoretical understanding has been turned the other way round, resulting in a mirror image of the developmental paradigm. Overcoming the understanding of childhood and adulthood as opposites and understanding childhood in terms of being appears to remain dependent on premises built into the developmental paradigm. Both childhood and adulthood are still treated as fixed and unitary categories, which are clearly separable from each other. The understanding continues to rely upon age-based determinism in order to deal with the dissolving and fragmenting tendencies in society which are calling for theoretical understanding.

The question of *difference*, both inside childhood and between childhood and other age groups, requires further elaboration. How should the question of difference in a society in which age seems at the same time to mean both less and more, be approached? Post-structural theorising seems on the one hand to downplay the meaning of age, age difference and predictability on the basis of age. On the other hand, we live in a society characterised by a heightened age consciousness. »The modern individual is highly conscious of his age; age consciousness is a central ingredient in modern time consciousness« (Julkunen 2003: 69). Like many other cultural categories, e.g. gender and ethnicity, age is not even thinkable other than in terms of difference, as similarities and contrasts. Age *is* difference.

Post-Structural Challenges to Childhood Theory

The aim of this chapter is to raise the question of age difference against the background of social change in late modern society. This will be done by discussing what childhood studies could learn from other branches of social theory, faced with similar theoretical challenges, and how they have managed to problematise difference, overcoming dualistic thinking and rigid assumptions about meaning. There are apparent parallels between the categories of gender and age as representations; like women, children also have been part of 'the others', defined as deviants from either the male or adult norm. In theorising ethnicity and migration, the parallels to childhood research become even more apparent: distant and unfamiliar cultures have not only represented 'the other', but also – like children – 'the undeveloped'. There are apparent parallels, then, between 'culture' and 'childhood' as systems of representation. The term *representation* refers to particular ways of conceiving of space and time that arise from social practices and then become a form of regulation of these practices (Harvey 1996: 212). Representations then have a particular relation to social practices.

It can be argued that both 'the other', when referring to migrants and refugees on one hand and children on the other hand, and 'development', when used in discussions of societies and cultures and then again when referring to childhood, are part of the same system of representations. It is valid to discuss childhood and ethnicity as parallels and to re-evaluate presumptions underlying 'the other' and 'development' in postcolonial discourse also in relation to childhood. Perhaps the 'othering' of childhood is not so different from other cultural forms of dividing people into 'us' and 'them' (Bauman 1990).

In order to do this, I will turn to poststructural sociological and anthropological theory. Among poststructural approaches, the postcolonial discourse (Bhabha 2000; Gupta and Ferguson 1997: 35) occupies a particular position when attempting to approach the question of identity and difference. Postcolonial discourse addresses the fixity in the ideological construction of 'otherness' as the sign of cultural, historical or racial difference. Postcolonialism intervenes in ideological discourses of modernity which attempt to give a hegemonic 'normality' to the differential, often disadvantaged, histories of nations, races, communities and peoples (Bhabha 2000: 66, 171).

Among the representations postcolonial discourse has intervenend in and critically revised, *'the other'* and *'development'* occupy a central position – constructions which have also acquired a central position in representations of childhood. The renewed interest in the application of postcolonial theorising to the dissolution of presumed connections between identity and place and to the location of culture and the ways in which culture is spatialised (Gupta and Ferguson 1997) is of particular interest when discussing connections between childhood and space. Critical re-evaluations of the meanings of difference in postcolonial discourse will be used in order to develop perspectives on what difference could possibly mean when we are discussing childhood and place. Before proceeding with this, however, I will in the next section establish the historical parallel between culture and childhood through representations of 'the other' and 'development'.

I will in this chapter lean against understandings in which postmodernism is rather regarded as an awareness and critique of modernity's assumptions than as a totally new epoch (Featherstone 1995; Bauman 1993). There is a temptation to become seduced by all the talk about change and dissolution penetrating every branch of society, to see fluidity over solidity, movement over settlement and instantaneity over sequence and duration. Some of the changes discussed in the chapter *are* relatively new and also profound, while others can rather be seen as a speeding up of processes, which have been already underway for a long time. And there are also tendencies in childhood, which point in the opposite direction, towards an increased separation of children's and adults' lives.

Identities arise in the intersection between existing systems and practices on the one hand, and the challenge that fluidity, movement and instantaneity pose to them on the other hand. Old and new practices coexist, making new combinations and comparisons possible. »In daily practice, nothing is replaced, it is merely overshadowed or altered by the imposition of the new« (Adam 2004: 120). In this chapter, the new will for analytical reasons be exaggerated and magnified.

Culture and Childhood as 'The Other'

How has the question of difference been dealt with in traditional representations of societies and cultures on the one hand and childhood on the other hand? What identity positions are created in these representations and what is their connection to place (culture) and age (childhood)?

There are apparent similarities between the construction of childhood as 'the other' and the Western notion of distant cultures as 'the other'. Western representations of 'the other' – represented by societies outside Europe – have been regarded as a prerequisite for the origin of the advanced, developed and industrial societies we have learned to know as the 'West'. The origin of the 'West' is, then, not to be understood as a result of an inner European process, but as the outcome of an experienced *difference* between 'us' and 'them', developed throughout centuries in Europe's contacts with societies and cultures outside Europe. The 'West' functions like an ideology, providing a standard model and criteria for evaluating other societies (Hall 1992b: 275-277). The concept of 'West', the meaning of which is virtually identical to 'modern', points to an idea and a historical construct rather than to a geographical construct or specific places (ibid).

The parallels between the Western construct of non-European cultures as 'the other' and the Western construction of childhood as 'the other' are apparent. In both, reference to distance, *separation*, experienced difference, mutual exclusiveness and to the ideological character of the construct is made. 'Othering' legitimates a cultural separation in space; 'they' are somewhere else, like children are in their childhood institutions.

The dichotomy typically built into the representation of 'the other' in colonial discourse can be found in representations of childhood as well. Like people from cultures different from ours, children have also been met with over-simplified conceptions of 'difference' and 'stereotypical dualism'. 'The other' is split into two opposing elements, the 'good' and the 'bad' (Hall 1992b: 280, 308). In the same way as the 'savage' in colonial discourse is represented as either 'noble' or 'ignoble', the 'child' of the Enlightenment has been pictured as 'innocent' or 'evil', 'angel' or 'devil' (James et al. 1998: 10-15; Meyrowitz 1985: 258-263). The 'innocent' child as pure, naturally good and uncorrupted, with needs, desires and even rights, corresponds to the 'innocent' and 'noble primitive' as the symbol for the natural, simple and uncorrupted life (James et al. 1998: 10-15; Marshall and Williams 1982; Hall 1991, 126-129). Both representations seem to fuel nostalgia and longing for a 'paradise lost'.

The 'evil' child conversely stands for the child in need of parental guidance and correction. Today the 'evil' child is found in the bad influence of peers and in discussions about whether young offenders should be protected or punished. 'Evil' stems from 'family breakdown' and 'the lack of adult control' (James et al. 1998: 11-12).

This picture corresponds to pictures of the 'savage' as 'hostile', 'brutal' and 'primitive' (Marshall and Williams 1982).

Through such *dichotomised* representations, a simplified conception of difference is constructed. Stereotyping is a main practice of attaching meaning to difference and of creating and upholding social and symbolic order. People are reduced to a few distinctive features which define their being, their essence. The Rest becomes defined as everything the West is not – its mirror image (Hall 1992b: 280, 308). This resembles how childhood in modernity has been understood as the opposite of adulthood, as being everything adulthood is not, or adult society's 'other'. The child became an instance of the Other, »a homologue for all such 'primitives' and a demonstration of the gulf that divided the 'civilized' from the 'uncivilized'« (Prout 2005: 46).

'Difference' is not only separation, it is *inferiority* as well. In the colonial discourse other cultures and peoples were not only 'different', they were also 'inferior'; they were seen as representing earlier stages of development. A central concern in social theory from the Enlightenment onwards was to seek to understand social relationships and state-society units in developmental terms. The development from traditional to modern societies was regarded as linear processes, which were assumed to have a universalising force. History was understood as having an inner logic and a direction understood as progress (Featherstone 1995: 87).

The similarities between the view of societies as progressing from lower to higher levels of development on the one hand, and modern constructions of childhood as a set of stages the child has to go through on the other hand, are quite apparent. Traditional developmental psychology is strongly built on presumptions about progress, linearity and universalism (Burman 1994: 48-51). Through the 'non-literate', the 'immature', the 'underdeveloped', 'the other', those who »need« to be represented by an outsider – all qualities that traditional anthropology has attached to 'primitive culture' (Clifford 1986: 113-115), childhood shares the fate of 'primitive culture', as it has been represented in Western discourse.

In this staging of societies and cultures, the American Indian for example has become the symbol of the underdeveloped, the »origin«. In their accounts of British conceptions of the world in the age of Enlightenment, Marshall and Williams (1982: 191) depict the American Indian as »men in an early stage of development, primitive Europeans in a sense«. »Rooted in their early stage of economic and social development, the Indians were classed by Locke alongside children, idiots and illiterates, in their inability to reason in abstract, speculative and comparative terms« (ibid.: 192). Could the parallel between (primitive) culture and childhood be more clearly drawn?

David Archard, on the other hand, connects the constructions of adulthood and the West: »First, his (Piaget's – H.S.) ideal of adult cognitive competence is a peculiarly Western philosophical one. The goal of cognitive development is an ability to think about the world with the concepts and principles of Western logic. In particular Piaget was concerned to understand how the adult human comes to acquire the Kantian categories of space, time and causality. If adult cognitive competence is conceived in this way, then there is no reason to think it conforms to the everyday abilities of even Western adults« (Archard 1993: 66).

Understood in this way, adulthood, as well as the binary construction of 'childhood' and 'adulthood' as opposites, does not in the first place refer to (biological) age, but to specific, historical and ideological forms of knowledge, attitudes and power. By removing Western assumptions, the meaning of age can consequently be reopened and de-stabilised.

Re-evaluating Difference

An increasing *sensitivity to differences* and a more positive evaluation of otherness and differences (but not necessarily a greater tolerance) has been regarded as one of the consequences of cultural globalisation, in combination with information and communication technology. It becomes more and more difficult to view 'them' through the long-distance lens implicit in such terms as 'the savage' or 'the native'. 'The other' seeks to speak back to 'us', and the margins move towards the centre (Featherstone 1995: 82-91). The child labour debate, in which Western standards for what constitutes a good childhood and Western solutions to the problem are increasingly questioned, represents a good example of how 'the other' speaks back.

One feature of modern life, which stands out as 'the difference which makes the difference', is the changing relationship between space and time (Bauman 2000: 8). One of its expressions is what has been called *time-space compression*: a compression of the time-space geography of the world, making it feel smaller and distances shorter, »so that events in one place impact immediately on people and places a very long distance away«. The world becomes »smaller«, distances shorter, boundaries are transcended and removed, and physical and social space is disconnected (Featherstone 1995: 93; Harvey 1989: 240-259; Hall 1992a: 300-301).

What happens then to separation and distance in space and in time – the main features in representations of childhood as 'the other'? These changes are closely intertwined with changes in the nature of space and time and in the relation between them, which will now be discussed.

Time and space are basic coordinates of all systems of representation. Different cultural epochs have had different ways of combining time-space coordinates. The rational ordering of space and time can be exemplified by the organisation of schools, hospitals and factories. Schools provide an ordered temporal passage from child to adult status, where curricula as spatial theories of development and timetables play a basic role and provide a model of 'cellular' discipline and control. The classroom is one of the most fundamental scripts for childhood. By rational ordering according to age, people of different ages and units of space overlap to a great extent (James et al. 1998: 41-45; Zeiher 2001; Gordon and Lahelma 2000).

Under the impact of modernisation and globalisation, the broken and fragmented time-space coordinates increasingly challenge the rational ordering of space and time in Western societies. Bauman (2000: 110-113) associates the beginning of the modern with the *emancipation of time from space*: time has increasingly become a factor of shortening or even eliminating distance. With the accelerating speed of movement and faster means of mobility, modern time has become more dynamic, flexible and expansive. There is, however, a natural limit to acceleration: when the time required for the movement is reduced to instantaneity it ceases to exist, eliminating duration, sequence and succession (ibid.; Adam 2004: 119-121). The global present comes into being: the capacity to partake in distant events as they are happening. Time, understood as linear, as duration, which presupposes that events take a certain time, is losing terrain, at the expense of time as instantaneity, as »moments about to be overtaken by the next moment« (Eriksen 2001: 123). As linear time is an important dimension of the faith in progress, the failure of linear time is accordingly part of the disappearing faith in progress (ibid.: 47).

Much of the 'instrumental rationality' which has been the operative principle of modern civilization has focused on designing ways to perform tasks faster, eliminating 'unproductive', idle, empty and thus wasted time (Bauman 2000: 113). This can be felt in all areas of modern life as a continuous increase of speed and acceleration, of performing tasks faster. Accelerating movement also means the enlargement of space, an experience shared not only by those travelling over long distances, but also in such everyday experiences as the daily commute to jobs and schools, and mass tourism to distant parts of the world. And we are all in our everyday life faced with what Thomas Hylland Eriksen (2001: 20, 76, 123, 150-153) terms an (unintended) »overproduction« of information, resulting from innovations in information and communication technology. Information technology removes distance, shortens time and fills the gaps with cascades of information, thus undermining linear time.

The weakening of temporality resulting from the altered relationship between time and space has far-reaching consequences for the status of childhood. Understanding childhood in developmental terms loses part of its ground as faith in linear progress from lower to higher levels of development weakens. The critique against understanding childhood as a series of more or less pre-determined developmental stages (see Morss 1996; Burman 1994) echoes the critique against modern social theory for its understanding of social relationships and state-society units in developmental terms. »It is this assumption of a destination for history, and of an inner logic of history which was understood as progress having a universalising force, which has been most strongly challenged by what have become known as postmodern theories« (Featherstone 1995:

87). Abandoning the notion of linear development and progress is, then, one of the cornerstones of postmodern understanding of historical time.

The »shrunken« time-space relationship thus hits at the core of the generational order of modern society and the distance in time between childhood and adulthood built into the developmental paradigm. Heinz Hengst (2003) addresses the changed preconditions for generational relations by using the concept *differential contemporariness*. The concept points to the shrinking »delay« of growing up in children's encounters with the world. The deregulation of generational order leads, according to Hengst, to the erosion of distinctive experience in the modern sense on the part of children. Children are first and foremost to be seen as contemporaries, which makes it difficult to identify them as a specific population group by their positioning in the generational order (ibid.). As 'immigrants' to a new (historical) age, children enter the present simultaneously with other people, regardless of age.

Contemporariness is connected to »presence«, present time. A feature characterising late modernity is that many things are brought to our reach at the same time, and with heightened intensity. To some extent, contemporaneity re-opens and even turns around the relation between childhood and adulthood in terms of competence, one of the cornerstones in the modern construction of childhood as a preparatory phase. In a world characterised by 'presence', children to a decreasing extent »grow into the culture« of adult society and take it over when they have grown up, as socialisation theory has taught us. The idealisation of everlasting youth, of innovation and trendiness, has reached previously unimaginable dimensions in our time.

The weakening of temporality also affects discourses about time use in everyday life. The concept of 'quality time', which has been much used in discussions about contemporary family life (Christensen 2002), would have been unthinkable in a society characterised by 'slow time'. One of the most pervasive discourses in later years has been about parents' 'lack of time' with their children. In the discourse, implicit comparisons are made to earlier times, when parents 'had time for their children'.

»The world is one place« has become something of a slogan in discussions of cultural globalisation. By stressing that the world is shrinking, theorists of cultural globalisation point to increasing contacts, cultural interchange and interdependencies inside and between nations and cultures. Flows of money, migrants, refugees, tourists, technology, financial information, goods, media images and information, ideologies and worldviews have the capacity to compress the time-space geography of the world. The boundaries of local cultures are seen to have become more permeable and difficult to maintain, with increased contact becoming unavoidable. More efficient and rapid means of communication have produced a higher density of interchanges (Appadurai 1997; Featherstone 1995: 86-93, 102).

Increased *mobility* in the world has raised questions about the relation between 'culture' and 'place'. Tendencies to equate 'culture' with 'place' have been criticised for treating space as naturally discontinuous, for territorialising national cultures and for separating cultures (Gupta and Ferguson 1997; Malkki 1997). Central to this critique is that cultures are not fixed in place and that all relations between place, people and culture are the results of historical and political processes. When Mike Featherstone (1995: 86) characterises interdependencies by arguing that »the flows of information, knowledge, money, commodities, people and images have intensified to the extent that the sense of spatial distance which separated and insulated people from the need to take into account all the other people which make up what has become known as humanity has become eroded«, we can almost imagine him talking about childhood: distance, spatial separation and insularisation are exactly the features which characterise modern institutionalised childhood.

While the consequences of electronic media for childhood have been discussed (see Meyrowitz 1985; Buckingham 2000), the idea of discussing childhood in relation to *migration* is perhaps less self-evident. The effects of mobility and migration on notions of home(lessness) and (up)rootedness have been a central theme in postcolonial discourse. Mobility and migration can be interpreted literally, as moving in or between countries or as living a transnational life. The concept of transnationalism refers to new kinds of migrant flows, to emergent migration processes in which people live lives across national borders (Basch et al. 1994).

However, the concepts of mobility, homelessness and uprootedness are not only restricted to migrants or refugees, who move very concretely between places. The concepts can be used also as metaphors to characterise globalised culture and life in contemporary society more generally. Liisa Malkki (1997: 52-53) speaks of a »generalized condition of homelessness« as characterising contemporary life everywhere (Edward Said in Malkki 1997: 53). Movement and migration have become fundamental to modern identity. Not only those who move are affected, but all of us: »Movement is the quintessence of how we – migrants and autochthones, tourists and locals, refugees and citizens, urbanites and ruralites – construct contemporary social experience and have it constructed for us« (Rapport and Dawson 1998: 24).

Play, Learning and Work 'on the Move'

In this section, I will examine some consequences for the generational order of the changed perspectives on time, space and movement discussed above. A cornerstone of the generational order of modern society is the progressive exclusion of children from working life and the placing of children in the physically and socially separate spheres of play and learning. Play and learning as proper childhood activities and work as an exclusive adult activity have become symbols of the opposition of adulthood and childhood in the modern. How are the spatial and temporal arrangements upholding modern relations between age groups effected by destabilising tendencies? What are the consequences for children's activities and places in particular? What follows are a few examples of ongoing discourses that are influencing the generational order. Relations between activity and place and time-space coordinates will be the primary focus.

Heinz Hengst (2001) has criticised childhood sociology for operating with fixed and oppositional categories of work and play and old assumptions about the place of work in society. According to him, the boundaries between play, learning and work have in contemporary society become blurred, and certain features of the activities have come to resemble each other. Aspects of playfulness are absorbed into work, and at the same time children's play has become serious business, which can less and less be thought of just as a preparatory activity.

Play and imagination

The identification of play and fantasy explicitly with childhood is strong in Western culture. In pedagogical theory play has been used as a pedagogical method for diagnosing children's developmental levels, and for controlling the child (Bernstein 1975: 117-121). When discussed in developmental terms, the serious business of dealing with the social order in their everyday life is easily hidden. Research conducted in day care centres (Corsaro 1985; Strandell 1997; Gulløv 2003) has unmasked complex social settings composed of activity and information flows, shifting social constellations and demands on time and space management, which is everyday life for many children. For the children this world is first and foremost »presence«, it demands dealing with social order here and now, rather than in a distant future. Underlining the fantasy of play is a much too narrow perspective for understanding the social challenges children have to meet in order to live in contemporary society.

On the other hand, new spaces arise in society which give room for and produce the stuff of playfulness and imagination – spaces which lack a clear connection to a specific age group. Discussions about the nature of the cultural sphere of contemporary society stress imagination as a constitutive feature of modern subjectivity. Electronic media provide new resources and new disciplines for the construction of imagined selves and imagined worlds. The cultural sphere offers a growing market for cultural and symbolic goods. »The culture of the consumer society is associated with play and hedonism, and an endless play with images, signs and symbols. Postmodernism is associated with »playful collaging of styles and traditions« (Daniel Bell in Featherstone 1995: 75-78).

Children's opportunities both to take part in and to represent themselves in this new play with images and signs are not in essence different from other age groups.

Children have extensive access to new electronic media (Suoranta and Lehtimäki 2004). That the opportunities for children to represent themselves had already increased with television has been given attention (Meyrowitz 1985: 243), and with the Internet these opportunities have multiplied. As Hengst has noted, children are less strangers in this world than adults and use media communication routinely as resources for play, conversation and social contact (Hengst 1987: 75; Suoranta and Lehtimäki 2004). Children are quick at 'reading' the signplay used, e.g. in playful advertising on TV or in communicative styles on the Internet.

Learning

New, informal learning environments have emerged, which compete with the school for children's time and engagement. *Informal learning* processes inside and outside educational institutions have acquired a new depth and quality in recent decades, which lends more and more importance to non-educational domains of everyday life (Hengst 2001: 15-16). The terms 'learning' and 'education' have been broadened in order to include new forms of knowledge acquisition. Learning can take place almost everywhere, in connection with many different types of activities, and is hardly distinguishable as a specific activity. In a society where we are flooded with information, learning is becoming an aspect of almost everything we occupy ourselves with, regardless of age (Bois-Reymond 2004: 189-193).

Information and communication technology has aquired a particular position as a new context for informal learning processes. One of many of the concepts developed in this context is 'mobile learning'. Mobile learning refers to the intersection of mobile computing and e-learning, or accessible resources wherever you are (Kynäslahti and Seppälä 2003: 55). When discussing whether mobile learning is a passing fad or serious pedagogy, Kynäslahti and Seppälä (ibid.: 51) distinguish between four properties of fads: their degree of novelty, the vigor and zeal with which they are embraced, the absence of longevity and low barriers of entry. With its strong references to 'fast time', mobile learning differs from more traditional and future-oriented school education.

Schools and other educational institutions are affected from the inside as well. Although the institutional context of learning in school imposes considerable restrictions to the dissolving of time-place coordinates, learning in school 'moves' as well. Individual curricula, flexitime, the increasing amount of group work and projects, freedom of choice and module-based study programmes are recent examples of dissolving tendencies. Eva Gulløv (2003: 24) shows that at least in some Danish day care centres there is considerable stress on children's choices and self-management, and a very special discourse on the child as an individual in modern society.

Work

The concept of work and what can be designated as work changes continuously, making the boundaries between work and other activities less distinct than before. In addition, the distinctions between sites for work and sites for learning are becoming more fluid. Work orientations and the meanings of work are becoming more pluralistic and complex (Hengst 2000).

A clear distinction between work and life outside work, or between working time and leisure time, was typical of industrial society, but is eroding in postindustrial society. Part of this phenomenon is the fragmentation of working hours and working commitment, and a growing need for flexible employees. Atypical working hours have spread and working has become more project oriented (Julkunen and Nätti 1999). In the service sector in particular there are many new types of jobs, which are part-time, seasonal, have irregular working hours and sometimes can be done anywhere and at any time. According to Richard Sennett (1998: 22-25, 30), 'no long term' has become the most tangible sign of new ways of organising working time, which corrodes trust, loyalty and mutual commitment. The capitalist economy is increasingly driven by continuous change, detachment and the short-term flexibility and flux produced by working in projects and networks.

The consequences of changes in working life for children's opportunities to participate in it have been discussed. Tendencies that are seen as creating instablity and unpredictability in working life (Sennett 1998: 16, 19) might increase children's opportunities in the labour market. They also give children's paid employment its distinctive character as short term and part-time; an in-between activity, in which children engage in the evenings, and on weekends and holidays, and which has to be adapted to school hours and school terms. Studies of children's participation in paid employment have revealed that the meanings of paid employment for children have changed profoundly since the days of early industrialisation. Paid employment is entering into new combinations with schoolwork, hobbies and other everyday activities (Mizen et al. 2001; Strandell 2003).

When discussing children's access to new physical and social space, it is difficult to make comparisons to a 'before'. At least part of the new social space which has been opened up for children simply did not exist before. It has emerged outside those activities which are referred to when discussing the modern childhood construction and the generational order, and it no longer fulfills the criteria that order rests upon. In addition to the emergence of new arenas for social action, old activities and arenas »move« and become displaced; their distinctive features become less pronounced, they become partly fused into other activities, and boundaries between activities become blurred.

Characteristic of many of the experiences of new spaces in children's lives is that their *reference to age is becoming blurred*. To various extents they have become 'ageless'.

Rather than entering into activities and spaces that they have been denied access to before, children, then, find themselves engaged in activities and spaces in which the reference to age is much less obvious than it used to be. To a growing extent they occupy spaces and activities in which they are not objects of adults' teaching, helping and controlling, and in which their social position is not basically different from that of adults. The equalisation or rapprochement of children's and adults' social positions has attracted attention as one of the outcomes of increasing age- and placelessness (Alanen et al. 2004: 195-201).

Electronic media, the erosion of a labour society and the rise of consumption as the main integrative force in society are to be held responsible for the growing similarities between play, learning and work. The growing similarities are one of the main arguments for the thesis of the liquidation of childhood, the *erosion of distinctive experience on the part of the children* (Hengst 1987, 2001).

Childhood as Difference

As discussed at the beginning of the chapter, childhood studies have had difficulty in discussing 'post', as reflected in increased mobility, fluidity, blurred boundaries and interdependencies in society, and in the development of social theory that these phenomena have given rise to. To move beyond fixed and binary categories and to deploy non-dualistic analytical resources, paying attention to the mixed, complex, impure, ambivalent, shifting, liquid and networked has been regarded as a growing challenge that social theory in general and childhood studies as part of it have to face in the future (Prout 2005: 59-67).

The dependency on dualistic concepts is reflected in the efforts made to make sense of the impact of social change on childhood. The change could be understood as resulting in a *homogenisation* of experiences between different age groups. In fact, a kind of homogenisation of experiences can be observed in the efforts to foresee what is happening or will happen in the future to childhood. The blurred reference to age has given rise to a considerable amount of public concern about the future of childhood and to predictions about the impending 'end' or 'death' of childhood, as the boundaries between childhood and adulthood become blurred, and childhood becomes 'invaded' by adulthood.

Neil Postman's (1982) account of the disrupting effects of television on childhood has been something of a symbol of the 'end of childhood' discourse. His conclusion is rather categorical: he relates childhood to print culture and anticipates the 'end of childhood' as print culture gives way to electronic media. Though Postman has been much criticised (see Buckingham 2000), the 'end of childhood' discourse lives strongly in public concern about the disastrous effects on children and childhood of new information and communication technology and other social phenomena, which dissolve the clear contrast between childhood and adulthood.

Nick Lee distinguishes in the new paradigm for social childhood research certain similarities to Postman's totalising view on childhood identities. »Though the new paradigm expresses rather different values from Postman, tending to celebrate, rather than lament, changing relations between adults and children, to some extent it also shares his 'revolutionary' model of social change« (Lee 2001b: 161). What both perspectives seem to have in common and what is important in this context is a rather homogenising view on childhood identities, or the possible identity positions of children. They also share a tendency to obliterate the childhood position in favour of the adult position, which is largely left untouched.

The post-structural and postcolonial discourse about the effects of cultural globalisation and the erosion of the division into 'us' and 'them' offers a slightly different approach to the question of homogenisation. The discourse tends to question whether the combination of increased mobility, cultural interchange and information and communication technology will have cultural homogenisation as its outcome. Rather than homogenising culture, globalisation creates »a *dialogical space* in which we can expect a good deal of disagreement, clashing of perspectives and conflict« (Featherstone 1995: 102). Instead of the homogenisation of experiences, cultural globalisation will, in this understanding, lead to greater diversity and increased sensitivity to differences, and to new spaces for the clash and mix of cultures, not only across the boundaries of nation-states, but within them too. People now draw on a wide range of cultural resources in the securing of their social identities (Featherstone 1995: 86-102; 1999; Appadurai 1997; Hall 1992a: 302-309; Hannerz in Rapport and Dawson 1998: 25).

Greater *diversity* and the expansion of dialogical space increases sensitivity to differences, among them differences *in* childhood. The fact that play, learning and work in late modern society have 'moved' in such a way that their reference to childhood versus adulthood has become more diffuse does not necessarily mean that age becomes emptied of meaning or neutralised. We live in a both-and society, which is at the same time highly age-conscious and permeated by conceptions about the meaning of age. Children themselves can be extremely aware of their own position on an age-scale and emphasise the importance of 'acting one's age' (Lallukka 2003). To a growing extent, age is defined as an individual act or choice instead of something taken for granted, which deepens age consciousness further (Julkunen 2003: 30). One of the resources for the collective 'work of imagination' in the cultural sphere discussed by Appadurai (1997: 1-16) could be thought of as playing with representations of age. Age representations can be combined in a multitude of ways, making it possible to act as both a child and adult at the same time.

On one hand, then, we have spaces and activities which are less age related than childhood space used to be, and on the other hand, a multitude of discourses in which age and age differences constitute an ingredient. The more age identities, under the influence of the global marketing of styles, places and images, become detached from specific times, places, histories and traditions (Hall 1992a: 306), the more cultural space there will be for trying out possible identities and for playing with differences. The field of possible identity positions has extended, opening up to possibilities of *combining* age identities. Today, children simply come into contact with a much larger spectrum of information, media images, cultures and worldviews than they used to only a few decades ago. All kinds of flows create dialogical spaces in which different and often contradictory ideas and images clash and mix to such an extent that there are no longer easy answers to what a person of a certain age should look like or how one should 'act one's age'.

Evidently all these changes and new ways of thinking do not enter children's everyday life unmoderated. They are filtered through social structures and practices, of which some are certainly resistant to new ideas and change only very slowly, if at all. Children still go to school, in buildings in which the time and space coordinates and the forms of social control have not changed much since the early days of the school institution; in part they are cemented already in the walls of the buildings. Institutional arrangements hold fast to the connection between age and place, contribute to keeping children 'in place' and resist change. New ideas and practices then do not replace old ones, but add to old ones and combine with them in various ways. The result is that there is simply more of everything. It is rather a question of both-and than of either-or.

The possibilities of combining elements from different time-space regimes and forms of social control give rise to *non-synchronous structures*, which can be compared to the multiplicity of involvements that transmigrants sustain in different places (Basch et al. 1994): elements stemming from different modes of thinking exist side by side in children's everyday life and combine in a multitude of more or less expected ways. Possible combinations of activities, places, forms of social control, and age-related experiences and acts are multiplied, giving rise to comparisons and to a necessity to process identity and difference. Non-synchronous structures existing side by side widen children's social experiences of and competencies in combining different time-space regimes and forms of social control.

Last, but not least: increasing mobility and uprootedness – both literal and symbolic – may result in a retreat from a felt threat of cultural disorder, a desire to return to some notion of 'home', to the familiar and safe (Featherstone 1995). A longing for the 'good old days' makes understandable why 'home', 'roots' and 'origin' seem to become so significant and emotionally loaded in our days – not least in contexts in which childhood is discussed. It is common to conceive of childhood as 'paradise lost'.

A sense of place and 'rootedness' increasingly become projects for reflection, social construction and nostalgia (Tuan 1980). In addition to longing for 'slow time', longing for 'home' in the unreflexive meaning of rootedness (ibid.) and worries about lacking social control can be identified in many public discourses in contemporary Western societies. Children's and their parents' (lack of) time together, parents' declining responsibility for controlling where, with whom and how their children spend their time, their TV watching habits and use of the Internet, and safety risks in public space are examples of dominant discourses in Western countries. The discourses can also be understood as reflecting a public concern for children who are seen to act too independently (James et al. 1998: 145-146).

Discussion

The aim of the chapter has been to examine difference in childhood research. Difference, as it is discussed here, refers neither to differences between children according to cultural or socio-economic backgrounds, gender or the like, nor even to age differences between children of a different age. The perspective is on childhood *as* difference, as a phenomenon, the boundaries of which have become more difficult to draw, as well as its relation to adulthood. Relations between age and place are becoming more diffuse.

The perspective on difference in childhood is an outcome of »odd« and somewhat unexpected uses of concepts such as mobility, migration, homelessness and uprootedness. These concepts are lifted out of the context of ethnicity and migration research, in which they are more routinely used, and introduced into discussions of childhood. The concepts are not used here to discuss real people's everyday reality, but instead understood as metaphors highlighting contemporary cultural and representational change, of which childhood is part, together with other social phenomena.

From metaphors, it is a long step to children's everyday life. It is evident that such representational change cannot have an unmediated impact on social practices in everyday life and that the connections are complex. However, discourses are not just ideas, they exert an influence on social practices as well. Metaphors structure our actions, they shape the ways in which we account for social action and provide us with strategic concepts to act with (James 1998: 139).

Representations manifest themselves mainly as discourses: the (postmodern) subject is conceptualised as being »formed and transformed continuously in relation to the ways we are represented or addressed in the cultural systems which surround us« (Hall 1992a: 277). All practices thus also include a discursive aspect. Hence, children must work with changed representations of childhood, age and difference. They cannot avoid running into new dialogical spaces, contradictory ideas and images, the mixing of cultures and representations, and non-synchronous time and space regimes. New ideas sometimes replace old ones, and sometimes just add to them giving rise to new combinations. There is a growing field of possible identity positions and choices, which presuppose reflexivity on the part of the children and also a degree of hardiness that enables them to live with uncertainty and unpredictability.

Late modern societies are *ambivalent* as to how much choice and freedom to make use of new opportunities children should be allowed. Children are quick to pick up new trends, ideas and technological innovations, to learn new things. On the other hand, a felt threat of cultural disorder is rather straightforwardly projected onto children and childhood in particular. The cultural destabilisation of childhood becomes easily translated into 'risk', which children should be protected from and prevented from encountering. The mix of emancipatory outcomes on one hand, and anxiety, uncertainty and unpredictability on the other hand, is met by likewise increasing demands on governing and controlling children (James and James 2005). What form that governing should take is a big question for late modern societies (see also Hanne Warming Nielsen's and Jan Kampmann's chapter and Anne Trine Kjørholt's and Vebjörg Tingstad's chapter in this book). Questions of social control have to be posed in new ways. A controversial situation has developed: how can children be controlled in spaces which are less age-specific and characterised by increasing mobility, blurred boundaries, flexibility and the enlargement of space?

References

Adam, B. (2004): *Time*. Cambridge: Polity Press.
Alanen, L. (1988): »Rethinking childhood«, *Acta Sociologica*, Vol. 31: 53-67.
Alanen, L., H. Sauli and H. Strandell (2004): »Children and childhood in a welfare state. The case of Finland«. A.-M. Jensen, Ben Arieh, A., Conti, C., Kutsar, D., Nic Ghiolla Phadraig, M. and Warming Nielsen, H. (eds): *Children's Welfare in Ageing Europe. Vol. 1*: Trondheim: Norwegian Centre for Child Research: 143-210.
Appadurai, A. (1997): *Modernity at Large. Cultural Dimensions of Globalization*. Minneapolis: University of Minnesota Press.
Archard, D. (1993): *Children: Rights and Childhood*. London: Routledge.
Ariès, P. (1962): *Centuries of Childhood: a Social History of Family Life*. London: Jonathan Cape.
Basch, L., N. Glick Schiller and C. Szanton Blan (1994): *Nations Unbound. Transnational Projects, Postcolonial Predicaments, and Deterritorialized Nation-States*. Basel: Gordon and Breach Publishers.
Bauman, Z. (1990): *Thinking Sociologically*. London: Blackwell.
Bauman, Z. (1993): *Postmodern Ethics*. Oxford: Blackwell.
Bauman, Z. (2000): *Liquid Modernity*. Cambridge: Polity Press.
Bernstein, B. (1975): *Class, Codes and Control, Vol. 3: Towards a Theory of Educational Transmissions*. London: Routledge & Kegan Paul.
Bhabha, H. (2000): *The Location of Culture*. London: Routledge.
Bois-Reymond, M. du (2004): »Youth – learning – Europe. Ménage a trois?« *Young* 12: 187-204.
Burman, E. (1994): *Deconstructing Developmental Psychology*. London: Routledge.

Buckingham, D. (2000): *After the Death of Childhood: Growing Up in the Age of Electronic Media.* Cambridge: Polity.

Christensen, P. (2002): »Why more 'Quality Time' is not on the top of children's lists«, *Children and Society*, Vol. 16: 1-12.

Clifford, J. (1986): »On ethnographic allegory«. J. Clifford and Marcus, G. E. (eds): *Writing Culture. The Poetics and Politics of Ethnography*. Berkeley: University of California Press: 98-121.

Corsaro, W. A. (1985): *Friendship and Peer Culture in the Early Years.* Norwood, NJ: Ablex Norwood.

Eriksen, T.H. (2001): *Tyranny of the Moment. Fast and Slow Time in the Information Age.* London: Pluto Press.

Featherstone, M. (1995): *Undoing Culture: Globalization, Postmodernism and Identity.* London: Sage.

Gordon, T., J. Holland and E. Lahelma (2000): *Making Spaces. Citizenship and Difference in Schools.* London: Macmillan Press.

Gulløv, E. (2003): »Creating a natural place for children. An ethnographic study of Danish kindergartens«. K.F. Olwig, and Gulløv, E. (eds): *Children's Places. Cross-Cultural Perspectives*. London: Routledge: 23-38.

Gupta, A. and J. Ferguson (1997): »Beyond 'culture': space, identity, and the politics of difference«. A. Gupta and Ferguson, J. (eds): *Culture, Power, Place. Explorations in Critical Anthropology*. Durham: Duke University Press: 33-51.

Hall, S. (1991): »Old and new identities«. A. King (ed): *Culture*. London: Sage.

Hall, S. (1992a): »The Question of cultural identity«. S. Hall, Held, D. and McGrew, D. (eds): *Modernity and its Futures*. Cambridge: Polity Press: 273-325.

Hall, S. (1992b): »The West and the Rest: Discourse and Power«. S. Hall and Gieben, B. (eds): *Formations of Modernity*. Cambridge: Polity Press: 275-320.

Harvey, D. (1989): *The Condition of Postmodernity. An Enquiry into the Origins of Cultural Change.* Oxford: Blackwell.

Harvey, D. (1996): *Justice, Nature & the Geography of Difference.* Oxford: Blackwell.

Hengst, H. (1987): »The liquidation of childhood. An objective tendency«. *International Journal of Sociology,* Vol. 17: 58-80.

Hengst, H. (2000): »Die Arbeit der Kinder und der Umbau der Arbeitsgesellschaft«. H. Hengst and Zeiher, H. (eds): *Die Arbeit der Kinder. Kindheitskonzept und Arbeitsteilung zwischen den Generationen*. Weinheim: Juventa: 71-97.

Hengst, H. (2001): »Rethinking the liquidation of childhood«. M. du Bois-Reymond, Sünker, H. and Krüger, H.-H. (eds): *Childhood in Europe. Approaches – Trends – Findings*. New York: Peter Lang: 13-41.

Hengst, H. (2003): »Childhood studies and differential contemporariness«. Paper presented at the *6th conference of the European Sociological Association*. Murcia, Spain, 23-26.9.2003.

James, A. (1998): »Imaging children 'at home', 'in the family' and 'at school': movement between the spatial and temporal markers of childhood identity in Britain«. N. Rapport and Dawson, A. (eds): *Migrants of Identity. Perceptions of Home in a World of Movement*. Oxford: Berg: 139-160.

James, A. and A. James (2005): »Changing perspectives, changing childhoods? Theorising the role of law in mediating the policy and practices of children's welfare«. Paper presented at the conference *Childhood 2005*, Oslo 29.6-3.7.2005.

James, A., C. Jenks and A. Prout (1998): *Theorizing Childhood*. Cambridge: Polity Press.

Julkunen, R. (2003): *Kuusikymmentä ja työssä*. Jyväskylä: SoPhi.

Julkunen, R. and J. Nätti (1999): *The Modernization of Working Times. Flexibility and Work Sharing in Finland*. Jyväskylä: SoPhi University of Jyväskylä.

Kynäslahti, H. and P. Seppälä (2003): »Mobile learning: Passing fad or pedagogy for the future?« H. Kynäslahti and Seppälä, P. (eds): *Mobile Learning*. Edita IT Press: 51-61.

Lallukka, K. (2003): *Lapsuusikä ja ikä lapsuudessa. Tutkimus 6-12 –vuotiaiden sosiokulttuurisesta ikätiedosta*. University of Jyväskylä: Jyväskylä studies in education, psychology and social reserach 215.

Lee, N. (2001a): *Childhood and Society*. Buckingham: Open University Press.

Lee, N. (2001b): »The extensions of childhood: Technologies, children and independence«. I. Hutchby and Moran-Ellis, J. (eds): *Children, Technology and Culture. The Impact of Technologies in Children's Everyday Lives*. London: Routledge Falmer: 153-169.

Malkki, L. (1997): »National geographic: The rooting of peoples and the terrotorialization of national identity among scolars and refugees«. A. Gupta and Ferguson, J. (eds): *Culture, Power, Place. Explorations in Critical Anthropology*. Durham: Duke University Press: 52-74.

Marshall, P.J. and G. Williams (1982): *The Great Map of Mankind. British Perceptions of the World in the Age of Enlightenment*. London: J. M. Dent & Sons Ltd.

Meyrowitz, J. (1985): *No Sense of Place*. New York: Oxford University Press.

Mizen, P., C. Pole and A. Bolton (2001): »Why be a school age worker?« P. Mizen, Pole, C. and Bolton, A. (eds): *Hidden Hands. International Perspectives on Children's Work and Labour*. London: Routledge Falmer: 37-54.

Morss, J.R. (1996): *Growing Critical. Alternatives to Developmental Psychology*. London: Routledge.

Postman, N. (1982): *The Disappearance of Childhood*. London: Allen.

Prout, A. (2005): *The Future of Childhood. Towards the Interdisciplinary Study of Children*. London: Routledge Falmer.

Rapport, N. and A. Dawson (1998b): »Home and movement: A polemic«. N. Rapport and Dawson, A. (eds): *Migrants of Identity. Perceptions of Home in a World of Movement*. Oxford: Berg: 19-38.

Sennett, R. (1998): *The Corrosion of Character: the Personal Consequences of Work in the New Capitalism*. New York: Norton.

Strandell, H. (2003): »'It's work that has to be done'. Children in working life«. Paper presented at the *6th Conference of the European Sociological Association*, Murcia, Spain, 23-26 September 2003.

Strandell, H. (1997): »Doing reality with play. Play as a children's resource in organizing everyday life in day-care centres«. *Childhood*, Vol. 4: 445-464.

Suoranta, J. and H. Lehtimäki (2004): *Children in the Information Society. The Case of Finland*. New York: Peter Lang.

Tuan, Y-F. (1980): »Rootedness versus sense of place«. *Landscape*, Vol. 24: 3-8.

Zeiher, H. (2001): »Children's islands in space and time: The impact of spatial differentiation on children's ways of shaping social life«. M. du Bois-Reymond, Sünker, H. and Krüger, H.-H. (eds): *Childhood in Europe. Approaches – Trends – Findings*. New York: Peter Lang: 139-159.

Time, Identity and Agency

Anna-Liisa Närvänen and Elisabet Näsman

The aim of this chapter is to scrutinize some of the ideas of post-modern society and to raise questions concerning both the conceptualizations on which these ideas are based and the empirical conclusions drawn. Our claim is that some of these ideas are erroneous due to their simplistic conceptualizations of time as well as of social identity. Furthermore, we suggest that there is a risk, due to the one-sided emphasis on processes of social change and discontinuity, that the *continuities of change* may be overlooked. We will also present conceptions that we see as more useful for analyses of time, identity and agency in present-day Europe. We will discuss the relatedness of the social meanings of time(s) to children's identities and agency in contemporary societies. We have chosen to illustrate this using social institutions that we consider to be still consequential in children's lives – institutions such as the life course, the social construction of the life phase childhood, and the material institutions of school and family.

Though ideas about contemporary society vary, some processes of social change are more commonly recognized, such as the pluralization of life worlds, the possibilities and choices in consumption, lifestyles, education, labour market and occupations. For example, childhood, and how it may be lived by children, changed remarkably during the end of the last century, particularly regarding performative arenas, consumption and lifestyles. Other changes as well, such as those in family structures, have had an impact on children's lives. Furthermore, with the advent of, for example, the Internet, children now have access to knowledge and activities that were earlier prohibited. Thus, in such contexts, we may talk about 'new' childhoods, offering a wide range of opportunities that impact on children's agency and identities. Yet, there is no general agreement on what consequences such social changes may have for social identities and life courses – or, indeed, whether we are witnessing a *new epoch*, post-modern society, or whether these changes are processes *within* modernity, forming instead a phase of late or high modernity.

When discussing modern society in contrast to post-modern society, Zygmunt Bauman writes somewhat suggestively: »From childhood through adolescence into mature age – this is how biography moved, never jumping stages either.« (1992: 165). He suggests that the modern type of biography-based, project-oriented identity no longer counts in post-modern society, which may also imply dissolution of the life course as an institution as well as of the social and cultural construction of the various life phases. The arrow of time, connecting past and future to the present in individual life plans, has lost its meaning, and what exists in post-modern society is the present present, the Jetztzeit. Continuity in life plans and in identities may only be reconstructed in retrospect, if at all (ibid.). Bauman, however, seems to be somewhat ambivalent as to whether or not there still exist what might be called identities. On the one hand, he refers to Giddens' discussion on self-identity in high modernity and, on the other, to Lyotard, who claims, in contrast to Giddens, that »there are no more identities, only transformations« (Bauman 1992: 184). Later on, Bauman questions the concept of identity in discussing the welfare state, consumerism and post-modern society (1998).

Anthony Giddens, in contrast to Bauman, stresses that contemporary changes are localized *within* modernity (1991). There is a »longue durée of institutions« (Giddens 1984). They give constraints that guide and limit action and that are consequential to social identities. Giddens argues that the past as well as the anticipated future is still important with regard to the trajectory of self, as well as »the cognitive awareness of the various phases of the life-span« (1991: 75). Also James A. Holstein and Jaber F. Gubrium, when discussing the social construction of the life course, its meanings and uses in everyday life, i.e. »how lives are organized in relation to time« (2000: 184), conclude that the »stage-like developmental model of the life course is, and will continue to be, the »reality of choice« for accomplishing organizational business just as it is our everyday preference for discerning the trajectories of our own lives« (2000: 213). The life course institution is a structure related to time, but also a typification that affects social identities and agency (Närvänen and Näsman 2004; forthcoming). In the following, we problematize these different views on time and present our choice of conceptualizations.

Multiple Times

One tendency in the social sciences has been to develop dualistic concepts of time, such as cyclical/linear, reversible/irreversible, repetition/change, social time/clock time and male time/female time. This kind of dualism also appears in Bauman's discussion on the jetztzeit in post-modernity, referring to the idea of different historical epochs, modern versus post-modern society (1992). The arrow of time, as he expresses it, between the past, present and future, i.e. the linear time conception of modernity, has lost its meaning.

These kinds of conceptions of time are deeply problematic, because they are too simplistic and thus deceptive and erroneous, overlooking as they do the multiplicity of time(s) and meanings of time(s) (Närvänen 1994; Adam 1995). Dualistic conceptions of time do not for example, recognize that repetition is progress, i.e. that cyclical time and linear time are not separable in reality (Elchardus 1988; Närvänen 1994; Adam 1995). As Barbara Adam argues: »cyclical processes by definition involve repetition with variation, linearity and progression« (1995: 38). She claims that seeing time and social life as reversible is impossible and thus an absurdity, being »no more possible than growing younger, ashes turning back into logs, the progression of a day moving from evening to midday, to morning« (1995: 35). Accordingly, »repetition and irreversibility are not separate or even separable concepts« (1995: 40). If it were the case, as Bauman claims (1992: 167), that the nomads of post-modern society, »hardly ever reach in their imagination beyond the next caravan-site« in their life itinerary, and that people in their lives are »always keeping options open« (1997: 88), all long-term planning for the future would not only be unnecessary, but unlikely or even impossible. Why are we still asking children what they want to be when they grow up? Why would a child engage in learning at school? Why would young persons invest a great deal of money and many years of studies in getting a degree if an occupational career no longer counts as a future-oriented project? Or, if Western standardized time no longer matters, how, for instance, is the organization of schools or public transportation possible? Also, in their exploration of young people's time perspectives, Julia Brannen and Ann Nilsen (2002) reveal sophisticated theoretical notions of time that do not reproduce dichotomies. They conclude that empirical work is needed to understand the various ways in which life may be planned: »We suggest there is considerable diversity in the ways in which young people conceptualize and consider their futures. This variation derives from young people's present perspectives as they relate to particular life-course phases and 'moments' which young people are in the process of negotiating, and the ways in which their expectations are shaped by their gender, ethnicity and educational and other resources, for example related to the social class of their families of origin« (2002: 520). While some young adults seem to live in the present, planning within the 'extended present', others do engage in long-term planning (2002). In contrast to, for example, Bauman's ideas about limited horizons of planning, thus living in the present, others, such as Anderson et al., claim that the evidence from their study »is better interpreted for large numbers of respondents in terms of a more linear and forward-looking approach«, planning their lives using long – even very long – time perspectives (2005: 146).

Bauman's dualism disregards how time is used, organized and understood in social reality; it fails to capture the complexities of time both in modern and in contemporary society. Adam rejects the dualistic idea that time in modern societies is irreversible and in pre-modern societies reversible. Her conclusion is that multiplicity of times characterizes both pre-modern and modern societies and, what is more, that the theoretical accounts of post-modern society disregard or even reject the importance of »the constitutive power of that totalizing and standardizing time« (1995: 157) when fragmentation and indeterminacy are emphasized. Such accounts have fallen back upon dualistic conceptualizations, and they not only lack empirical evidence, but »falsify the contemporary experience«, producing theory that is no longer »adequate to its subject matter« (1995: 156). In accordance with Adam, we suggest that this is a serious problem. Even though theories may never be able to capture and accurately mirror social reality in all its complexity, they should »be adequate to the reality they seek to encompass, explicate and constitute« (1995: 153). A conception of time should capture the multiple times and meanings of times, i.e. express how time is reckoned, experienced, understood, talked about and organized in any society or context. We will now present some interrelated key concepts that we feel may be useful, though not exhaustive, in discussing the multiple times and meanings of time in social reality. Firstly, we draw on Mark Elchardus' points about the concept *temporality*, which focuses on processes. The properties of temporality are, according to Elchardus, repetition and sequence (1988; Närvänen 1994; 2003:1). More technically formulated,

»the following two conditions must be simultaneously fulfilled:
- some, potentially unique, events must be constituted (classified) as, or taken to be, repetitions or equivalences (i.e. instances of a more general class of events); and
- these events must be sequentially ordered, at least by the elementary distinction between before and after.

A concept of time is a concept that expresses these properties and a temporal meaning is a dimension of meaning that interprets reality by using these properties« (Elchardus 1988: 45-46).

The definition also implicates timing, duration and rhythm.

This conceptualization encompasses the simultaneity of the cyclic aspect of time (recurrence) and the linear (succession). A calendar year, for example, recurs when we have passed through the previous year, sequenced in seasons, months and days, i.e. constituting a temporal order of what has been before and what is coming after, and yet it is not the same year, but a new year to come. Also, in everyday life, we talk about the life cycle of birth and death, the life course sequences of childhood, adulthood, etc., knowing that for each of us this cycle is unidirectional (Elchardus 1988; Närvänen 1994). It should also be noted that repetition should not be understood here in terms of recurrence of sameness. As Elchardus discusses, recurrence or repetition involves »relative« invariance« (1988: 46), which allows some change.

Social norms and regulations are linked to temporality. At school, for instance, the temporal organization and ordering of schedules, including timing, duration and rhythm of lectures and breaks, is also a normative order, communicated and interpreted, and thus has social meaning and is consequential to children's agency. As Elchardus notes, »the timing and the duration of an event will be part of the complex aspects on the basis of which the event will be interpreted, attributed to an actor and made into an act that calls for specific expectations and reactions« (1988: 52). There is, in other words, a right time or good time for action as well as a wrong or bad time (cf. Adam 1995). Norms define what is to be seen as on-time or off-time, and thus also what is judged as normal or as deviant based on temporality (Holstein and Gubrium 2000). Teen-age pregnancy, for example, may be regarded as an off-time for having a child in Western societies, while there are societies in which childbirth at the same age is conceived of as perfectly normal. This example also demonstrates the contextuality of timing.

An overall *temporal order* is the division into the past, present and future, i.e. into what has been, what is and what may be coming. Adam calls this »a *time-frame* within which we organize, plan and regulate our daily existence« (Adam 1995: 21, italics original), for example in terms of the sequencing of our lives or of history. The past, present and future, hence, also constitute a *temporal orientation* (Närvänen 1994; 2003:1). Consciousness of the time passing, of the irreversibility, unidirectionality and finitude of life-time, and of the expected future, has meaning for our plans, actions and interactions (ibid.; Adam 1995). The present, in terms of age and localization in the life course, and the anticipation of the expected future, as well as experiences in the past, may be a basis for deciding whether or not to have a child, whether to engage in education or work, etc.

It may be obvious, based on the above, that the recognition of temporality is important in understanding agency. This is in line with Mustafa Emirbayer and Ann Miche's temporal-relational conceptualization of agency »as a temporally embedded process of social engagement, informed by the past […] but also oriented toward the future […] and toward the present« (1998: 962). Agency, as understood here, is situational, but also relational, agency is »always agency *toward* something, by means of which actors enter into relationship with surrounding persons, places, meanings, and events […] agency entails actual interactions with its contexts« (1998: 973).[1] The past, present and the anticipated future are significant in our definitions of the situation and in our interpretation of opportunities and constraints for action (Närvänen 1994; 2003: 1). The past is significant for our present definitions of the situation in terms of, for example, »sedimentations of social order through the processes of institutionalization and socialization«, of traditions, habits, norms, laws, social hierarchies and social typifications, and also in terms of idiosyncratic biographical experiences (Närvänen 1994; 2003: 1 and 15). Every individual has a unique set of experiences, which may be part of his/her definition of how to act in the present, but, as George Herbert Mead asserted (1932), action is first and foremost future-oriented, i.e. our anticipation of the future is part of our actions in the present. The action is in the present, but it presupposes reflective interpretation and definition of the present situation, through use of experiences and knowledge from the past as well as through anticipation of the future, in terms of intentionality of the action, imagined possibilities, outcomes, purposes, desires, etc. (Närvänen 1994; 2001: 3; Närvänen and Näsman 2004). Returning to Bauman, if jetztzeit, the present present, is all there is, is action in these terms possible at all? We now turn to the issue of identity as related to temporality.

Social Identities and Temporality

In the theorizing about modernity versus post-modernity, identity too is conceptualized in terms of radical change. Robert G. Dunn recognizes several theoretical weaknesses in post-modernist and poststructuralist theories of identity that focus on self-identity, fragmentation and/or the power of discourses: »discussions of identity have been severely limited by lack of attention to the ways it is formed within a field of social relations and the processes governing interacting selves« (1998: 18), and, »The tendency to deprivilege or neglect the social processes of identity formation in favour of discursive effects is fairly widespread in contemporary theory« (1998: 32). Related to these problems is the problem of the subject and subjectivity. Some theoretical accounts seem to deny subjectivity and individuality, the subject no longer being »an individual but a fluid set of effects produced by processes of […] discourse« (1998: 65). This last remark also points to the problems of conceptualizing and understanding agency when using these approaches. When Bauman (1992; 1998) discusses issues of identity in post-modernity, he emphasizes ephemerality, fragility and even the threat of extinction of what may be called identity, in contrast to what appears as unitary and stable identities in modernity. Against such a position, Dunn has argued that the idea of unitary, stable identity in modernity has acquired »the character of myth« (1998: 53). Given the processes of pluralization of life worlds, institutional processes of differentiation, technological development, individualization, diversification and globalization, accompanied by other social changes *characteristic of modernity*, »the modern (European and American) individual, thus, was always implicated in a number of different projects of self-realization and change« (1998: 54). This suggests continuity of change, rather than disruption. Moreover, Giddens argues that the idea that there may no longer be anything that might be regarded or experienced as identities is exaggerated (Giddens 1991). Some empirical phenomena even show a tendency in the opposite direction. In Europe and the US, there have been growing social movements such as nationalism during the past decade, a revival of ethnic affiliation and loyalties and growing social movements claiming legitimacy for identity formation such as those associated with sexuality (cf. Dunn 1998). There has also been an increasing nostalgia, in terms of an interest in local history, autobiographies, heritage trails, family genealogies, etc., which all may be seen as ways to create identities – and continuity – through connecting past and present. There is an increasing interest and investment in celebrations of transitional events such as student graduations, anniversaries and weddings. All these examples may be interpreted as creating continuity in identities, some concerning continuity between biographical and historical time, others continuity across the life course (cf. Hockey and James 2003; Dunn 1998). Post-modern theorizing on identity seems to reject or neglect what might be identified as continuities between modernity and contemporary society.

Our raising of these critical comments is not to be interpreted as a total rejection of poststructuralist theories. Rather, we argue for the need to develop comprehensive theories of identity formation, encompassing both the significance of discourses and of the social processes involved in understanding the production and reproduction of identities. As a contribution to this and to theoretical frameworks concerning the relations between social identities, temporality and agency, we will now discuss some ideas about identity formation, focusing on social processes.

We consider identities as social and relational, emerging in interaction with others. They may be seen as both an individual enterprise of reflexivity and of social interaction and relatedness to others. It is through these interrelated, entangled processes that the individual defines and re-defines herself/himself and others across the life course (cf. Jenkins 1996). Social identities are also embodied: »Identities are brought into being through embodied action; they are recollected, enacted and imagined by people« (Hockey & James 2003: 205).

We do not understand the self as an inner entity, but rather as a continuous process of action, interaction and reflexivity. The self is situational, performed in activities and acts, and may be confirmed or rejected by others. If the definition of self is contested and rejected, the individual may in some circumstances reconstruct or modify her/his social identity, and vice versa, definitions of self that are confirmed may strengthen the identities enacted. This presupposes the capability to perceive oneself from another person's perspective, by seeing oneself through the eyes of the other, i.e. role taking. The self is then an object both to itself and others (Mead 1934), and it is this that makes the self a self, »that is, the reflexive capacity of self-consciousness« (Dunn 1998: 32). The self is both a subject and an object.

According to Richard Jenkins, the formation of identities, whether individual or collective, is to be understood in terms of an internal-external dialectic of identification. Jenkins defines self as »each individual's reflexive sense of her or his own particular identity, constituted vis-à-vis others in terms of similarity and difference, without which we would not know who we are and hence would not be able to act« (1996: 29). This means that identity formation is not a question of an individual's self-determination, but a dialectic relation between an individual's sense of her/his specific identity (internal identification) and of how others see and define her/him (external identification). Here the conceptualization clearly relates social identities and agency.

Social identities may be ascribed on the basis of social categorizations (such as gender, ethnicity, age, class, etc.) and social positions (child, student, parent, teacher, etc.), which constitute the basis for collective social identities. Social categorization is the external definition of collective social identities, while group identification, in terms of belonging or membership and/or through recognition or creation of similarity within the group and, thus, difference with respect to others, is the internal identification (cf. Jenkins 1996).

Jenkins differentiates between the nominal dimension of collective social identities, encompassing how the group or category is defined in discourse, and the virtual dimension that refers to how its members behave or are treated by others (1996: 87). This enables an analytic distinction between identity ascriptions in the form of discourses, how such ascriptions are defined, by whom, how they are mediated and interpreted, on the one hand, and the individual experiences of such ascriptions, on the other, which allows the stance-taking individual to relate to discourses, make choices, reflexively plan lines of action, etc.

Category-based identities may confirm an individual's sense of self, but they may also contest it in an upgrading or degrading way (Närvänen 2003: 1). This is then a question of an internal-external dialectic of identification. If the ascribed identity is contradictory to the definition of self, the individual may resist, oppose, or find other strategies, with the purpose of escaping such ascribed negative identities.

These issues are connected with issues of relative power, but also with the meaning of context. Whose definitions of social identities count in what contexts and under what circumstances? Can such definitions be contested and, if so, by using what strategies? Social institutions and organizations, for example the family or the school, are sources of social identities through varyingly predefined positions, social hierarchies and activities, but they may vary in their capacity to influence an individual's identities (Närvänen 2003: 1; Jenkins 1996; Goffman 1961). Because identities emerge, are produced, reproduced and changed through social relationships in various contexts, power and agency need to be studied in everyday interactions and in various contexts. There are, for example, several discourses on the age-related life phase childhood, picturing and ascribing typical social identities to persons occupying this life phase. Such discourses, however, do not determine behaviour, but rather, children may reflexively relate to such ascriptions. They may also use such discourses for their own purposes, for example in a strategy to escape demands from adults, to create a scope of action or to justify a questionable action by legitimating behaviour as typical of their age and thus not to be worried about, while knowing that such behaviour is actually not accepted (cf., Raby 2002; Näsman and von Gerber 2003; Närvänen amd Näsman 2004).

Temporal orientation is inherent in this conceptualization of the self and social identities. Reflexivity presupposes consciousness, retrospection and projectivity:

»As consciousness alternates between action […] and reflection […], a self emerges from the dynamic interplay of present, past, and future. Looking backwards at past events, the self has a biographical history, but the 'facts' are subject to (re)interpretation from the standpoint of the present. Looking forward to goals and purposes of one kind or another, the self constructs a line of action in the present by anticipating, and thereby bringing into being just those events which seem to call for an intended response. Far from being the static and structural entity, that is so often depicted, the self is more accurately understood as a momentary stance toward past and future events« (Flaherty and Fine 2001:157).

This account can obviously be related to the temporal-relational conceptualization of agency we referred to above, highlighting relations between the self, social identities and agency. »Who am I?« is a question posed concerning identity, »How will I act in this situation as the person I am and as the person others think I am, given my past experiences, and given what I want and wish to happen in the future?« is a question connecting agency and social identities. What does this mean in childhood? Because the family and educational settings are the contexts in which children live most of their lives, we will focus, in the following sections, on how the social meanings of time are mediated to children at home and at school in relation to children's agency, but as we agree with Allison James and Alan Prout (1997) in their claim that children's experiences of time must be understood while acknowledging the meanings of age and life course, we will first discuss these time-related concepts (Närvänen 2004).

Social Meanings of Age and Life Course as Time-Related Concepts

Childhood is an age-based phenomenon and 'child' an age-based social position. Age has, however, no inherent meaning. It's meaning is socially constructed. Age may be understood as individual biographical time, encompassing chronological and biological age. Age is also a structural concept (ibid.). In other words, age is an individual experience of time passing and life changing, relating individual time to historical, on the one hand, and a social structure, comparable to other structures, on the other. As a structure, age is institutionalized in the life course institution, consisting of interrelated, age-based, socially and culturally constructed sequences of life phases. The life course is, in other words, a temporal periodization of life-time, a structuring of the life-time (Närvänen 2004; Närvänen and Näsman, forthcoming). The life course structuring is both an ongoing process and a product of various processes, such as powerful professional discourses on stage-like development and maturity, and political, ideological and economic discourses (Närvänen and Näsman, forthcoming). In everyday life, the life phases work as typifications in understanding and structuring life, relating oneself and others to time, assessing the past, present and future and in guiding action (Holstein and Gubrium 2000; Närvänen and Näsman 2004). Age and position in the life course constitute a possible basis for social categorization and ascription of category-based social identities »through which people define and identify individuals and groups within society« (Pilcher 1995: 1). This concerns, for example, what a child is and what is or is not expected of a child at a certain age. Such understandings may form more or less taken-for-granted knowledge, in interaction with children, at the same time as such understandings mediate how childhood is understood and define what is expected, approved or rejected as correct or appropriate behaviour: »age or life course location can provide the basis for interpreting a person's behaviour as seriously »inappropriate« and hence, psychologically unhealthy«, or deviant (Holstein and Gubrium 2000: 80).

Age is a social position vis-à-vis others and should be understood in terms of status differences and differences in relative power or powerlessness. There is an age order (analogous to gender order), i.e. a social hierarchy of age categories and life phases, in which these are ascribed different social status in relation to one another (Närvänen and Näsman 2004). Age and the localization in the life course structure constitute one basis on which rights, obligations and responsibilities are distributed in a society and thus also a basis for inclusion and exclusion with regard to activities, resources, places, etc. There is an institutionalized separateness of childhood, i.e. an »increasing division between the world of the child and the world of the adult« (Pilcher 1995: 39, Närvänen and Näsman forthcoming). »For children, the power of calendrical time to restrict their access to social space is a daily experience« (Hockey and James 1993: 162). Such asymmetrical power relations can be discussed in terms of the ideological dominance of adulthood with regard to other life phases, such as old age, youth and childhood (Hockey and James 1993). We may understand the 'aged' order of time-place-activity patterns in terms of power relations and as part of a process of age-based typifications comparable to the idea of separateness due to gender (Hirdman 1990). Because age may be related to other 'orders' such as gender, class, ethnicity and disability, there are various childhoods, for instance in the sense that social definitions of a child, of the life phase childhood and ideas about processes of growing up may vary depending on such categorizations.

Age and the position in the life course are consequential to agency (cf. Närvänen and Näsman 2004). This point is emphasized by James and Prout: »Age fixes the limits and boundaries to western conceptions of childhood and, although these limits are largely context specific and may vary, 'age' nevertheless exerts a powerful and constraining force on daily activities of children« (James and Prout 1997: 232 f.). Children's lives are regulated by formal and informal age-related regulations and norms to an ever increasing extent, pointing out the significance of specific ages in childhood and in children's relations to others (Närvänen and Näsman 2004; forthcoming). Chronological age is used as a basis for permitting or prohibiting certain activities and access to certain places, and it also shapes »age relationships, empowering some individuals and disempowering others« (Pilcher 1995: 118).

The age-based ascriptions of identities and appropriate behaviour may shape children's sense of selfhood. Children are defined, for example, in terms of difference, i.e. what they are not as compared to adults regarding such things as competencies and capacities (Hockey and James 2003; Näsman and von Gerber 2003). That their age has specific meanings for children is obvious also in children's accounts of their chronological age, which are most often expressed very exactly, in years, months and even weeks (Hockey and James 1993: 162). »I am eight years and seven months old« is a kind of answer showing that age indeed matters in childhood, as adults would not express their age with such accuracy.

Children may contest the age-based ascriptions by referring to examples of incompetence among adults, but also accept the ascribed identity of human becomings as part of their own understanding of who they are and what the social meaning of a child position is. Children may describe childhood as a stepwise development of competences by age and experience, and thereby themselves delimit their scope of agency (Näsman and von Gerber 1996; 2003). Ageing in childhood may be seen as an identity career in an age-based hierarchy.

Age, then, has social meanings on several levels. There is, however, a dialectic relationship between structure, culture and agency (Närvänen and Näsman 2004). The meanings of age and localization in the life course are mediated through structural aspects such as age categories, age-related formal regulations, life-phase-directed welfare policies and state interventions, and at the same time mediated and produced through interaction and social practices in everyday life (ibid.). In the following, we will exemplify an application of our theorizing about time in a discussion on family and school mediation of the social meanings and conceptualizations of time (age) to children. Naturally, this issue is in itself part of the age ordering, because how and at which age mediation takes place may be based on social and cultural understandings (discourses) of age and ageing in terms of, for example, development of cognitive capabilities, maturity and/or psychological needs.

Mediating Meanings of Time and Children's Family-Time

James and Prout note that »it is during childhood […] that time and perceptions of time have perhaps the greatest social significance« (1997: 231). Because time has no inherent meaning, social meanings of time are mediated by various actors and in various contexts and 'learned' successively while growing up. As Adam has written,

»The dominant approach to time, the way time is conceptualised, related to and used, tends to be established during childhood« (1995: 7). Institutions, such as the family and the school, are important arenas in which the social meanings of, for example, time, and thus also of what it is to be a child, are mediated. This encompasses, for example, the temporal organization of time in everyday life, duration, rhythms and timing of activities and the interrelatedness and synchronization of family members' activities. It encompasses furthermore social meanings of time in relation to life phases and ages, such as the meanings of childhood or adulthood discussed above. In fact, such meanings are interrelated. The temporal order can be conceived of as related to temporal orientation: The future-oriented discourse of childhood and the discourse of parenthood and childhood in the family institution imply that parents have the obligation to socialize their children into successively understanding and acting in accordance with the temporal order. The normative aspects of timing mean that a child's ability to enact the time demands constitutes good behaviour (normality) and indicates a competent parent, while a child staying up late or a teenager not coming home at the agreed-upon hour are seen as indicating deviance and lax parenting. Another aspect of this is the idea of children's vulnerability to a lack of time order. The understanding of a good family environment for children's successful development includes the idea of regularity and routine, i.e. a repetitive activity pattern in the family, creating continuity, stability and security. Flexibility and a temporal scope of action are seen as endangering the development of a child. Time discipline is thus seen both as nurturing and healthy. Such hegemonic discourses on childhood still work within families, between children and parents as well as in society at large, creating continuity in how childhood is constructed, produced and reproduced, and how it may successively be changing, thus creating continuity in time conceptions (Närvänen and Näsman 2004).

Temporal order is mediated in the family, through the rhythms of everyday life, with reference to activities and cultural norms and understandings associated with them. The Western standardized time is one part of the temporal order mediated in the family. Time, however, may not in the first place be talked about and explained to very young children in terms of clock-time, but rather in terms of activities such as play-time, dinner-time, bath-time, after-lunch-nap-time or bed-time. Likewise, the disciplining of young children in terms of hurrying and getting finished will not be effectively done through arguments concerning clock-time and minutes passing. Specific dates and the standardized clock-time may be seen as irrelevant and even incomprehensible to young children, just as concepts related to linearity of time, such as being late and hurrying, may be hard for young children to understand (Jacoby and Näsman 1989). Successively, this kind of structuring of time and talking about time is complemented by standardized clock-time also within family life, for example by defining appropriate bed-time on school nights as nine o'clock in the evening, but on

Fridays and Saturdays as eleven o'clock. The child also comes to understand that time schedules in the family vary by age. A child goes to bed earlier than his/her parents, a young child earlier than an older sibling. Getting older in childhood means that temporal norms in the family change and become more similar to those of the adults. 'Learning about time' is more than gaining knowledge of clock-time and calendar-time. Children's lives are regulated by both informal and formal age-related norms, which mediate children's position vis-à-vis others. Such norms are not only about time, but also about location in the life course and social identities. Social identities, based on age categories, and mediating age order, are inherent in 'learning' the social meanings of time.

A specific aspect of social meanings of time is timing, which we discuss in relation to temporal orientation and order. The hegemonic future-oriented discourse on childhood as stage-like development and maturity implies norms about being on-time, for example with respect to chronological age. Timing can refer to doing things at the appropriate time, appropriate age in a specific context as well as to, for example, synchronizing activities and taking others' time into account. There is, for example, a need to synchronize time in families: parents' working hours, child-care hours, school-time and time for leisure activities, i.e. a need for periodization of time at various places and in periods of transport between these places, as well as a need for coordination of the family members' various times. There is, in other words, a jigsaw puzzle of time in family life and a 'time bind' within the family (cf. Jacoby and Näsman 1989: 105; Hochschild 1997). The family comes to be linked to other organizations with their respective temporal order and demands on the time family members spend at home, such as spill-over from the parents' work or children's homework (Jacoby and Näsman 1989: 272). Children's school-time and organized leisure activities, for instance, create a rhythm and, thus, temporal pattern of synchronization, dependence and waiting, for both themselves and their parents (Lareau 2000). The degree of fitness between these time patterns and norms and the degree of flexibility when the timing in the jigsaw puzzle for some reason breaks down varies, for instance, as a function of working life conditions related to the gendering and social class hierarchy of the labour market (Jacoby and Näsman 1989: 124, Näsman 1997). Here, the power dimension involves a combination of the relation parent/adult versus child and the child-related adult position as parent versus that of a paid worker.

One consequence of the time bind between family members, for example, is that there may be a need to negotiate whose time schedule counts in the family. An example of such a time bind and its consequences is given by Allison James, Chris Jenks and Alan Prout, who show the limited control young people have over their leisure time, due to the structuring of their time at school and due to »the temporal rhythms of the household« (2001: 76), which make it difficult to develop friendship, as friendship and »trust takes time to develop, time together« (2001: 77). The time coordination involved in the sharing of a child's time by separated parents highlights children's lack of control of their own agenda. Power relations may then be enacted through parental regulation of children's activities in time and space, which also marks the social position of children in relation to parents: »Children get to know their 'age' and place through being allowed access to certain times and spaces« (Hockey and James 2003: 173). The child position, in relation to parents and other adults, may mean relative powerlessness, as adults operate and control children's time and »define whether children are 'too young' or 'too old' to engage in certain activities or behave in certain ways« (Pilcher 1995: 46), i.e. whether or not the timing of their activities and behaviour is to be seen as age appropriate.

This, however, is not to say that children are totally powerless in relation to parents or other adults. Parents may choose their workplace and plan their working hours with the children's times in focus (Jacoby and Näsman 1989), and in families where children are engaged in several organized leisure activities, children's time may dominate the overall planning of the family's temporal organization (Lareau 2000). Formal regulations as well as informal norms about the age at which children may be left alone at home, have access to public places, or whether or not children should take part in organized leisure activities, and then on their own or accompanied by a parent, may be a basis for children's influence on parents' time irrespective of the children's own actions, but children may also in some situations be successful in negotiating time and space.

Jenni Harden's study (2000) on children, risk and safety demonstrates children's capacity to negotiate with their parents to overcome restrictions on access to various public places, but also an array of other strategies, such as information control or breaking the rules. The transfer from one context of adult surveillance to another may open a scope of action of this kind, if it means a gap in adult control. This calls for a discussion of children's agency within the family and in relation to parents.

As mentioned, we see agency as a temporally embedded process (Emirbayer and Miche 1998). Agency is about being able to make choices and influence the present situation, by interpreting the situation, opportunities, constraints and resources at hand. Knowledge and past experiences are used in reflection over this. Whether or not and how to act also involve anticipation of the future, i.e. the anticipated consequences of an act or of not acting. Because agency presupposes time for acquiring knowledge and gaining experiences as the basis for reflexivity, interpretation and action, it is obvious that age makes a difference with regard to children's agency. Young children's agency is, consequentially, limited, and they may be more easily persuaded or even forced by parents. The scope of agency, as conceptualized above, increases successively with experience and knowledge, strengthening, for example, children's abilities to negotiate with adults. Anne Solberg's research on ten year old children shows how children quite successfully negotiate with their parents about time spent at home after school without parental supervision as well as about age-related activities, i.e. what may be expected of a ten year old child. According to Solberg, children of this age »are in a position to influence the outcome of the negotiating process in directions which they perceive to be favourable to them« (1997: 127).

Solberg argues that children also may modify parents' prior conceptions of age and what childhood means by negotiating age-related activities (ibid.) This could be interpreted as children 'doing being older' by displaying independence and capability in managing afternoon hours at home on their own. They are influencing not only access to time of their own and access to space, but also how their parents perceive them (cf. Närvänen and Näsman 2004). Solberg suggests that the children whose mothers were full-time housewives were probably acting in a more childish manner than were the children in her study, which also supports our interpretation of these children 'doing being older', i.e. acting older, in an accountable way, than their chronological age would suggest: »When parents of the new 'homestayers' see their children carry out the responsibilities placed upon them, they experience their children to be 'growing' older socially with respect to their biological 'age'« (1997: 141).

Mediating Meanings of Time and Children's School-Time

In comparison with the family, the education system may be an equally important or even more important institution with regard to mediating social meanings of standardized time, but also meanings of the position as a child. During childhood, a great deal of time is spent within the education system, and the school explicitly or implicitly mediates meanings of time through educational practices, even though these meanings first and foremost may be seen as »a part of the hidden curriculum of education« (Adam 1995: 59). The school and its educational practices define children as different from adults in many respects, thereby also defining what it is to be a child in relation to others, such as younger children, older children, or to youth, ascribing age-category-based social identities. Children are, »defined through their bodies, bodies which are seen to develop and mature in relation to externally derived conceptions of their social, intellectual, physical and moral competencies« (Christensen, James and Jenks 2001:203). We discuss children's time both in relation to the temporal organization at school and the temporal orientation implicit in educational practices.

The temporal ordering and organization of activities by clock-time and the social meanings inherent in it are mediated in several ways: educational practices, structuring of school work through scheduled times and locations for lectures, breaks, lunch-time etc., ordering in years and stages, scheduling and quantifying of school work as topics and courses, use of achievement tests and so on (Adam 1995). The structuring of school work through timetables, schedules, clocks and calendars mediates the »universalized, decontextualized and quantitative time« (ibid.: 61) that »gets habituated during childhood« (ibid.: 64). The structuring of school work communicates to children an understanding of time as a finite resource, and thus something that should be used efficiently. They see that time is allocated to various activities and may be managed and exchanged, that there is such a thing as a deadline with regard to access to time for activities, and that time may be controlled. In other words, time is seen as a material commodity: »through a temporal disciplining of the body in the everyday social practices of the classroom – a discipline wrought upon the body by the self or by others – time becomes understood by children as a commodity which is subject to an exchange relationship based on both discipline and/or liberation« (Christensen, James and Jenks 2001: 203).

The temporal organization and structuring of children's time at school encompasses time-related norms such as punctuality, but also norms of appropriate behaviour at school in its various locations and with respect to teachers, including the expectation of norm conformity (Närvänen 2003: 1; Bergström and Holm 2005). Deviating from such expectations may be punished by teachers and also used as a basis for a definition of the child as problematic. Consequently, the structuring of school work constitutes mediating power relations. Disciplinary power is inherent in this temporal and spatial organization of school work and operates through it, subjecting both children and their teachers to time control. Yet children also learn that there are social hierarchies and differences between positions, such as the asymmetrical power relation between teachers and children. Teachers may follow the scheduling at school, but it is the children's achievements that are assessed and evaluated in a time-related way. It is their speed of achievement that is measured, for instance when teachers arrange time-based school work competitions in the classroom, set time limits for examination or evaluate children according to age-related standards. Teachers control children's presence, behaviour at school and progression in achievement, which is followed by decisions about and distribution of punishments and rewards to children, some of which are time-based (Närvänen 2003: 1; Christensen and James 2001; Adam 1995). Denying children their free-time (play-time) if they have been 'misbehaving' or extending their school day with extra detention hours are examples of temporal sanctions (Christensen and James 2001).

There are also differences between staff and children with respect to opportunities and constraints, i.e., differences in agency (ibid.; cf. Närvänen 2003: 1; James, Jenks and Prout 2001). As some studies show, children experience that they have little control or choice concerning time at school (Christensen and James 2001). The temporal and spatial organization of the school work sets limits for what children are allowed to do at school, as it highly determines not only the activities but also their duration and location. The temporal and spatial organization, consequently, controls and delimits children's interactions and relations with one another (Närvänen 2003: 1;

James, Jenks and Prout 2001). Even when a school officially aims at offering children a range of choices in terms of time and place at school, this choice may end up being conditioned by the children's conformity to norms of behaviour and achievement (Bergström and Holm 2005)

Research that focuses excessively or unilaterally on the spatial and temporal mechanisms of disciplinary power may, however, as Sarah Holloway and Gill Valentine point out, run the risk of paying far too little attention to children's agency (2000). Children may question, oppose and negotiate the formal organization of time and space and the power embedded in it, and they do not always use spaces in the ways intended by adults (Philo 2000; Bergström and Holm 2005) and, hence, do not submit entirely to the temporal order (Närvänen 2003: 1). Playing hooky, being late to class in the mornings or after breaks, finding reasons to leave the classroom during lessons may be used to create some free-time. Deviating from the teacher-initiated activity during school hours constitutes making time one's own. The break-time at school may also be used to escape supervision, creating free zones or group territories, which are part of children's agency and of importance for their relations with one another and their opportunities to form and confirm social identities other than the identities ascribed by the school staff (ibid.).

As shown above, the temporal ordering and organization of school work and the disciplinary power inherent in it concern understanding the multiple times – and the multiple meanings of time – and how these may be related to agency and social identities. In the following, we add to this the mediation of temporal orientation in the education system.

The school is a future-oriented institution and a future-oriented setting in which »the past and present take a special meaning in terms of what they might indicate about forthcoming behaviour« (Holstein and Gubrium 2000: 84). Key concepts used within the education system, such as teaching, learning, assessment, student records or profiles, achievements etc., are concepts of temporal orientation, invoking the past, present and future (Adam 1995). Records are kept and used to assess a child's present performance in light of past performances, and children's performances, assessed and interpreted by teachers, constitute a basis for judgements about their future achievements, the present thus being temporally extended, encompassing the past as well as the anticipated future (ibid.). As Holstein and Gubrium claim, »From the very first days, then, children are 'constructed', their pasts typified and their futures tracked« as »teachers and other school personnel categorize students and project their futures in the organization with regard to the working interpretive contingencies of schooling« (2000: 100). An important basis for interpreting children's performances are lay and professional theories about children and what may be expected of them in terms of development of maturity and competence in relation to age, pointing out development towards greater maturity, responsibility and rationality (ibid.; Christensen, Jenks and

Prout 2001; Näsman and von Gerber 2003). Such theories have been incorporated »into educational practices as unquestioned and unquestionable 'fact'« (Adam 1995: 68), which encompasses conceptualization of the child in terms of stage-like progress in capabilities and competencies related to age and, thus, to the body (cf. Christensen, James and Jenks 2001). Curricula are based on »assumptions about a 'right age', a pre-existing 'appropriate base' upon which to build, and about proper sequencing« (Adam 1995: 68), as part of the underlying discourse of stage-like development and the social significance of norms related to time. The evaluation of children's achievements according to criteria for what they should have learnt given a certain period of time encompass time-related norms concerning both duration and age. Children are seen as 'on-time' or 'off-time' in relation to the discourse of development. It is through this powerful discourse that children are defined as human becomings, rather than beings and, thus, as 'naturally' deficient compared to adults. The everyday typifications of children related to specific ages and life phases offer a basis for how to approach, interpret and judge children in terms of normality or deviance in relation to the past and to the anticipated future (Holstein and Gubrium 2000).

»The entrenched status of such developmental models is nowhere better witnessed than in the everyday interactions of the school classroom. Here a stratification and disciplining of the child population is achieved through the marking out of levels and stages of competence and achievements, essentially measured in relation to the steady progress of chronological age and achievement of developmental tasks« (Christensen, James and Jenks 2001: 210).

Through assessment of children's progress and decisions made on the basis of such interpretations, teachers are »creating an interpretive trajectory of a student's life«, thus affecting the options available for children with regard to both their future education and their occupational life (Holstein and Gubrium 2000:89). Children who fail to achieve in accordance with the predefined stages of progress may be regarded as deviant, being 'off-time' (Holstein and Gubrium 2000), defined by teachers as lagging behind, slow-learners or under-achievers, and some of them are seen as requiring special education, which may mean that the child is separated even spatially from children in his/her class (Närvänen 2003:1). Some are not allowed to move up to the next form and, thus, are identified as belonging to a collective of chronologically younger children. The metaphor of a developmental ladder is here supported by the expression 'moving up'. Being regarded as 'off-time' in relation to achievement may even affect children who are defined as especially gifted or bright students, pointing out these students as being different from others (James, Jenks and Prout 2001: 72-73; Adam 1995). A child who is ahead of his/her age on the developmental ladder may be problematized as precocious, i.e. premature and negatively deviant. An eventually demonstrated competence may be questioned as not genuine or superficial – »They do not really understand...« (Näsman and von Gerber 2003) or they are seen as being pressed to achieve off-time by their parents and, hence, »not allowed to be the children they really are«.

School is an institution that may then be a powerful source for various aspects of children's identities. At school, children are ascribed age-category-based identities, through which they are normally defined as similar to others of the same age and different from children older or younger than themselves, as well as different from teachers. Children may also be categorized on the basis of achievement or on other bases, such as social background. Such definitions of children can be understood as internal-external processes of identification. Ascriptions of an identity to a child, such as slow-learner or precocious, may affect the child's relations to others, teachers as well as classmates and affect how the child will be defined by them, which may in turn affect the child's definition of itself, and thus the child's identity. Some children adopt the age-based definitions as part of their own understanding of childhood as a developmental ladder, referring to their ageing and/or status shifts in the education system as relevant to stepwise increases in competence, rights and responsibilities (Näsman and von Gerber 2003). This means also acknowledging a status difference whereby a child is higher up in the hierarchy than younger children, who may be described in degrading ways, but lower than older children, who may be looked up to or feared (ibid.). Children may, as already mentioned, also use the understanding of themselves as human becomings in order to negotiate a scope of action and free themselves from responsibilities (ibid.; Hockey and James 1993).

Social identities based on social categorizations are not necessarily internalized, even though they may be consequential for identity. A category-based social identity, such as the category child, is a nominal identity, while the individual experiences of that social identity may vary. There are for example »local differences in typification and practice with respect to institutionalised identities« (Jenkins 1996). Such local differences may be identified in studies of different schools – or indeed families – with respect to identity ascriptions, children's experiences of such ascriptions as well as children's agency. An individual may reflexively and interpretively relate to ascribed category-based identities and not necessarily accept being defined by others or act as is expected. As already mentioned, there may be resistance to such categorizations. Thus, the processes of identification and agency have to be understood in the light of interpretive practices (Närvänen and Näsman 2004). Cultural representations and typifications of a specific life phase, and thus of the characteristics of the incumbents of that life phase, are reflected upon and become meaningful through interpretation. Such processes are fundamental with regard to the definition of self, the situation and, thus, agency. Social and cultural discourses on, for example, childhood and, thus, representations of childhood are »neither monolithic nor totalizing« (Holstein and Gubrium 2000: 207). For example, there may be a local culture that »supplies orientations and resources for interpretation« (ibid.: 207). Furthermore, children may spend most of their time at school and at home, but these are not the only contexts in which identities are constructed and re-constructed. Age identities and meanings of the life course position may be negotiated and constructed elsewhere, through relationships with others, children as well as adults.

Concluding Remarks

Our chapter started by criticizing, on theoretical grounds, some ideas in post-modern society, because these dualistic conceptualizations cannot capture the multiple times or the relatedness of temporality, agency and social identities. They neglect or cannot explain the meaning of social processes in constructing and re-constructing identities or the social meanings of time with regard to identity formation. Conceptualizing and understanding the relatedness of temporality, social interaction, social identities and agency constitute a challenging task that has not been dealt with sufficiently within theories of post-modern societies. As a contribution to future theorizing, we have conceptualized time in terms of temporal order, pointing out temporal structuring and organization, and in terms of temporal orientation, pointing out the meanings of past, present and future – dimensions of importance for understanding the temporal complexities of everyday life. We also shortly discuss other time-related concepts such as duration and timing. We argue theoretically that the complex interplay between contexts, relationships, meanings of the biographical past, the present situation, the anticipated future and interpretive practices is of importance for understanding social identities and social identifications as well as agency. Social identities are certainly displayed, for example, through consumption, but if there were no one there to observe this consumption, no one to reject the social identity thus displayed or to verify it, would it not be quite meaningless as a performance or dramatization of an identity? The temporal-relational perspective may highlight the meanings of contexts, local cultures, etc., as interpretive resources, thereby also highlighting the diversity of identity formation as well as agency.

The temporal-relational perspective outlined here presupposes that multiple times and multiple meanings of time are recognized. It also presupposes a relational understanding of social identities, as created interactionally and contextually. Furthermore, both identity formation and agency are understood here in terms of interpretive practices concerning the past, present and future. Reflexivity and interpretive practices are necessary in order to understand processes of social identification as well as agency (cf. Närvänen and Näsman 2004). This article, however, constitutes only one step towards creating a temporal-relational perspective on social identities and agency.

Our criticism of the ideas of a post-modern society also concerns the lack of empirical support for the claims about a radical change into a new era. Our main claim is that research on and theorizing about contemporary society has to deal with change in terms of both continuities and discontinuities. The empirical and theoretical challenges are found, for example, with respect to the multiplicity of times – to exploring 'how time works' in contemporary society rather than assuming the dualistic notions of time in modern versus post-modern society. There is also a paucity of evidence for the idea that identities hardly exist any more, or if recognized, that identities are only a product of self-determination or self-reflexivity, or mainly temporarily displayed through consumption or lifestyles. Again, the challenge is to conceptualize what is actually meant by social identities and the processes through which such identities may be produced and performed.

We do not deny, however, that there is empirical support for talking about processes of social change in relation to the phenomena discussed here. There are, for instance, discussions on the growing processes of globalization that encompass compression of time and space, due to changing communication techniques and increased travelling. This means, for instance, faster dissemination of ideas through mass media and the Internet, establishment of transnational social relations and dissemination of material products globally – just a few examples of processes of social change that characterize contemporary life and are consequential to, for example, social definitions of identities. But the fact that such processes as the globalized dissemination of lifestyles and products for consumption are consequential does not mean that we know what the consequences may be in local contexts. Paradoxically, globalization in this sense may contribute, for example, both to homogenization of the ideas of childhood and to diversification of childhoods due to the enlarged range of products that, as Alan Prout has claimed, are providing »new cultural niches and leading to the emergence of new identities« (2005: 30). To this should be added the notion that cultural ideas as well as products are the objects of local interpretations and locally grounded transformations that also contribute to diversity. In accordance with Prout, we argue that globalization »does not in itself provide an explanation of social and economic trends » (2005: 16), but has to be described, analysed and specified. Research on how globally disseminated ideas, cultural products, transnational relations as well as the ideas of globalization as such are locally used and interpreted becomes, therefore, an urgent issue. Our understanding, however, is that these changes are taking place within modernity, making late-modernity a better label than post-modernity. There are continuities in change between modernity and contemporary society in several respects, such as in some of the ways in which the concepts child and childhood are socially and culturally defined and how such social constructions work in everyday practices, as illustrated through our discussion on family and school as well as on the social meanings of age. Such definitions are still consequential for children and how childhood is understood, and may be a source of tension with respect to other social processes that may imply partly changing conceptions.

In summary, we do acknowledge that childhood is changing in several respects, but also that, in other respects, childhood may instead be becoming strengthened as a conception. The idea of the blurring of boundaries between childhood and adulthood within theories of post-modern society, hence, should be subject to sophisticated analyses. As David Buckingham has claimed: »The boundaries have indeed become blurred; yet in several respects, they have also been reinforced and extended« (2000: 74), pointing out the increasing institutionalization of children's lives and the domestication of leisure as examples of processes that reinforce and extend childhood, which is in line with our discussion in this article.

Our conceptualization of time in terms of temporality is not exhaustive, but we find it useful in discussing the multiplicity of times in social reality, in this case in children's lives, and in problematizing some ideas about post-modernity. The challenge for the future is further development of approaches to theorizing about and understanding contemporary social changes, taking into account both the discontinuities and the continuities of change.

References

Adam, B. (1995): *Timewatch. The Social Analysis of Time*. Cambridge: Polity Press.
Bauman, Z. (1998): *Work, Consumerism and the New Poor*. Buckingham, UK: Open University Press.
Bauman, Z. (1992): *Mortality, Immortality & Other Life Strategies*. Cambridge: Polity Press.
Bauman, Z. (1997): *Postmodernity and its Discontents*. Cambridge: Polity Press.
Buckingham, D. (2000): *After the Death of Childhood. Growing up in the Age of Electronic Media*. Cambridge: Polity Press.
Bergström, M. and I. Holm (2005): *Den svårfångade delaktigheten i skolan. Ett ungdomsperspektiv på hinder och möjligheter*. Linköping: Linköping University.
Brannen, J. and A. Nilsen (2002): »Young people's time perspectives: From youth to adulthood«, *Sociology*, Vol. 36: 513-537.
Christensen, P. and A. James (2001): »What are schools for? The temporal experience of children's learning in Northern England«. Mayall, B. and L. Alanen (eds): *Conceptualising Child-Adult Relations*. London: Falmer Press: 70-85.
Christensen, P., A. James and C. Jenks (2001): »'All we needed to do was blow the whistle': children's embodiment of time«. Cunningham-Burley S. and K. Backett-Milburn (eds): *Exploring the Body*. New York: Palgrave: 201-222.
Dunn, R. G. (1998): *Identity Crises. A Social Critique of Postmodernity*. Minneapolis: University of Minnesota Press.
Elchardus, M. (1988): »The rediscovery of chronos: the new role of time in sociological theory«. *International Sociology*, Vol. 3: 35-59.
Emirbayer, M. and A. Miche (1998): »What is agency?«, *AJS*, Vol. 103: 962-1023.

Giddens, A. (1984): *The Constitution of Society. Outline of the Theory of Structuration*. Cambridge: Polity Press.

Giddens, A. (1991): *Modernity and Self-Identity. Self and Society in the Late Modern Age*. Cambridge: Polity Press.

Flaherty, M.G., and G.A. Fine (2001): »Present, Past, and Future. Conjugating George Herbert Mead's Perspective on Time«. *Time & Society*, Vol. 10: 147-161.

Goffman, E. (1959): *The Presentation of Self in Everyday Life*. Middlesex: Penguin Books.

Goffman, E. (1961): *Asylums. Essays on the Social Situation of Mental Patients and other Inmates.* Middlesex: Penguin Books.

Harden, J. (2000): »There's no place like home. The public/private distinction in children's theorizing of risk and safety«. *Childhood*, Vol. 7: 43-59.

Hirdman, Y. (1990): »Genussystem«, SOU: *Demokrati och makt i Sverige*. 1990: 44.

Hochschild, A.R. (1997): *The Time Bind: When Work Becomes Home and Home Becomes Work*. New York: Metropolitan Books.

Hockey, J. and A. James (1993): *Growing Up and Growing Old. Ageing and Dependency in the Life Course*. London: Sage.

Hockey, J. and A. James (2003): *Social Identities across the Life Course*. New York: Palgrave.

Holloway, S. and G. Valentine (2000): »Spatiality and the new social studies of childhood«. *Sociology*, Vol. 34: 763-783.

Holstein, J.A. and J.F. Gubrium (2000): *Constructing the Life Course*. Second edition. New York: General Hall Inc.

Jacoby, A.L. and E. Näsman (1989): *Mamma Pappa Jobb. Föräldrar och barn om arbetets villkor*. Stockholm: Arbetslivscentrum.

James, A. and A. Prout (1997): »Re-presenting childhood: time and transition in the study of childhood«. James A. and A. Prout (eds): *Constructing and Reconstructing Childhood: Contemporary Issues in the Sociological Study of Childhood*. London: Falmer Press: 230-250.

James, A., C. Jenks and A. Prout (2001): *Theorizing Childhood*. Oxford: Polity Press.

Jenkins, R. (1996): *Social Identity*. London: Routledge.

Lareau, A. (2000): »Social Class and the Daily Lives of Children. A Study from the United States«. *Childhood*, Vol. 7: 155-171.

Mead, G.H. (1932): *The Philosophy of the Present*. Amherst New York: Prometheus Books.

Mead, G.H. (1934): *Mind, Self & Society: from the standpoint of social behaviorist*. Chicago: University of Chicago Press.

Närvänen, A-L. (1994): *Temporality and Social Order*. Linköping: Linköping University (diss.).

Närvänen, A-L. (2003): *Time, Space and Identities – a Dramaturgical Approach*. Linköping: Institute for the Study of Ageing and Later Life, Linköping University.

Närvänen, A-L. (2004): »Age, Ageing and the Life Course«. Öberg B-M., A-L. Närvänen, E. Näsman and E. Olsson (eds): *Changing Worlds and the Ageing Subject*. Aldershot: Ashgate: 65-80.

Närvänen A-L. and E. Näsman (2004): *Age Order and Children's Agency*. (Paper presented at COST A19, Croatia, Zagreb, October 2004).

Närvänen, A-L. and E. Näsman (forthcoming): *Challenging Postmodern Life Courses?*

Näsman, E. (1997): »Föräldraskapets synlighet i arbetsplatskulturer«. J. Bonke (ed): *Dilemmaet arbejdsliv-familieliv i Norden*. Nordic Council of Ministers, TemaNord 1997:534.

Näsman, E. and C. von Gerber (1996): *Mamma Pappa utan Jobb*. Stockholm: Rädda Barnens Förlag.

Näsman, E. and C. von Gerber (2003): *Från spargris till kontokort. Barndomens ekonomiska spiraltrappa*. Linköping: Linköping University.

Philo, C. (2000): »'The corner-stones of my world'« (editorial introduction to special issue on spaces of childhood). *Childhood*, Vol. 7: 243-256.

Pilcher, J. (1995): *Age and Generation in Modern Britain*. Oxford: Oxford University Press.

Prout, A. (2005): *The Futur of Childhood. Towards the Interdisciplinary Study of Child*ren. London: Routledge Falmer.

Raby, R.C. (2002): »A tangle of discourses: girls negotiating adolescence«. *Journal of Youth Studies*, Vol. 5: 425-448.

Solberg, A. (1997): »Negotiating childhood: changing constructions of age for Norwegian children«. James, A. and A. Prout (eds): *Constructing and Reconstructing Childhood: Contemporary Issues in the Sociological Study of Childhood*. London: Falmer Press: 118-137.

Notes

1   Temporality and agency are discussed more thoroughly by Närvänen and Näsman (2004), related to the wider discussion of dialectical relations between structure, culture and agency.

ENLARGEMENT OF SPACE

Metamorphoses of the World Within Reach

Heinz Hengst

Rethinking the Space-Time Continuum

In the fields of social science and cultural studies, a growing awareness for 'space' as a category of analysis can currently be observed. Attempts are being made to redefine space in relation to time, and to attach greater value to space in this context. Manuel Castells, a social geographer, deserves special mention in this connection. In the first book in his trilogy on »The Information Age«, clearly distancing himself from most classical social theory, he notes that »The dominant trend in our society displays the historical revenge of space, structuring temporality in different, even contradictory logics according to spatial dynamic« (Castells 1996: 497). Castells is not alone with this new perspective of the space-time continuum. Peter Sloterdijk, in his new book entitled »Im Weltinnenraum des Kapitals« (2005) (Inside Capital's Inner World) has provided a significant counterpart to Hegel's well-known definition, according to which philosophy is »its own time apprehended as thought«. For Sloterdijk, philosophy is »its own space apprehended as thought«. He understands his book as a farewell to what he calls »the era of one-sided idolization of time«. Karl Schlögel (2004) refers to a 'spatial turn' in historical and cultural studies. What Sloterdijk would like to jettison as 'one-sided idolization' is for Schlögel 'spatial atrophy'.

Perhaps this is one of the areas in which the clocks of social-scientific childhood research run differently than in present-day social theory and cultural studies discourses. In any case this type of childhood research cannot be accused of having suffered from any 'spatial atrophy'. The locating of children in society, the core theme of such research, has always focused an eye on children's spaces as well. How this is so is clearly illustrated by the first sentence in a study on »Die Orte und Zeiten der Kinder« (Children's Places and Times): »Where children find room in the spatial world shows specifically what sort of place society assigns them« (Zeiher und Zeiher 1994: 17). While Helga and Hartmut Zeiher likewise enquire in their study into children's times *and* spaces, childhood research in the social sciences, cultural sociology and ethnology has a definite spatial bias. This slantedness – many spatially related studies, but relatively few studies on temporal relations – in the German-speaking research community has been described by Armin Klein (Klein 1993: 100). I believe that, also from an international perspective, one can say that childhood research has tended to have more of a spatial bias than a temporal one. This may have something to do with a continued, subliminally reductionist image of children as bodies, and the concomitant fixation of the experiential relevance of the world within physical reach. In one of the broadly recognized comparative studies on the change in the experience of space of children (Behnken et al. 1989), one can find the thesis that:

> »Socialization takes place to an essential extent in *the* space that is open to direct access by our body, our senses. In the adult town dweller, the 'primary space' tends to be congruent with the routine space of the everyday acting. The 'primary space' as the 'world within reach' (A. Schütz; Th. Luckmann 1975), due to the experienced physical presence and continuity of the current acting, becomes a social space of highest subjective certainty. In that part of the social world, there is forming the notion of social reality that is trusted by the individual; here the identity of the individual person finds its spatial anchoring« (ibid.: 402).

As research into *present-day* children's spaces, *sociological* childhood research has concentrated its focus in recent decades above all on a boost from modernisation that severely changed the relationship between inside and outside. It often operated (in Germany at least) in tune with the most diverse of local government initiatives. Such activities indicate an end to indifference towards 'environmental issues' that – at an international level – are also expressed in many 'urban studies'. The spatial themes of such childhood research have not been finished, and the key demands of these initiatives have been fulfilled in exceptional cases only.

Nevertheless, I consider a 'spatial turn' to be necessary in childhood research by social science and cultural studies also, a turn in the sense of 'rethinking' the prevailing concepts of social space and interpreting the changes that are occurring. By 'turn' I mean the notion that it is possible (indeed imperative) to have many ways of seeing one and the same subject-matter, and ways very different to the established ones. A 'turn' in this sense does not mean replacing one research object with another (e.g. time with space), but taking dimensions, in this spatial dimensions (in childhood research) and opening them up, widening them, pluralising them.

The society in which I 'locate' the object of childhood research by social science and cultural studies is a society undergoing structural transformations. Given such a transitional situation, I think it makes sense to see children as contemporaries first of all, and to conduct childhood research by analysing 'differential contemporariness'

(Hengst 2004). In other words, even if contemporary societies allocate children a place in (their) generational orders, one should refrain from fixating all too rigidly on children as a population group. The context of the following reflections on the spatial experience of contemporaries is above all a highly mediatised and globalised society. The basic assumption being made is quite simply that all contemporaries (all generations living today) must make arrangements – under such conditions – with complex social spaces.

Looking at recent studies on the children-childhood-space complex, one can identify a certain sensitisation for broadening our understanding of social spaces in the context of current trends towards globalisation, commercialisation and mediatisation (for example, some of the papers in the »Special Issue: Spaces of Childhood«, Childhood 2000, and of »Children's Places. Cross-cultural perspectives«, Olwig and Gullov 2003). This broadening and opening of perspective is also reflected in new notions like 'imaginative geographies' (Holloway and Valentine 2000), 'thirdspace' (Kondo 2004; Matthews et al. 2000) and 'heterotopia' (Mitchell and Reid-Walsh 2002; McNamee 2000). Some important new ideas for rethinking relations of external and internal spaces are emerging from a research approach in the field of children's media (Livingstone and Bovill 2001; Livingstone 2002; Mitchell and Reid-Walsh 2002) that examines media as 'environments', and the ways they are used in different spatial contexts. The need to root the issue of children and social space at the macrosocial level is seen in the final remarks in the editorial introduction by Chris Philo to »Special Issue: Spaces of Childhood« (Philo 2000: 253) and in Karen Fog Olwig's and Eva Gullov's introductory paper entitled »Towards an anthropology of children and place« in »Children's Places. Cross-cultural perspectives« (2003).

Domestication, Insularisation and Institutionalisation

As a better marker of the intended 'turn', I will begin my observations with a few remarks on discussions of children, childhood and space in Germany. In recent decades, investigating the places and spaces of children has been a central theme for German childhood research in the wider sense. In the 1960s, the theses applied by German researchers to the caesura in children's experience of space, referred to new processes of 'domestication', 'insularisation' and 'institutionalisation' (which is related to the other processes). 'Domestication' refers to the shifting or relocating of children's experiential space and children's activities away from the street, from unregulated external spaces to protected (by fences, walls and supervision) internal spaces. The concomitant 'institutionalisation' refers to the increasing organisation of children's culture within specialised bodies and institutions (pre-school centres, after school centres for schoolchildren, sports clubs, music schools, painting schools, ballet schools and what have you). 'Insularisation' means that the unitary space available to earlier generations of children is now fragmented – children's spaces are scattered and can only be reached if the children have greater mobility of their own, or with parental help. Distances and modes of passage between one island and the other in private and public transport mean that smaller children, in particular, can no longer have a concept of contiguous space. The organisation and experience of their habitat are 'insularised'. All these trends are manifestations and effects of transformations in society as a whole, fostering pluralisation and the individualisation of childhood.

The prevalent understanding of domestication, insularisation and institutionalisation is derived from modernisation theory. And it is beyond question that important changes in children's and childhood places can be reconstructed with the modernisation thesis (cf., among others, the comparative European study conducted by Manuela du Bois-Reymond et al. 1994). Arguments based on the modernisation thesis become problematic when the latter is applied one-dimensionally or in a universalising sense. In any case they are likely to gain from additional analyses that take the pluralisation and expansion of social spaces into consideration. One could refer in this context to the need for spatialisation on the conceptual level. By spatialisation I then mean a retraction of the diachronic perspective in favour of concentration on synchrony, simultaneity and co-presence(s). Emphasis is laid on the analysis of everything that is simultaneously appropriated as social space and becomes existentially important as social space.

An initial impression of the potential gains to be had from such a change of perspective is provided by the design and results of an ethnographic study conducted a few years ago by Jan C. Oberg (2000). Oberg studied the social spaces of children and youths in a place on the Amalfi coast (Costiera Amalfitana) in the south of Italy, and addressed the question as to where the children he studied can be located (all of them having family members and/or relatives who live as migrants in northern Italy or in other northwest European countries):

> »Socialised on the street 'in the home village, traditionally', they may have well stocked children's rooms in the region where they have arrived, are members of the local football club or other clubs, have social networks extending from Italy to northern Germany, not to speak of social competence due to the situation of having to come to terms with two cultures and languages simultaneously. Being highly mobile, they routinely commute with their families back and forth between the two regions, feel just as close to 'traditional' local village culture as they feel equally close (or distanced) from some elements of global mass culture.« (Oberg 2000: 10).

This picture may open up a broader perspective for looking at the 'bandwidth' and the implications of co-presences, overlaps and crossovers between the real and the virtual that are constitutive today for the experience and construction of social spaces. For children living on the Amalfi coast, 'the North' that they know from stories, from the media and from travel is of similarly great importance as the social loci (family home, school, the street, the piazza, the bar, the church — all multidimensional social spaces for them), in which they move in day-to-day life. They view the place where they live, their region, through the eyes of tourists who frequent the same places. Like the holidaymakers, they orientate themselves using the cultural patterns offered by the tourist industry. In other words, they perform a 'second localisation' with the help of global scripts. They are connected to universal popular culture through the entertainment media, and they participate, not least, in a transnational virtual peer group.

The little detour into the social spaces of children on the Costiera Amalfitana can sensitise us not only to approaches based on modernisation theory which are in need of completion — particularly as regards spatial issues. It also leads (as does a study by the Danish anthropologist Karen Fog Olwig on migrant children of Caribbean origin, 2003) into a world for which Ludger Pries (1998) coined the term 'transnational social spaces', into a world of international migration processes that can be understood less and less to any appropriate extent from the perspective of the regions of origin and arrival. Pries refers to social intermeshing contexts that have developed a kind of »autonomous gravity« »which constitute new social spaces that — in contrast to …. habitual forms of social space — are delocalised and geographically diffuse« (ibid.: 69).

Although the example of the Amalficoast children produces a particularly strong impression due to its obvious multidimensionality, one does not have to conduct ethnographic studies on the Amalfi coast to discover similar patterns of expanded social spaces closer to home. They are found soonest among many migrant children living in various European countries. Less pronounced, perhaps, than in a particular corner of southern Italy, but there is indeed a great deal of significance in what is propagated with the term 'circulating territories'. The families of migrant children are visited by relatives from their 'home' country, and visit that country themselves in the holidays, moving in transnationally woven networks. Some aspects of these spatial experiences and spatial constructions are obviously not present in the case of non-migrants. That said, the 'multilocal, multigeneration family', or the 'extended family' discussed in current family research — family types that are realities for many children today — also confront us with something like 'circulating territories'.

Extended Social Spaces in Social Theory, Media and Cultural Studies Discourses

The Amalfi example should also sensitise us to two basic approaches for investigating expanded social spaces and changes in the world within reach:

- ethnographic and micro-studies of social spaces and new spatial dimensions or elements in our time, and
- social, cultural and media theory approaches with a global perspective.

In the following, I use each of these approaches in turn. The core of my analysis concerns the consequences of modified social spaces for the conceptualisation of contemporary experience. I would like to begin my little tour d'horizon by presenting some pertinent approaches in social and media theory.

One of the impacts of globalisation is described in current debates as 'deterritorialization' (Tomlinson 1999). What is meant here is that enhanced mobility and the new electronic communication system weaken the bonds that tie production, consumption, culture, politics and identities to fixed locations. Some researchers have developed extended concepts of space in order to analyse the effects and mechanisms of deterritorialization and despatialization. Gupta and Ferguson (1992), two anthropologists, speak of 'global space', and Arjun Appadurai has coined the term 'global ethnoscapes' to refer to spaces or communities of people with shared identity, but without firm ties to (only) one place (cf. Appadurai 1998). Mention can also be made here of Homi Bhabha's (1994) model of an extended experiential and existential space between cultures, which he calls 'thirdspace'. Recent migration research takes into account (as already noted in the Amalfi episode) the fact that migrational trajectories are increasingly found to be circulatory movements coordinated through transnational networks (cf., among others, Pries 1998; 1997).

Deterritorialisation

One key concept in the discussion of modified experience of social spaces under globalisation is 'deterritorialisation'. For John Tomlinson (1999), 'deterritorialisation' is an integrative concept embracing other concepts such as 'delocalisation' and 'displacement', which can help us to understand the extensive transformations taking place »in the place-culture relationship in the context of global modernity«. He defines deterritorialisation as »the loss of the 'natural' relation of culture to geographical and social territories«(ibid.: 107). In this view, the 'global' functions as a kind of cultural horizon within which we 'frame' our existence (with different emphases). Tomlinson stresses the double-edgedness of this trend, which consists in the dissolution of forms of security provided by local environments, on the one hand, and on the other hand in our being offered a new understanding of experience in larger, ultimately global contexts. People are starting to include remote events and processes more routinely in their perception of what is important for their own life.

I find Tomlinson's ideas about the social range of deterritorialisation to be especially important. He knows, firstly, that globalisation is a process that produces and/or reinforces inequalities, that globalisation has its 'winners' and 'losers' (ibid.: 131). At the same time, however, he emphasises the universal nature of deterritorialisation, showing clearly how wrong it would be to see deterritorialisation as something that only occurs above a certain socioeconomic level, with those below that level living in a different experiential order, excluded from the globalisation process. Tomlinson refers in this context to the transformation of local cultural milieus, the closure of old industrial factories in working-class areas due to relocation of production to other parts of the world or – within the same process – the location of new industries with different work cultures in the old industrial districts, the transformation of a district primarily inhabited by (white) workers into a multiethnic district as a result of labour migration. None of these changes implicitly involves the use of communications technology. It should also be noted that deterritorialisation takes place at a relatively low level of technological development. If this aspect is taken into account, then the ones excluded are that tiny group that never make a phone call or watch television. Even marginalised groups for whom being tied to their locality is fate, experience a transformed locality increasingly penetrated by the global world. Even when they are the losers of globalisation in every respect, this does not mean that they are excluded from its impacts. On the contrary: the poor and the marginalised – for example those who live in inner-city districts – are often the ones most exposed in everyday life to some of the turbulent changes and hence the ones with the least protection, whereas the wealthy can afford to withdraw to the (remaining) rural areas that still have at least a semblance of a (still) intact and stable locality. This means that deterritorialisation in developed Western societies entails a basic level of commonality. The risk involved in deterritorialised culture is not the level of prosperity first and foremost, but a way of living that is dissociated from its locality as a result of the various forces operating in the global modernisation process. This outcome, moreover, is not confined to the population(s) of the first world (ibid., especially: 106-149).

Media as environments and hybrid social spaces

Important though it may be to realise that globalisation and deterritorialisation are not reducible to mediatisation, it is evident – and Tomlinson leaves not a shred of doubt – that the new media and technologies are an important means of transport. Media form an important interface between local circumstances and global (cultural) elements. Media and communication systems are 'disembedding' mechanisms, to use Giddens' (1991) terminology. Today's electronic media, especially television, are important carriers, brokers and producers of cultural patterns. Models for all kinds of identities – age-related, gender-based, generational, national and regional – are transported in the soaps, sitcoms, talk shows etc., and in news about national and global events. The media also supply scripts for occupying, using, appropriating and reconquering real, physical spaces (cf., with reference to children and youth, Hengst 2005 and 1997). Their addressees work them into their local discoveries and experiences, into their spatial concepts und cultural practices. When reference is made in the following to 'media', then a differentiated, continuously expanding mixture of old and new media is implied that is symbiotic (especially through networked media systems) with an entire universe of commodities, which interferes in all everyday social spaces.

Television

Tomlinson has correctly pointed out that deterritorialisation already occurs at a relatively low level of technological development. This level has meanwhile been reached for most people (at least in the West). So it may make sense, even in an age in which computers, the Internet and mobile communication are entering the everyday lives of more and more people, to not remove television from the research agenda of social science, culture studies and media studies – particularly as far as children are concerned.

One of the few media researchers who have dealt in a differentiated manner with the decoupling of geographic and social space (in his terms: of physical environment and media environments) for human acting is Joshua Meyrowitz. In a first conclusion, his (hardly recognized) work can be reduced to the thesis that, with the establishment of television, a new type of generation has become established. I consciously choose the formulation type of generation in order to make clear that it is problematic to assume clearly distinguishable generations and corresponding habits in the given connection.

Meyrowitz is not a children's media researcher. His subject is a 'new social landscape', specifically the influence of electronic media and media environments on three decades of social changes in the USA. He does not only think about the change in the difference between children and adults, but also asks for that between masculinity und femininity and between public and privacy under the conditions of the trend towards decoupling of geographic and social spaces. He sees his particular approach as a synthesis of Goffman and (a demystified) McLuhan. As far as McLuhan is concerned, he sees himself like the former as a 'medium theorist', essentially sharing his (media determinist) view that the medium (less the content) is the message. Meyrowitz proceeds on the basis that the electronic media have brought about »a very clearly recognisable restructuring of the social 'stages' on which we play our roles«, and a change in what appears to us as »appropriate behaviour« (Meyrowitz 1987: 15).

Meyrowitz develops his concept, among other things, by dealing with Erving

Goffman from whom he differentiates himself because the latter, just like many other sociologists, only considers the everyday role play with regard to the physical places, the stages at and on which it takes place. Meyrowitz argues that the electronic media have destroyed the traditional relations between physical and social environments and caused new configurations including both physical spaces and information environments. I only take up one of Meyrowitz' central thoughts. It is the way he thinks about similarities, differences and the specific interaction of medial and physical environments. As far as the similarities are concerned, he stresses that media, just like walls and windows, can separate or either hide or display something or someone (ibid.: 17-18). On the other hand, the assertion of permeability of medial and physical space is a central aspect of his argumentation. He speaks of a new kind of permeable border, a new borderline (ibid.: 42). In summary: Physical and media environments are not completely different, but two sides of a coin. This is what makes Meyrowitz' variant of an extended concept of space (ibid.: 39). It is the – under aspects of experience relevance – most important 'relationship' between physical and media environments that the electronic media reduce the differences between direct and media-imparted interaction. With regard to television, it implies that the speech and external appearance of other persons are also 'visible' for, i.e. accessible to people who are not at the same place. »And just like the viewers may have the feeling that they have 'met' one of the persons they have watched on TV, they may get the impression that they have 'visited' the places shown to them« (ibid.: 98).

Having information about a certain environment, says Meyrowitz, »partially means to be 'in' that environment«. Moreover he is of the opinion that the access to information also opens the door to physical access (ibid.: 138). Not least, the latter is important because Meyrowitz states an undermining of the traditional relations between social and physical spaces, but at the same time knows that there still exist separate places and that the place, as a physical space, continues to be »an important determining factor for many types of interactions« (ibid.: 137). Meyrowitz finally sticks to an important difference between direct and indirect experience when he is convinced that, even though the electronic media have mixed many social situations in the outlined meaning, the direct physical presence and the mutual observation continue to be the most important means for gathering social experience. He does not really clarify the difference between the importance of physically present and of (only) medial participation to the constitution of experience. But he makes clear that we do not have to deal with two different 'worlds' in the age of electronic media. Moreover, he is sensitive to the changed relation of cultural scripts for the selection and acquisition of physical stages. They are fed from many sources. So one has access to a lot more of scripts than stages and it is the cultural work to filter appropriate scripts out of the variety of offers for one's own performances.

An important element for understanding Meyrowitz' extended or mediatised understanding of space is the concept of Self he borrowed from Symbolic Interactionism and G.H. Mead, because this provides him with a different way of accessing the experience of social space than the one favoured by childhood research, borrowing from phenomenological sociology (Schütz and Luckmann 1975) (cf. the references at the beginning of this article). Self is not defined by the physical boundaries of the person's body. Rather it is a reflected concept that develops in the same measure as one learns to see oneself as a social object. Self comes into being through perceiving that one is perceived by others. G.H. Mead refers to 'generalised others', by which he means that people observe and evaluate their own behaviour from the perspective of other people. One characteristic element in Meyrowitz' thinking is that the media have broadened the range of generalised others to such an extent that the people we experience as significant others are no longer confined to those we know from direct, unmediated interaction within our own communities. Members of other communities and inhabitants of other places can also function as mirrors for the self. The dependence of self-concept on place and its respective inhabitants is weakened (but not wholly eliminated) by the 'mediatised generalised other'.

Meyrowitz extends Mead's concept not only by introducing the generalised other communicated by the media. He also provides a spatial variant of the generalised other (later, as well): the 'generalised elsewhere'. He assumes that the media generate awareness of the »generalised elsewhere« by giving us perspectives that are external to the respective place we find ourselves. This 'generalised elsewhere' serves as a mirror in which we perceive and evaluate our own, constructed, place. This is how we experience where we live not only as *the* community, but as one of many possible communities; »not only as the centre of our experience, but as a place that is further north or west and more liberal or conservative than other places« (Meyrowitz 1998: 178).

Meyrowitz' thesis that the electronic media torpedo group identities that are based on a 'joint presence' and that they create many new forms of access that have little to do with the former localization (Meyrowitz 1987: 111) is of importance with regard to the positioning of children as a distinctive part of the population in society. Especially for children, the easiness of 'leaving' a place via electronic media makes it possible to bypass the information channels and hierarchies of their physical environment. Under the impact of the electronic media, he argues, there have been changes in the sequence of gaining information from 'stage behaviour' (which only ever conveys the ideals of a group) and 'background information': »Candidates for group membership learn a great deal about the background behaviour of a group before they become full members« (ibid.: 119). »Children, for example, learn a lot about adulthood through the electronic media, more than they ever used to through the print media. In fact, television is the first mass medium that allows small children a detailed look into their parents' 'background'« (ibid.). Meyrowitz' argumentation comes down to the assertion that, in the age of electronic media, there can neither exist something like childhood as a distinct homogenous field of experience nor something like adulthood. And he reads that development as a (kind of) delocalization of what he calls stages of life:

> »The ability to see the own life as a series of transitions requires a 'view from above', elevated, from the angle of some special stage of life. We are not restricted to the information system of the respective stage of socialization that we are in. The television conveys to all of us a better feeling of how it 'feels' to be in another stage of life. Paradoxically, it makes people more conscious of the transitions in life because the stage of life is less space-related, less all-embracing.« (Meyrowitz 1987: 121).

The Internet and the discourse on 'additional technosocial spaces'

Meyrowitz' analysis of modified spatial experience in mediatised societies relates primarily to television. The same subject is now discussed with reference to the Internet, above all. Within that discourse the 'two worlds' theory has been abandoned in favour of analytical perspectives that allow greater differentiation. Besides the distinction between present and absent, there is a further distinction, namely that between presence and remote presence. There are modes that mix online and offline reality, and the analyses of these mixed modes focus attention on new ways of linking global and local contexts, new fields of intercourse between the local and the remote. These analyses corroborate a pluralisation of the levels on which we operate in order to establish relationships with people and artefacts, to acquire and evaluate experience. Reference is made, for example, to the loss of geographical markers, and to the perforation of private and public spaces. Daniela Ahrens, a German sociologist, views technologies for electronic networking as mirrors that call on us »to realign and renegotiate the local dimension in everyday contexts of life with new, global, transboundary spaces, with the knowledge, the cognitive styles, modes of reflection and aesthetics from remote, unconquered worlds« (Ahrens 2003: 184). This is Meyrowitz' 'generalised elsewhere', through which we view our own place and construct it as a »second locality«.

> »The value of the local becomes renegotiable in new ways. The necessity arises to redefine the local in its relationship to global, transboundary spaces. (…) Just as world society becomes something we can experience *in situ* with new technologies, these technologies also provoke new configurations of the local« (ibid.).

If one accepts the analyses by Tomlinson, Meyrowitz and Ahrens, then – as an initial summary – we are not witnesses to the dissolution of everything modern, but of complex and complicated restructuring processes. In their studies on deterritorialisation, television and the Internet, the significance of physical locality is not called into question. Markus Schroer (2003) has given some thought to the conceptualisation of how the real and the virtual are linked, and favours a line of thinking in which real and virtual space mutually influence each other, and applies a term taken from systems theory, 'interpenetration' (Schroer 2003: 218-219).

Imagined social spaces

If the question of contemporaries and space is to be discussed in relation to welfare aspects and with adequate consideration of our time, then it is important to know, first of all, where the scripts come from that people are interested in, and secondly that, through media, they today usually have access to many more scripts (of possible lives) than they do to stages where they can acquire such scripts (cf. Meyrowitz). Arjun Appadurai (1998) has made some comments on this aspect that are worth reflecting on. He writes:

»In present-day social life (..) the imagination has acquired a peculiar, additional effect. More people than ever before, in more parts of the world than ever before give consideration today to more variants of 'possible' lives than ever before. One important source for this change lies in the existence and role of the mass media. They represent a rich, constantly changing repertoire of possible lives, some of which can be successfully adopted in the lived imaginations of normal people, others not (Appadurai 1998: 21).«

Appadurai explicitly points out that this 'fact' need not be seen as something positive and encouraging, that it does not suggest at all that »the world is now a happier place providing more 'choices' (in the utilitarian sense of the word) for a greater number of people who could also lead a fulfilled life – since people now possess greater mobility«. He is only interested to point to the fact »that even the most mediocre or hopeless existence, that even the most brutal and inhuman conditions, the worst inequality that can be lived and experienced are now open to the game of imagination« (ibid.:21ff.). People experience that their local living conditions are limited compared to the kind of material affluence globally on offer. In his opinion, this will prompt them to work in their everyday activities at bridging this gap, i.e. at globalising the local and in this way pursue a second form of localisation.

The consequences that Appadurai draws for ethnographers from these trends should be transferred to research into children's social spaces. Appadurai demands (namely) that researchers »can no longer assume that local peculiarities are something 'down to earth', that they can no longer assume when choosing the locus as a research object that they will encounter something that, compared to a larger perspective, is more fundamental, more random and therefore more 'real'«. Today, complex and partially imagined lives would have to form the foundations of ethnography, »at least of an ethnography that wants to be heard in a transnational, despatialised world« (ibid.: 23).

Not Quite Here and Not Quite There

The range of extended social spaces with which today's children (must) make arrangements is very broad and applies to each of the three key locations of modern childhood: the family, the school and the street (in the widest sense). On the one hand, it is impossible to consider them all equally in a short paper, on the other hand, systematising them would imply adherence to a logic that is also questioned or cancelled to a certain extent by deterritorialisation and mediatisation. I will approach this complex with some thoughts on the mediatised and commodified interior spaces of today's children. Interior spaces constitute a terrain that, until only a few years ago, did not feature in childhood research as the study of the spatial dimension of childhood, despite the 'domestication' thesis (for reasons for this exclusion, see Buchner-Fuhs 1998). I will then concentrate on studies that illustrate variants of the physically absent and virtually present with reference to new media and technologies. After that, I will introduce two concepts applied by childhood researchers to explain changes in the world within reach. In doing so, I bear in mind the childhood-adulthood, male-female and private-public dimensions postulated by Meyrowitz. Finally, I shall pursue the traces of mediatised and commodified criteria and concepts of social space in children's thinking.

Dealing with media-rich homes and (digital) bedrooms

Given the transfer of culture between generations, it is essential, it seems to me, to focus intensively on the fact that the importance of the family lies not only in the management of dependency, but also in the fact that it creates a more or less common culture based on the sharing of resources. The space in which this culture ensues is not just the family apartment or house (Livingstone 2002: 183). In consumer society, the family home is (not least) a marketplace. It is a triviality that the family, like many public leisure spaces outside the family, has turned into an arena for private (commercial) interests. The latter is true especially of children's bedrooms today. At the same time, they are also a central location of identity work. Sonia Livingstone points out (echoing Meyrowitz) that the bedrooms of children and youths are used in very different ways to overcome spatial boundaries and limits on identity. The following aspects are significant in connection with the differentiation of presence. The child's bedroom is a space that enables participation in a shared peer culture in two different ways: 1. it is a place where one can be together with friends, and 2. it is also a place where a child can experience and cultivate bonds to the peer group when alone in the room, not least because the child is involved with media (products) and toys that are highly valued among its peers.

> Bedroom culture, writes Livingstone »represents a new opportunity for targeted advertising and marketing, as the media-rich child's bedroom is both a site for commercial messages and a location for the display and use of consumer goods. While the bedroom is thus a key site for the increasing commercialisation of childhood and youth, it also supports the development of identity in ways that may be, but are not necessarily, exploitative« (ibid.: 156).

One other aspect is worthy of mention here, namely the shift in the ways that boys and girls appropriate space. Until now, childhood and youth researchers have viewed and continue to view 'indoors' as being a female domain, and 'outdoors' as being a male domain. Livingstone states with regard to bedrooms (and claiming functional equivalents to street culture) that the boundaries between male and female culture become blurred. Owing to the deteriorated conditions for street childhood and to the increasing mediatisation of children's bedrooms, boys are also ascribing increasing importance to their bedrooms. They, too, need spaces in which to develop their identity and engage in relationships. »One may even speculate that for boys, some aspects of street corner culture may be reproduced in the bedroom in the direction of the traditionally male culture of the street« (ibid.: 157).

Technosocial situations as moratoria and compensational spaces

Internet activities
In some recent studies, there is increasing reference to the virtual spaces that children and young people inhabit. It was in this context that the term 'digital bedroom' was coined (Sefton-Green and Buckingham 1998). Internet activities are a special focus of interest. In the relevant research work, one occasionally encounters the thesis that the Internet functions as a stage where people can experiment with alternative identities (Turkle 1998). Yet real Internet activities provide little corroboration for this thesis (cf. Hengst 2002). Online spaces do not constitute alternative spaces for children and young people, but are extensions of the 'spaces' in which they act in 'real', everyday life. Children do not take part in online life without a connection to daily, physical life in local, physical spaces. As Maczewski noted, »The body sitting at a keyboard is the place where online and onground experience is negotiated and integrated« (Macze-

wski 2003). Addressing the issue of what the Internet means for children and young people, Chris Abbott noted a few years ago that, for many young people, the 'Web' was above all an environment where the pressure is off, and in which problems could be explored in relative safety – an environment that enabled complementary rather than alternative experience (Abbott 1998: 97). Many findings enable the Internet's communicative potential to be identified as complementary or 'supplementary' in function (Fix 2001).

If the communicative focal points set by young people are to be interpreted, in a non-traditional manner, meaning not as developmental tasks for specific phases in life, then a more generationally specific interpretation, is a possible alternative – the Internet as a moratorium, as a new, by no means only youth-specific place for acquiring experience under relatively 'safe' conditions and with an reduced level of risk – e.g. being able to say something cheeky or forward without having to worry too much about the consequences.

I would like to note that we are not dealing here with something entirely new. At the least, there is such a thing as a basic significance in linking the near and the far, the virtually present and the physically absent, that was valued and demanded by children and youths prior to the Internet. In interviews with children and youths about how important telephoning is to them, they have always mentioned the importance of the relief they feel by not being (physically) present while phoning. Older children emphasise the non-committal, playful aspect, the 'experimental' or 'rehearsal' element in phone calls they make (cf. Hengst 1989). They are looking, Liede and Ziehe (1983) write, for »immediacy from afar« or »a closeness that is simultaneously distance and that commits one to nothing«, in which – as emphasised again and again in interviews – nothing has to be expressed in a logical, conclusive manner.

'Simsen' (sending/receiving SMSs)

Quite obviously, these options are greatly expanded and differentiated by the spread of mobile phones, which have now advanced to become *the* medium used by young people. In Germany, 90 percent of 12- to 19-year-olds have a mobile phone (Tully and Zerle 2005: 11). What is interesting in the case of mobile phones is that the disparities in access to technology that are found in respect of ownership of and access to computers and the Internet are reversed. Whereas the latter technologies correlate closely to higher social status of the parents, more youths with parents of low social status have mobile phones. Gender-related differences are likewise reversed. More girls than boys have a mobile phone. They use their phone more often and spend more money on it. Girls are more active at sending SMSs, especially (ibid.: 15).

One of the undisputed findings in childhood and youth media research is that young people favour mobile equipment and storage media much more than adults do. The reason for this is that such devices make them independent of time and space constraints, and thus confer a certain amount of autonomy. Mobility is a key requirement for living an independent life. »Mobile communication leads to the surmounting of spatial constraints by being reachable, to personal bonding and hence to 'being in touch'« (Selmer 2005: 27). As the huge increase in SMSs shows, there is more to mobile phone use than just making phone calls. In 2004, more than 30 billion SMSs were sent – about two thirds of that total by mobile phone users (ibid.: 12). A number of studies have shown the role played by mobile phones in the sub-differentiation of young people's communication spectrum. SMS communication is primarily used to nurture existing contacts. For young people, the mobile phone is a medium for short-range communication. One can observe not only an enlargement of social networks, but also and above all an intensification. SMS communication, like online chatting, is no substitute for face-to-face communication, but supplements conventional forms of communication. In an increasingly individualised society with a high level of leisure mobility, SMSs are used to a significant extent for organisational purposes, e.g. for (spontaneously) arranging and postponing meetings (Döring 2005). One crucial advantage of SMS communication compared to phoning – according to youths in one study – is that one has even more control over the process. It is not just the unencumbering aspect as such that makes this combination of interaction and physical absence so attractive. A more important aspect of SMS'ing is that the interaction is non-synchronous, which means one does not have to concentrate all of a sudden, and can disconnect and avoid getting bored without having to be impolite – something that would be difficult to avoid in the case of a telephone conversation (Schulz 2005). So there are variants and degrees of stress avoidance.

As part of an ethnographic study conducted with youths and young adults, Mizuko Ito and Daisuke Okabe (2005) produced a typology of the different ways that 'electronic and traditionally located architectures' interact or interpenetrate through the sending and receiving of SMSs. They were investigating interactive situations they called 'hybrid technosocial situations'. To that extent, Ito and Okabe are closer to Goffman's situationist approach than to Meyrowitz, whose object of focus is the transformation of 'information systems'. They distinguish between 'mobile text chat', 'ambient virtual co-presence' and 'augmented flesh meet'. 'Mobile text chat' takes place in very different places – at home, in the classroom and in public transport. Like chatting on the Internet and in phone calls, 'mobile text chat' occurs when two parties are interested in communicating about a particular subject. What Ito and Okabe find unique about this type of SMS communication is that it can be used to fill »even small 'communication voids', gaps in the day where one is not making interpersonal contact with others, particularly in settings such as public transportation where there are prohibitions on voice calls«. 'Ambient virtual co-presence' refers to a social setting that differs significantly from phoning and from face-to-face, one-to-one interaction. These are messages intended for a small circle of close friends (only). Ambient virtual co-presence imparts a sense »of persistent social space constituted through the periodic exchange of text messages«. These messages also define »a space of peripheral background awareness that is midway between direct interaction and non-interaction« (ibid.: 263). 'Augmented flesh meet' refers to extension of the boundaries constitutive for physical meetings, specifically by supplying information about the time and place of a specific meeting before, during and after the meeting itself to friends who cannot be at the meeting place, and in this way bring them closer to the meeting (ibid.: 265).

New Childhood Research Concepts of Social space

In some English-speaking research papers in recent years a sensitisation for new thinking regarding the spatial experience of today's children is also reflected in new concepts. The concepts in question are Foucault's (1986) concept of 'heterotopia' and Homi Bhaba's (1994) and Edward Soja's (1996) concept of 'thirdspace'.

Heterotopia

In one of his smaller works, Foucault (1986) identified the existence of social spaces that function as a kind of counter-proposal to the respective existing worlds. He therefore calls them 'other spaces', and distinguishes between two main types – the utopian and the heterotopian. Utopias by definition are non-spaces, and perfect social dream worlds. Heterotopias do actually exist, in contrast, but they are also counter-worlds and different to any real places.

Sarah McNamee (2000) has taken this concept of Foucault and applied it among other things to video games. They allow a different space, a secret space, to be created – a heterotopy, in other words: The children are located in a real place (their bedrooms) and engaging with a real machine (the computer), the space where they experience the adventure is not there but in one of Foucault's 'other spaces'. Residing in such a heterotopy is fun to the extent that it enables one to break out of the controlled world of everyday life. These heterotopies are compensational spaces (quite as Foucault would understand them). »Through entering into some of the 'other' spaces I have discussed, it is possible for children to escape the boundaries around childhood« (ibid.: 490).

Claudia Mitchell and Jacqueline Reid-Walsh (2002) view the girls' homepages and websites as heterotopia. What is interesting about their analysis is first of all the way in which they detail the blurring of boundaries between the public and private spheres. Secondly, they see the websites that children construct and maintain as a perfect example of today's youth and popular culture – not least because the activities involved do away with any age barriers. At the end of their paper, they reflect on the changing power relations between the generations and add a new perspective by questioning the centrality of oppositional reference, and illustrate with 'their'« medium, the website, that as soon as we are dealing with more than purely physical spaces, but with virtual ones as well, we are faced with more complex relationships between freedom and coercion.

Whereas Foucault assumes that certain contrasts continue to exist despite all the changes to social spaces and concepts of social space, or at least the contrast or opposition between the public and the private, Mitchell and Reid-Walsh are convinced

> »that the space of the Web and the homepage may 'unsettle' and indeed begin to overturn this opposition. Moreover, the opposition between outer and inner psychic space may be unsettled as well by the web, for it is on the publicly accessible, personal homepage that one may find the expression of an author's innermost secrets, dreams, and passions« (Mitchell and Reid-Walsh 2002:156).

Thirdspace

The second concept is 'thirdspace'. Thirdspace is a particular species of hybrid social space. The term goes back to Homi Bhaba (1994) und Edward W. Soja (1996) and is used by Matthews et al. (2000) to refer to the street as a 'terrain between childhood and adulthood', as a field of experimentation in which the novelty of hybrid identities can be articulated. Matthews et al. speak – with specific reference to shopping malls – of medially and commercially extended social spaces, i.e. social space such as the commodified streetspace, for which teenagers join international youth culture in order to appropriate it, and reinforce their efforts to be recognised as full members of society. The researchers emphasise the security of the framework in which activities occur, including activities that challenge adults by challenging their notions of well-behaved children. Commodified streetspace, according to the authors, is an appropriate modern location for those in transition to adulthood.

> »We use the concept of thirdspace to make sense of young people's place use. According to Soja (1996), those 'who are territorially subjugated by the workings of hegemonic power have two inherent choices: either accept their imposed differentiation and division, making the best of it; or mobilise ... and struggle against this power-filled imposition (Soja, 1996: 87). Both of these choices are inherently spatial and inevitably result in 'division, containment and struggle'« (Matthews et al., 2000: 290).

Matthews et al. lay emphasis – quite in keeping with Bhaba's ideas, which were developed with reference to anti-colonial resistance – on the struggle of young people for their right to independence and autonomy. From this perspective, the street becomes a thirdspace, a »dynamic zone of tension and discontinuity where the newness of hybrid identities can be articulated« (ibid.: 282). In the context of the present paper, it is important above all that experiences with thirdspace, especially as a result of the all-pervading commercialisation of malls, allow teenagers access to cultures and values that »supersede the parochial« (ibid.: 291). It is probably beyond question that the shopping mall exemplifies the experiences that today's children have with the street in the widest sense, and with commodified outdoor spaces.

Children's Place Concepts and Criteria

We know hardly anything about how the changes briefly outlined here are actually manifested in children's criteria and concepts. This issue is usually of no key importance in the few studies conducted in this direction. It is rather the case that analyses not explicitly or primarily related to social space sometimes produce results which permit conclusions about new elements in the children's notions of social space. This is the case, for example, when the focus of interest is on children's problems with (collective) identity and group membership. The results of one study on children's images of family (Ulich and Oberhuemer 1992) can be interpreted here as showing that the majority of the four-, six- and eight-year-olds interviewed in the study have 'despatialised' their notions of family. One of the key findings of this study was that, for the older children, 'living together' in the concrete, visible sense was not (or was no longer) an imperative criterion of family. Like most of their contemporaries in other age groups (cf. Bertram 2000), the children distinguished both explicitly and implicitly between family and household. The 'ideal' families described in the study are not nuclear or small families, but comprise many people – seven and more – in the majority of cases. The children's extended families are primarily social networks. If we apply Karen Fog Olwig's line of thinking, then Jan Oberg's findings on the multiple social worlds of children on the Amalfi coast have a correlation in notions of places of belonging and identification that Karen Fog Olwig (2003) explored among children whose parents or grandparents had emigrated from the Caribbean to the USA or to Europe. Olwig's biographical (life story) interviews show that these children identify with very different places than their own. They show clearly that, due to their experience of life so far, they assign existential importance not only to local and national but also to transnational 'places of belonging' (ibid.: 232).

The specific role played by media and the world of commerce in today's children's concepts of social space was demonstrated by a study carried out by Sarah Holloway and Gill Valentine (2000). Holloway and Valentine take Edward Said's term 'imaginative geography' in its broadest possible sense to include a consideration of how children from Britain and New Zealand imagine each other's nation in terms of place, people and patterns of daily life (Holloway and Valentine 2000: 338). They show, how the importance of television and the entertainment media more generally is shaping children's understandings of other places and point to the considerable influence of the global entertainment media, and global cycles of consumption, in shaping the ways in which contemporary children envision the world (ibid.: 353). The children's »images of other places stem, at least in part, from the ways children have read media, thus confirming the suggestion in a range of educational and psychological studies (…) that popular culture is an important source of environmental imagery for children« (ibid.: 348).

Cedric Cullingford has shown vividly how efficiently the media are able to influence children's concepts of society and their ideas about how societies function. The main reason I mention his study here is because he talks more than in the other studies mentioned so far about the appropriation process to which children owe their criteria and concepts. In his book on »Children and Society«, Cullingford (1992) has reconstructed images that children create of the society in which they live, and provided an interpretation of approximately two hundred interviews with 8 – 11-year-old English children. In their images of society, Cullingford discovers an underlying conservative attitude, an 'essential conservativism' which consists in their having little trust in people's ability to improve things. Their notions of society are essentially that the way society operates is better explained in terms of fears rather than guilt. For precisely that reason, children consider the threat of punishment to be justified (as the only effective deterrent). But what is interesting in general, above all in the present context, is the explanation that Cullingford provides for the source of such basic images of society. Above all, he considers such images to be a 'response' to what present-day children filter out, casually, from the endless chatter that bombards them daily, especially from television. They make sense of society by using the means at their disposal – the decontextualised messages about law and order, guilt, horrors, wars and competitive struggles that circulate in the media, at home and in school.

Transformations of the World within Reach: Preliminary Conclusions

I would like to conclude this paper with a few summary thoughts on experience as communicated by the media. Alfred Schütz and Thomas Luckmann (1975), whose ideas about the 'spatial layering of everyday lifeworlds' are gladly referred to in studies of social space in order to ground the primacy of the world within physical space, explicitly stated in those days that technological development has resulted in a 'qualitative leap in the scope of experience and an extension of the range of action'. They draw a very differentiated picture of relationships between primary and secondary reach, primary and secondary range of action and emphasise that these relationships are highly dependent on the current state of technological development. In the field of communication studies, these interrelationships have always been a subject of dispute, as has the difference between direct and indirect experience. Like no-one before, Manuel Castells has pilloried the dichotomising of real and virtual experience that can still be found in cultural critique (and in childhood research as well) (Castells 1996: 403f.). He describes notions entertained by critics of the electronic media, according to which the new symbolic environment does not represent reality, as »an absurdly primitive notion of 'uncoded' real experience that never existed« (ibid.: 404). At this juncture I shall not be dealing with Castells' concept of 'real virtuality' and its application to current communication relationships, but will keep to the term I mentioned at the beginning for designating a normative basis for important work in childhood research relating to children's social spaces, namely the 'world within reach'. Angela Keppler (2002) has contributed some clarifying thoughts on the metamorphoses of the world within reach in a context of intensive mediatisation. She confronts the term 'medial experience' with the conventional notion of 'existential experience'. For her, existential experience is a process of acquiring individual orientations on which people can base their way of life. In the conventional understanding of experience, it is assumed »that experience of life is always gained *from* the situations *for which* it creates orientations«. In the media age, the interrelationship between experienced situation and the situation of experience has been severely loosened. One of our everyday experiences is to encounter situations in which we have never been and never will be. One important metamorphosis of the world within reach is thus the following: »Medial experience is experience of a temporarily or permanently unreachable world within the reachable world, and at the same time a permanent projection of one into the other«(Keppler 2002: 55). This projection is the only sense in which medial experience becomes orientational – and hence genuine – experience. The situation that is perceived beyond the world within physical and practical reach must be charged with meaning by being related to one's own life – it has to be appropriated. Medial experience is »an experience of situations *beyond* the reach of one's own action, and *within* the reach of one's own lifeworld situation« (ibid.: 56). According to Keppler, medial experience can only be understood appropriately when consideration is also given to its having 'intersubjective topicality', that it is shared with others, and that others simultaneously ascribe meaning to it. In the present mass media age, people experience themselves as actors who live in one present despite their different positions. Angela Keppler refers to participation in a medially configured cultural age (ibid.: 57).

There is clearly a need for further differentiation here, particularly of notions of intersubjective topicality and medially configured cultural age, for example if one thinks of Internet chatting, eMailing and the use of mobile phones. So it is no coincidence that the examples used by Keppler in support of her arguments are situations into which TV programmes project, and not, for example, interactions with mobile phones. She devotes little attention to the problem concerning the experiential content of hybrid, 'technosocial' interaction – in other words the kind of interactions mentioned in the second section of this paper, which have always been medially instrumented. There are two aspects of her attempt at explanation I find important: 1. the distinction between lifeworld and practical physical reach, or the range of one's own action and 2. the emphasis on appropriation.

The manifold interlinkages of virtual and real elements in situations, interactions and lifeworlds in general is an aspect that Markus Schroer (2003) had in mind when he coined the term 'interpenetration' as a means of conceptualising the mutual influencing of virtual and real space. Schroer recommends this term, but not without asking, whether the picture of permanent penetration is not too simple for understanding the multilayered relationship between the real and the virtual (ibid.: 219). The fact that this multilayered-ness has implications for appropriation should need no further explanation.

Sensitivity to this complexity is evidenced in some microsociological writing. Authors of studies examining the virtual worlds and constructions of social space among children, almost always refer to an amalgam of sources for the geographical knowledge of today's children. This knowledge is acquired *casually* along the way. One might be tempted to borrow (in very unconstructivist style) from Karl Mannheim (1928/1965) and say that this knowledge filters down to children (so to speak) as one of the effects of milieu. Cedric Cullingford (1992) has described this 'infiltration' in vivid – and very constructivist – form. Whereas Cullingford emphasises the major role played by omnipresent media in everyday life, the output from which is registered by children in a similarly casual way, Arlie Russell Hochschild (2003) shows the other variant of this theme. She points out how children in the USA always notice quite incidentally, when consuming media, that their parents have to organise their being looked after, and how they do so: »In the end, while children may be playing a video game, watching TV, or reading a comic, they are doing something else: eavesdropping« (Hochschild 2003:181). Both variants confirm that the everyday reception of media is usually not an exclusive activity, but is almost always mingled with other activities, and that the media have become an (audiovisual) environment within and with which we endlessly interact.

In summary, we can conclude that the transformations of the world within reach referred to in this paper lead to ambiguous experiences in which empowerment and vulnerability, options and risks are combined in complex mixtures. We can generalise and say – like Tomlinson has shown with the example of deterritorialisation – that for potentially all contemporaries there is a new basis where major differences arise in the appropriation of new environments. The extent to which children's forms of appropriation and experiences differ from those of other age and population groups is something that requires investigation, taking that shared basis into consideration. One of the key tasks of studies guided by the 'differential contemporariness' concept is to clarify the issue concerning the importance of generational membership in the winner/loser split.

References

Abbott, C. (1998): »Making connections: Young people and the Internet«. J. Sefton-Green: (ed): *Digital Diversions. Youth Culture in the Aage of Multimedia*. London: UCL Press: 84-105.

Ahrens, D. (2003): »Die Ausbildung hybrider Raumstrukturen am Beispiel technosozialer Zusatzräume«. C. Funken and M. Löw (eds): *Raum, Zeit, Medialität. Interdisziplinäre Studien zu neuen Kommunikationstechnologien*. Opladen: Leske + Budrich: 173-190.

Appadurai, A. (1998): »Globale ethnische Räume«. U. Beck (ed): *Perspektiven der Weltgesellschaft*. Frankfurt: Suhrkamp: 17-40.

Behnken, I., M. du Bois-Reymond and J. Zinnecker (1989): *Stadtgeschichte als Kindheitsgeschichte*. Opladen: Leske + Budrich.

Bertram, H. (2000): »Die verborgenen familiären Beziehungen in Deutschland. Die multilokale Mehrgenerationenfamilie«. M. Kohli and M. Szydlik (eds): *Generationen in Familie und Gesellschaft*. Opladen: Leske + Budrich: 97-121.

Bhabha, H. (1994): *The Location of Culture*. New York: Routledge.

Buchner-Fuhs, J. (1998): »Das Kinderzimmer in der sozialwissenschaftlichen Kindheitsforschung«. P. Büchner, M. du Bois-Reyond, J. Ecarius, B. Fuhs and H.-H. Krüger: *Teenie-Welten. Aufwachsen in drei europäischen Regionen*. Opladen: Leske + Budrich: 147-243.

Castells. M. (1996): *The Rise of the Network Society*. Oxford: Blackwell Publishing.

Childhood (2000): Special Issue: Spaces of Childhood«, *Childhood*, Vol. 7., No. 3.

Döring, N. (2005): »Handy und SMS im Alltag«. *Medien und Erziehung;* Vol. 49: 29-34.

du Bois-Reymond, M., P. Büchner, H.-H. Krüger, J. Ecarius and B. Fuhs (1994): *Kinderleben. Modernisierung von Kindheit im interkulturellen Vergleich*. Opladen: Leske + Budrich.

Fix, T. (2001): *Generation @ im Chat. Hintergrund und explorative Motivstudie zur jugendlichen Netzkommunikation*. München: kopaed.

Foucault, M. (1986) »Of other spaces«. *Diacritics,* Vol. 16: 22-27.

Giddens, A. (1990): *The Consequences of Modernity*. Cambridge: Polity.

Gupta, A. and J. Ferguson (1992): »Beyond culture: Space, identity and the politics of difference«. *Cultural Anthropology*, Vol. 7: 6-23.

Hengst, H. (2005): »Complex Interconnections: the Global and the Local in Children's Minds and Everyday Worlds«. J. Qvortrup (ed): *Studies in Modern Childhood. Society, Agency, Culture*. Houndmills, Basingstoke: Palgrave Macmillan: 21-38.

Hengst, H. (2004): »Differenzielle Zeitgenossenschaft«. D. Geulen and H. Veith (eds): *Sozialisationstheorie interdisziplinär. Aktuelle Perspektiven*. Stuttgart: Lucius & Lucius: 273-291.

Hengst, H. (2002): »A**R**e yo**U** **M**ale **or F**emale? Der Computer, das Internet und der kleine Unterschied«. J. Steitz-Kallenbach and J. Thiele (eds): *Medienumbrüche*. Bremen and Oldenburg: Universitätsverlag Aschenbeck & Isensee: 53-69.

Hengst, H. (1997): »Reconquering urban spots and spaces? Children's public(ness) and the scripts of media industries«. *Childhood*, Vol. 4: 425-444.

Hengst, H. (1989) »'Secondary Orality' in der Kinderkultur«. Erlinger, H.D. (ed): *Kinderfernsehen II*. Essen: Die blaue Eule: 125-141.

Hochschild, A. R. (2003): *The Commercialisation of Intimate Life. Notes from Home and Work*. Berkeley and Los Angeles: University of California Press.

Holloway, S. and G. Valentine (2000): »Corked hats and *Coronation Street*: British and New Zealand children's imaginative geographies of the other«. *Childhood*, Vol. 7.: 335-357.

Ito, M. and D. Okabe (2005): »Technosocial situations: Emergent structurings of mobile email use«. M. Ito, M. Matsuda and D. Okabe (eds): *Personal, Portable, Intimate: Mobile Phones in Japanese Life*. Cambridge MA: MIT Press: 257-273.

Keppler, A. (2002): »Begrenzung und Entgrenzung. Zur Dialektik medialer Kommunikation«. J. Fohrmann and A. Orzessek (eds): *Zerstreute Öffentlichkeiten. Zur Programmierung des Gemeinsinns*. München. Fink: 53-64.

Klein, A. (1993): *Kinder, Kultur, Politik. Perspektiven kommunaler Kinderkulturarbeit*. Opladen: Leske + Budrich.

Kondo, Kaoruko (2004): »Global and Diasporic Media and Children's Hybrid Identities. The Case of Japanese Children in London«. *Medien und Erziehung*, Vol. 48: 59-71.

Liede, M. and Ziehe, T. (1983): *Über Telefonitis, die Liebe zu alten Klamotten und den Hunger nach Intensität. Gespräche über die junge Generation*. Reinbek: Rowohlt.

Livingstone, S. (2002): *Young People and New Media*. London: Sage.

Livingstone, S. and M. Bovill (eds)(2001): *Children and their Changing Media Environment: A European Comparative Study*. Mahwah, NJ: Lawrence Erlbaum Associates.

Maczewski, M. (2003): »Kids online. Identitätsentwicklungen bei der Vernetzung von Online- und Onground-Erfahrungen«. H. Hengst, and H. Kelle, (eds): *Kinder, Körper, Identitäten*. Weinheim und München: Juventa: 245-266.

Mannheim, K. (1965): »Das Problem der Generationen«. L. von Friedeburg (ed): *Jugend in der modernen Gesellschaft*. Köln und Berlin: Kiepenheuer & Witsch: 23-48.

Matthews, H., M. Taylor, B. Percy-Smith and M. Limb (2000): »The unacceptable *flaneur*: the shopping mall as a teenage hangout«. *Childhood*, Vol. 7: 279-294.

McNamee, S. (2000): »Foucault's heterotopia and children's everyday lives«. *Childhood*, Vol. 7: 479-492.

Meyrowitz, J. (1987): *Die Fernseh-Gesellschaft. Wirklichkeit und Identität im Medienzeitalter*. Weinheim (Orig.: *No Sense of Place* 1985).

Meyrowitz, J. (1998): »Das generalisierte Anderswo«. Beck, U. (ed): *Perspektiven der Weltgesellschaft*. Frankfurt: Suhrkamp: 172-191.

Mitchell, C. and J. Reid-Walsh (2002): *Researching Children's Popular Culture. The Cultural Spaces of Childhood*. London: Routledge.

Oberg, J.C. (2000): *Il mondo tra I monti. Eine ethnographische Studie über soziale Räume von Kindern und Jugendlichen im süditalienischen Tramonti* (unpublished masterthesis, University of Bremen).

Olwig, K.F. (2003): »Children's places of belonging in immigrant families of Carribean background«. K.F. Olwig and E. Gullov, E. (eds): *Children's places. Cross-cultural perspectives*. London and New York: Routledge: 217-235.

Olwig, K.F. and E. Gullov, E. (2003) (eds): *Children's Places. Cross-Cultural Perspectives*. London and New York: Routledge: 1-19.

Philo, C. (2000): »The corner-stones of my world. Editorial introduction to special issue on spaces of childhood«. *Childhood*, Vol. 7: 243-256.

Pries, L. (1998): »Transnationale Soziale Räume. Theoretisch-empirische Skizze am Beispiel der Arbeitswanderungen Mexico – USA«. U. Beck (ed): *Perspektiven der Weltgesellschaft*. Frankfurt: Suhrkamp: 55-86.

Pries, L. (1997): »Transnationale Migration«. *Soziale Welt: Sonderband 12*. Baden-Baden: Nomos: 15-44.

Schlögel, K. (2004): »Kartenlesen, Augenarbeit«. H. D. Kittsteiner (ed): *Was sind Kulturwissenschaften? 13 Antworten*. München: Wilhelm Fink Verlag: 261-283.

Schroer, M. (2003): »Raumgrenzen in Bewegung. Zur Interpenetration realer und virtueller Räume«. C. Funken and Löw, M. (eds): *Raum, Zeit, Medialität. Interdisziplinäre Studien zu neuen Kommunikationstechnologien*. Opladen: Leske + Budrich: 217-236.

Schütz, A. and T. Luckmann. (1975): *Strukturen der Lebenswelt*. Neuwied: Luchterhand.

Schulz, I. (2005): Zwischen Reiz und Risiko. »Jugendliche über Handys und Mobilfunkangebote«. *Medien und Erziehung*, Vol. 49: 17-23.

Sefton-Green, J. and D. Buckingham (1998): »Digital visions: children's »creative uses« of multi-media technologies«. J. Sefton-Green (ed) (1998): *Digital diversions: Youth culture in the age of multimedia*. London: UCL Press: 62-83.

Selmer, L. (2005): »'Nicht nah, aber immer für dich da!' Erreichbarkeit im Familienalltag«. *Medien und Erziehung*, Vol. 49: 24-28.

Sloterdijk, P. (2005): *Im Weltinnenraum des Kapitals*. Frankfurt: Suhrkamp.

Soja, E.W. (1996): *Thirdspace. Journeys to Los Angeles and Other Real-and-Imagined Places*. Oxford: Blackwell.

Tomlinson, J. (1999): *Globalization and Culture*. Cambridge: Polity.

Tully, C.L. and C. Zerle (2005): »Handys und jugendliche Alltagswelt«. *Medien und Erziehung*, Vol. 49: 11-16.

Turkle, S. (1998): *Leben im Netz. Identität in Zeiten des Internet*. Reinbek: Rowohlt.

Ulich, M. and P. Oberhuemer (1993): »Und sie machen sich ein Bild… Familie aus der Sicht von Kindern«. Deutsches Jugendinstitut (ed*): Was für Kinder. Aufwachsen in Deutschland. Ein Handbuch*. München: Kösel: 120-126.

Zeiher, H.J. and H. Zeiher (1994): *Orte und Zeiten der Kinder. Soziales Leben im Alltag von Großstadtkindern*. Weinheim und München: Juventa.

Mobile and Uprooted? Children and the Changing Family

An-Magritt Jensen

As a little girl I used to travel to my grandparents. They lived in a village in the very bottom of a long fiord, with a travel distance of seven hours by boat. I must have been around seven years when starting to travel alone. The boat left very early in the morning. The combination with a latent seasickness and the early rise always – as I remember it – left me vomiting over the boat's gunwale as the journey began. But I never thought of this as a problem and full of expectations I looked forward to my next visit. As a mother I never sent my son on such travels, just as present-day parents tend to state that they put larger restrictions upon their children's mobility than they experienced themselves in their childhood. But there is one exception and that is for children travelling to visit their father.

My 'mobile childhood' in the early 1950s differs from present children's travelling. My parents never doubted that I was safe among strangers. They knew I would be my grandparent's guest for a few, precious days. The mobility that is the focus of this article is that of children who travel between two parental homes as a result of changing family patterns. Such mobility takes place in context where public space is perceived as a threat to children. Furthermore, the children may be sent between homes where parental relations are not on good terms, and where conflict may dominate. These mobile children transgress the parental fear of public space and sometimes concern for their wellbeing in the other home, for the sake of a greater goal: time with the father. As more children grow up in single-mother families increased attention is given to children's need of fathers. The fatherless society is featured as *the crisis* of today as described in the bestseller of David Blankenhorn (1995). On the internet a multitude of father organisations homepages pop up in a split second, claiming that the fatherless society derives from gender wars and underscoring children's need of time with the father. I shall refer to this as the 'needed father' ideology.

The issue raised in this article is if the needed father ideology can conflict with children's rootedness in space? I shall argue that childhood is positioned between diverging interests of adult society. On the one hand parents, mothers and fathers, claim their share of the children's time. On the other I shall argue that a market society – although not explicit – may gain from enhancing flexibility in the future labour stock. I shall use children's commuting between homes as my case. This commuting is justified by the best interests of children. Maybe the benefit is located in adult society?

Children's Mobility in a Liquid Modernity

Children's mobility has undergone some paradoxical changes over time in terms of an expansion and shrinking at the same time. Even if there are historical accounts of young children travelling long distances alone, as described in 1856[1] in 'Tom Browns School-days' by Thomas Hughes, mobility has become a part of children's lives to an unprecedented extent. Increasingly children will follow their parents on charter-trips during holidays to distant places as visualized in the South-Asian tsunami catastrophe during Christmas 2004. Children are reaching wider, but not necessarily on their own initiative. Present-day parents avoid exposing children to unsupervised areas, often by the justification of heavy traffic and 'stranger danger'. As a result public space is increasingly defined as adult space and children's everyday space outside the adult gaze is shrinking (Valentine 1996). The street and neighbourhood is substituted by organized activities to which children depend on transport, often in a family car. Helga Zeiher (2001) describes how children shape their social life through moving between 'islands' of unconnected spaces defined through their activities (2001). Pia Christensen et al. (2000) challenge concerns over increasing fragmentation of children's outdoor spaces. They find that it is through »the dynamic and fluid movement of children in, out and around the home that their own sense of belonging to the family and the home is constituted« (ibid.: 153). But the family and the home remain the centrepiece in children's sense of belonging. With new family patterns children's homes are part of their spatial 'islands'. Children shape their family life through moving between parents living apart. Spatial belonging is substituted by fluid movement between parents.

Children are seldom included in descriptions of the 'liquid modernity'. Zygmunt Bauman (2000) portrays the 'upper circuits of global capital' (mostly men), travelling only with cabin luggage: attaché case, mobile phone and a portable computer, while Saskia Sassen (2003) describes the 'survival circuits' of the same economy, where maids, nannies, and sex-workers migrate from poor to rich countries (mostly women). But neither of these authors take account of children. Nonetheless, children are not excluded from social structures; they are part of society at large (Qvortrup 1990). I shall argue that the 'liquid modernity' has become an important feature of childhood. When parents live apart children's exposure to the dangerous 'outside' is subsumed by the greater importance of spending more time with the father. In the process they learn to cope with differing challenges, shifting routines and varying relationships.

Children's mobility is primarily a result of adult's decisions; where to live, to spend their holidays, the structuring of everyday life between home and work. Hence, children are brought into the world of travellers by other people's decisions and most important for my topic by their parents' decisions of not living together. The often referred notion of Ulrich Beck and Elisabet Beck-Gernsheim (2002: 91) that »family life no longer happens in one place but is scattered between several different locations« captures a childhood condition about which little is known. This is not to say that the relationship between home and movement remains unexplored.

Children's commuting between parental homes symbolises modern childhood where, as John Gillis (2003) tells us: »… family time has become one of the chief means by which adults connect not just with children, but with childhood itself, now commonly thought of as a principal source of regeneration« (ibid.: 150). It was space, not time, which defined family relationships. To children with parents living apart family time is ensured through commuting between homes. The commuting signifies a shift from space to time in family relationships. Commuting separates a child spatially from one house, one locality and one community while attaching them emotionally to the parents through time. At the same time the commuting challenges the image of childhood. First of all it stands in contrast to the domesticated childhood. Through commuting new public spaces are opened to children. Furthermore, commuting challenges the image of a familiased childhood, resting metaphorically on the dependency and immobility of the child in a home (James 1998). Family life is detached from a common home, and attached to individual relations to the mother and the father. Finally, it defies the private and non-regulated aspects of family life. Commuting organizes time according to a regulated, agreed-upon schedule. Children can not just change their mind. While 'home' is associated with basically private and individual routine, memory, and identity (Rapport and Dawson 1998), commuting between two parents may represent a focal point of struggles and conflicts. Commuting may be imperative for a child's time with both parents, but it may also be detrimental to their sense of belonging.

Through travelling children sustain their relations with both parents, but they may pay a price in their everyday life with friends, a neighbourhood and leisure activities. There are both possible gains and losses of this mobility, but the degree to which this is perceived as a problem depends on the importance adults place on the benefits that are achieved through the travelling. Since the large majority of children with parents living apart have their daily life with the mother, and visits to the father (as we also shall see later) I will term my issue time with the father rather than 'the other parent'. I shall put my searchlight on the interface between the ideology of the needed father and children's possible losses in their everyday life. I give more emphasis on the losses than the gains since the importance of time with the father is well researched in a host of studies, while the losses to children's everyday life are largely silenced.

Common Trends and Varying Contexts – a European Look

Changes in children's family patterns are common trends in European countries. More children are born to an unmarried mother, more children experience family dissolution and more children live in a single mother family for a substantial part of their childhood. But large variations in family types prevail. The international survey Health Behaviour among School Aged Children 2001-2002 (HBSC) shows that in all countries most children live with both parents (Currie et al. 2004).[2] In a majority of countries the proportion of children (aged 11, 13 and 15 years) not living with both parents fluctuates around 20 to 30 per cent. The broad picture indicates a South – North line, where children in the South (and Israel) are more likely to live with both parents, than children in the North. About 10 per cent of Italian children do not live with both parents, compared to 30 per cent in the Scandinavian countries, and even more in England.

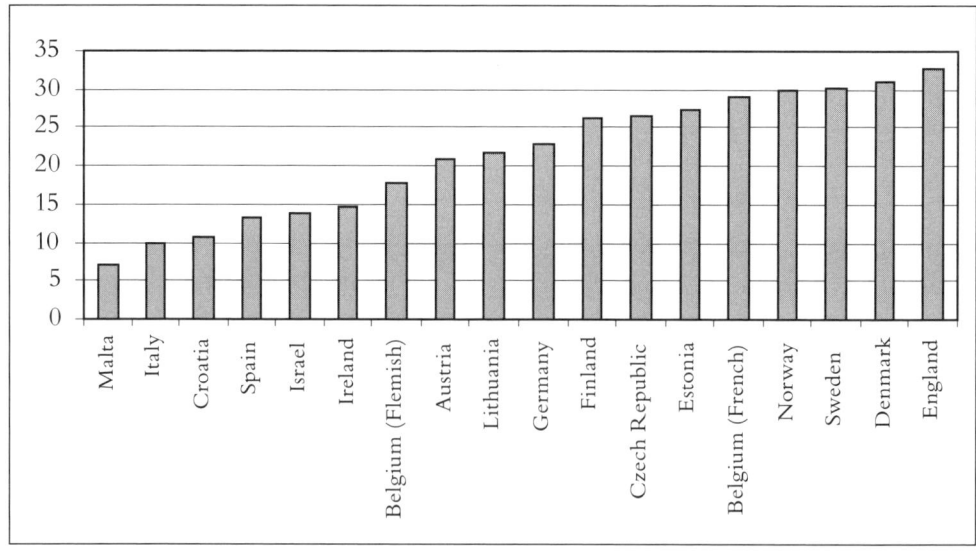

Figure 1. Children 11 to 15 years not living with two parents. %
Source: HBSC 2001-2002

In the European research-network Children's Welfare[3] 13 countries have delivered a 'Country Report' (I shall refer to these as 'report' below) on family changes and children's access to space (among other issues). Among the common trends summarised from the reports, are emerging single-mother families (Jensen and Qvortrup 2004). In all countries an overwhelming share of children stay with the mother if parents live apart. But father's involvement in childcare varies. In countries with a more stable family structure children live with the father, but do not necessarily use much time with them. A 'needed father ideology' may surface where modern family patterns are widespread. The involved fatherhood is likely to appear where the patriarchal, married, nuclear families are substituted with open structures of cohabitation and single parenthood coupled with ideologies of gender equality, Elizabeth Thomson tells us (2003). These countries are likely to be found in the northern Europe, and in particular among the Scandinavian countries.

Single parenthood gains terrain, but the traditional gender order in responsibility for children remains. Children continue to live with their mother and are parted from their father. Where family patterns are unstable, more children have parents in two homes and when father involvement increases, children commute more. Hence, the ideology of the needed father seems to vary in strength. Among countries with traditional family patterns fathers seem to take a more distant role towards their children. A few examples from the reports may illustrate the variation.

In Italy almost all children live with both parents, but fathers are only marginally involved in child care. It is still highly unusual among fathers to participate in daily care of their young children. About one in five feed their small children, put them to bed or change nappies even if such collaboration is increasing (Conti and Sgritta 2004). Similarly, in Croatia, where 90 per cent of the children live with both parents, most non-resident fathers (and fathers of extramarital children in particular), single mothers indicate, rarely contact their children. Even when living nearby, only a minority of the fathers have seen their child during the last year (Raboteg-Saric 2004). To a large degree, this is also the situation in Ireland, another country where an overwhelming majority of the children live with both parents. However, over the recent years the rise in extramarital births has been spectacular in this country. Most children born outside marriage have parents living apart, and every second father has not been in contact with their child. Only a minority of non-resident fathers play any role in their children's lives (Devine et al. 2004). In Austria children complain that they want more time with their father, both if living with the father and after a divorce. But the fathers are unable or unwilling to dedicate time with children due to their commitment to work (Beham et al. 2004). In Germany it is noted that parents' separation accelerates child mobility. Among these children some move more or less on a regular basis between the two homes, and have their own room in each. However, in rare cases children spend an equal amount of time in both homes. About half of the affected children in ages 5 to 10, and fewer among the older children spend every second week-end in the other parent's home (Jurczyk et al. 2004). Only scattered information on children's visits between homes is found, but in countries where traditional family patterns prevail, the need of much time between children and their fathers does not seem to have a strong place in public discourse.

By contrast in the Nordic countries many children do not live with both parents at the same time as the support to gender equality is strong. Fathers are expected to take part in child care while living with the child, and to spend much time with children they do not live with on a daily basis. These are countries with a stronger impact of the needed father ideology. But gender equality in parenting should not be overstated. As noted in the Finnish report, a public concern over the lone child is phrased in gender neutral terms and is centred on working patterns more than children's need of time with the father. The existence of small children in a family has amazingly little impact on fathers working life and very few fathers use their right to parental leave. In 1998 about 200 000 Finnish children had their parents in separate households, at an average distance of about 55 km. Many children may have a substantial travel distance to visit the other parent's home (Alanen et al. 2004). The attention on the needed father is directed to fathers not living with their children. The focus has gained strength over recent years although scepticism is now surfacing. This is described for Denmark where children increasingly are switching between two homes. The Danish report informs us that visiting agreements are ill-balanced between parents and children. Children's desire to have more time with their friends, or to have a more coherent life without frequent travelling, has turned out not to be sufficient reasons to overrule the father's right to see his child. On the other hand, if the father does not turn up at the agreed-upon time the child has few rights (or sanctions) to deny the father's visiting schedules (Kampmann and Warming Nielsen 2004). Among Norwegian children it is estimated that about 40 per cent of the children born by the beginning of the 1990's will not live with their father at their 16th birth day. Intensive debates over the best interest of the child, understood as children's right to two parents, prepare the ground for a time-share system of parenting.

The picture that emerges from the Country Reports is one of increasing shares of children not living with both parents, although the levels and rate of changes vary. Observations on children's commuting between two homes are scattered. Still, we get glimpses of a situation in which problems may be looming. In some countries, the problem seems to be a lack of contact between children and their fathers in general. In other countries, strong ideologies of fatherhood involvement have surfaced. We find this most pronounced among the Scandinavian countries, where modern family ideologies have gained a foothold. Paradoxically father involvement increases in countries where children are more likely not to live with the father on a daily basis.

The involved fatherhood has gained a strong ideological position in Scandinavia. Children's commuting between two homes has some very delicate borderlines where contact with two parents is judged against other needs of children. Conflicts between children and parents, and between mothers and fathers, are looming. An important issue is whether children's rights to set their own priorities may be jeopardised if these are in conflict with their parent's rights. I shall explore the Norwegian case below (Jensen et al. 2004b).

Children's Travelling in Numbers

Traditionally a high cultural value has been given to children's free and unrestricted outdoor play and children have been walking or bicycling to the school, alone or together with friends. As my personal introductory story tells, some fifty years ago my own parents had little concern when sending me for rather long journeys alone. They trusted that other adults would help if needed. Most parents thought so. However, in the course of time strangers have shifted to potential dangers.

Several studies have confirmed that Norwegian children now increasingly spend their time indoors. A parental concern about outside danger is a driving force in this development. 40 per cent of the children now are taken to school either by public transport or in the family car. One in every forth child in the first years of schooling are driven in the family car even if the distance is rather short (between 500 to 1000 meters). A great majority (80 per cent) of parents of school-aged children estimate that their own children are more restricted in their access to outdoor areas than they were themselves as a child. A protective attitude to children's movement outside the home prevails, but an ever increasing share of children has parents living apart. To these children movement outside the home, and often alone, is necessary to visit the father.

Norway is not an easy country for travelling. Geographically the country covers a large area. If turned upside down from the most southern tip, the northern part will reach Rome. Mountains, fiords and difficult roads complicate the matter. Being situated close to the polar circle winters are long and dark while summertime, of course, offers daylight almost for the 24 hours. Still, in the Northern part there is hardly daylight during November through January. Winter storms, snow and fog cause delays and unpredictable travelling. The country is also sparsely populated, with it's about 4,5 million people there is only 13 persons per km². With a regional policy emphasising that all parts of the country should be populated, many children have parents living far apart with long distances and challenging travels.

Family life with both parents is still the most common. Among all children (0-18) 75 per cent live with both parents and for the youngest children (0-6 years) the proportion is 84. Almost every second child in Norway is now born outside marriage – the majority of these in a consensual union. Since the end of the 1980s family instability has increased and children born in consensual unions are at high risk of a parental break-up. Despite the modern aspect of consensual unions as a family type, an overwhelming proportion of the children live with the mother (85 per cent) after break-up. Only a minority of all children in single parent households, 7 per cent, live with the father and these are usually teenagers. Over time no increase in this proportion has taken place, but more children live with both parents in two homes (8 per cent). Since 1996 a doubling has taken place in time-shared (equal basis) parenthood and given the broad support in public opinion and family policy, the increase is likely to continue.

Joint legal responsibility between parents living apart is a major manifestation of the involved fatherhood. Until recently it was common for single mothers to have sole responsibility, and particularly among parents in consensual unions. Recently an increase in joint parental legal responsibility is taking place (now at 47 per cent). When parents have joint parental responsibility children are much more likely to live with both parents, they are much more likely to visit the father often (8 to 12 days a month) and they are more likely to have shorter distances between the homes compared to when the mother has sole responsibility (Jensen 2005a).

Previous studies have confirmed that family change is a main factor behind children's moves in general (Jensen and Clausen 1997). In depth interviews with children suggest that many feel they have little influence on relocation of home, surroundings and playgrounds after divorce (Moxnes 2003). But children's travelling between homes has not been mapped until Statistics Norway carried out the Survey on Visiting Arrangements and Child Allowance in 2002 (Sætre 2004). The survey (I shall name this the Survey on Visiting 2002) contains information on 2600 children under 18[4] who do not live with both parents. The information is given by a parent. I shall use these data to illustrate three aspects of children's mobility between homes. First, how far is the geographical distance? Second, what kind of emotional zones are children moving in? Third, are the conditions under which children visit varying with the distance between homes? Table 1 shows the geographical distance between parent's home.

Almost one in four children has walking distance between the homes, and an additional 40 per cent of the children are living in short distance (less than ½ hour) by public or private travel means (mostly bus or car). Hence, the children living with rather short distance constitute two thirds (66 per cent) of all children. Among those travelling for longer time, about the same proportion go by private car (14 per cent) and by public means (16 per cent). Seven per cent of the children are travelling by air. For about four per cent of the children there is no information on travelling.

Travel distance	0-4 years	5-9 years	10-14 years	15-17 years	All
Walking distance	18	23	23	24	23
Short – public/private car	49	47	42	36	43
Long – private car	19	17	14	9	14
Long – public (air, bus or train)	11	10	17	25	16
No contact/NA	3	3	4	6	4
Total	100	100	100	100	100
Number	273	746	1003	451	2473

Table 1. Travel means and distance between parent's home by age of the child, per cent.
Source: Survey on Visiting 2002.

Tabel 1 illustrates variation in travelling patterns by the children's age. Younger children are more likely than older children to travel by car. Older children are more likely to travel long distances by public means. Still, of importance for the argument of this article is to note that only one in four children have parents living within walking distance. The implication is that great majority of children do not have parental homes with a shared neighbourhood. Friends and leisure activities for many of these children will be out of reach when visiting the father.

Almost every second among those children sharing the time equally between two parents has walking distance between the homes (not shown in table). This implies, at the same time, that even in this group of children every second child can not just walk between the homes. In most cases the homes are not far between. The majority travel short distances (less than half an hour) by car. But five per cent travel long distances by air, bus or train (Jensen 2005b). Among children living in two homes on an equal term, long distance travelling is not common. But not having a shared neighbourhood is as common as having one.

Do children commuting over longer distances have parents who are on good terms? Are they moving between emotional zones where conflict is prevalent? The survey on visiting 2002 has four alternatives of the level of conflict: no conflict, a little, some conflict and high conflict. I have merged this into two groups, one of no conflict or little, and the other on some conflict or high. While no or little conflict between the parents dominates (about 55 per cent), a substantial proportion of the children have parents with conflict and 18 per cent at a high conflict level. Does the level of conflict vary with the travel distance between homes?

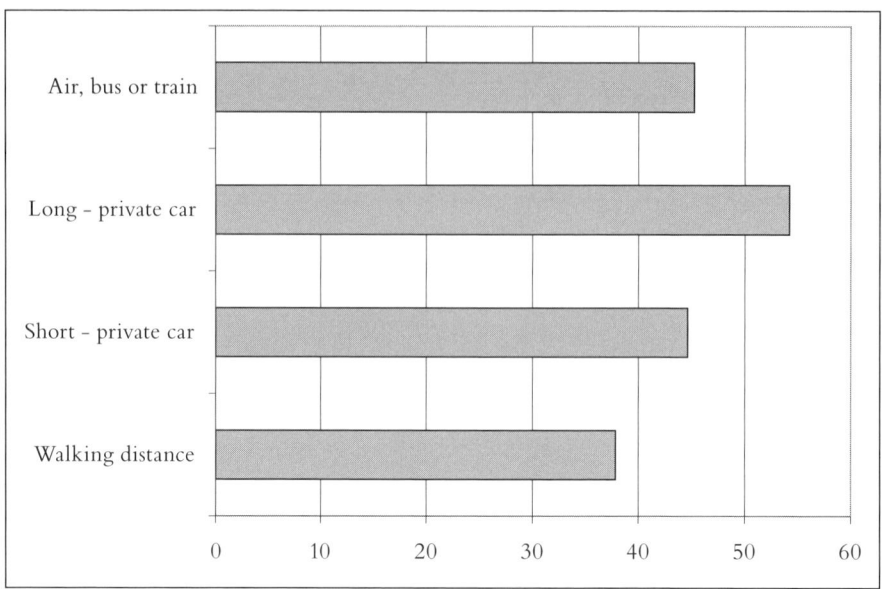

Figure 2. Children with parents having some or much conflict by travel means and distance between homes, per cent.
Source: Survey on Visiting 2002

Children living within walking distance have parents with less conflict (38 per cent) while the highest level of conflict is found among children travelling long distances by car (54 per cent). Children with long public travelling (air, bus or train) and short distances by private car have parents with some or a high level of conflict in 45 per cent of the cases. Commuting does not only indicate a distance in geographical space. A substantial proportion also commutes between strained emotional zones.

Two patterns are emerging: one pattern includes children with two homes in walking distance, and the other children who commute over long distances by car. Children with two homes in walking distance maintain a shared neighbourhood and parents have less conflict. Further analyses show (not included in Figure 2) that these children frequently visit the father. The other group of children travel long distance by private car and have more often conflict between the parents. To these children the visiting is parting them from an everyday life of friends and leisure activities while adding a situation of tense emotional zones between parents in conflict.

The general picture emerging from Figure 2 is one where conflict between parents are not negligible. Even among children living in walking distance more than one in three have parents with some or high levels of conflict between them.

Children travelling long distances by air, bus or train have a lower conflict level between parents than children travelling long distances by car. But also here almost every second move between parents in conflict and their travel activity is substantial. One out of three children with long public travels (37 per cent) visited the father at an ordinary monthly schedule (4-7 days) or more (8 days +). Assuming that they travel on average every second month (a conservative estimate), and adding a couple of travels for holidays, we arrive at about 6 to 8 long distance travels per year. The air companies estimate about 100.000 child-travels per year.[5]

Children's mobility is justified with the best interests of the child. It is a general agreement that the most significant problem for a child with parents living apart is the threat of loosing contact with the non-resident parent (father). Seldom the question is raised about how much time is needed and under which conditions? Do we know that the more time, the better off is the child? Is a fifty-fifty sharing between the parents necessarily better than a thirty-seventy sharing? Figure 3 illustrates the conditions under which children visit. It indicates that long distance between parental homes is challenging to several aspects of children's social welfare.

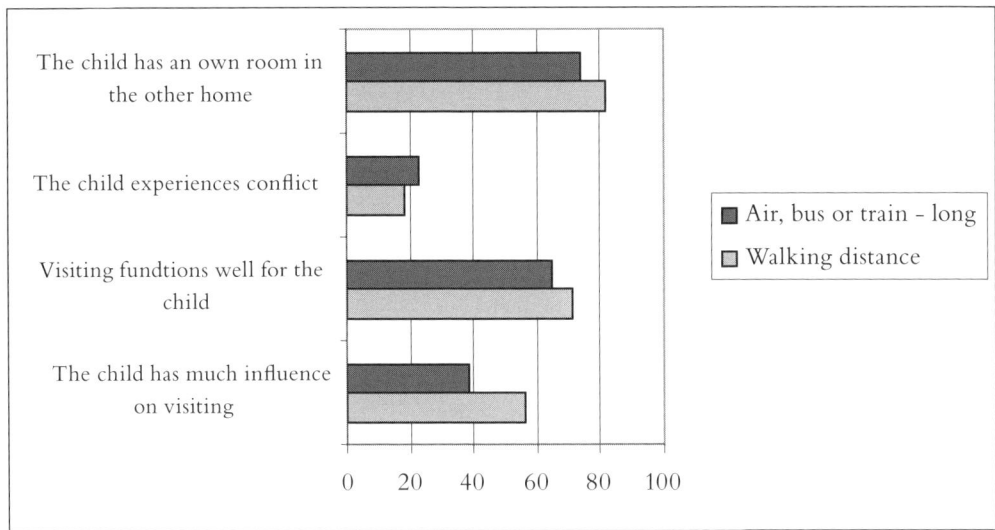

Figure 3. Indicators of children's social welfare by distance between the homes, per cent.
Source: Survey on Visiting 2002

Interpreting Figure 3 we should be reminded that we do not get children's own stories. The interviewed person is a parent. Nonetheless, our interest here is the different pictures according to the distance between the homes and maybe we can assume that parent's accounts are not influenced by distance. We find that the children commuting long-distance have less often a room on their own, they more often experience their parent's conflicts, and they are less satisfied with the visiting system. Most notably in

Figure 3 is the difference in children's own influence on the visiting frequency. The child's influence is much lower among children travelling long distances (40 per cent) as compared to children with walking distance (58 per cent). Following this, a pattern emerges where contact with the father may conflict with other components of children's welfare. Commuting does not solve all problems; it may even create some new.

We have looked into geographical distance, emotional zones and conditions of children's visits. The majority of children have to move out of their own neighbourhood to be with the father, many move between troubled emotional zones, and long distance travelling challenges children's welfare, in particular their lack of influence on the visiting. Some of the challenges of the travelling are illustrated in the stories below.

Mobile Children – Some Possible Risks

The mobile children are a new feature filling the empty spaces of waiting halls, bus stations and airports, Zygmunt Bauman argues (2001). They are scattered, but visible once your attention is turned to this phenomenon. My attention to this issue was through a personal experience some years ago. I was visiting a family of five, the mother, step-father and three children. The daughter at 10 was at home with a friend. The two girls were in the sofa, enjoying a children's song contest on the TV. The two other children, a boy of 8 and another daughter of 13 had gone to visit the father, about one hour train-travel away. Shortly after my arrival, the phone rang and I could hear a boy's yelling »You forced me!«, hanging up the receiver. The mother explained herself that the daughter at home had 'escaped' the regular visit to the father because she was invited to a birthday party the following day. The boy in particular had objected to going. There was no conflict between the children and their father. The boy's problem was that he wanted to relax at home. The mother from her perspective, fearing of being accused of breaking the agreed upon visiting scheme, an accusation – if proven – could result in losing the daily custody, had coerced the boy to go. The 10-year old daughter, in this case, had a valid reason not to go on the agreed-upon visit, while the 8-year old son had not. A couple of years later, when I met the family again, the whole situation had deteriorated. At this stage the father had remarried a Filipino woman and now all three children resented the regular visiting schemes. They saw some extenuating circumstance when comparing themselves to other friends, the mother explained, because their travel distance was too long for more frequent visiting than every fortnight. By this, they were able to take part in their other weekday's activities, such as riding and ballet. The children disliked the break-up in their other activities and in this case the travel distance was a protection against larger claims on their time.

Since this incident I have collected other experiences on my own travels. To give some ideas of the kind of situations that may emerge I shall give some examples below.

The long flight
The little boy could be 7 years old, travelling on a Saturday evening from the north to the south of the country. The journey would take about 2 ½ hours and the boy was bored after the first 10 minutes. I was seated next to him, but he showed no sign of wanting contact. His attitude was repressive with no smile in his face. The stewardess came around with crayons and a little booklet to all children, but this was finished in short time. A little relief was offered as he was allowed to play with his 'game-boy', similar to the rest of the children. But even this did not last long. He was up and down – with his seatbelt on, to the floor and again in his seat. Having tried out his limits of movement he finally turned to me and asked for the time. The question was repeated after a short while, and we were into a game where he guessed the time before I gave the answer, always guessing that more time had lapsed than the real watch-time showed. Still being very reserved, we had a little conversation around this game and he told me that this was not his first travel. Actually he made this travel quite often.

The lone flight
This was also a little boy, maybe 8 or 9 years old. While the other children were picked up by their respective mother or father, no-one waited for him. After a (rather short) while a policeman (in full uniform) came to assist the boy in picking up his luggage. No, the boy did not remember what his suitcase looked like, but since only one was left at the luggage band they agreed it was his. What happened later I do not know, but guess that the policeman was able to trace the parent and bring them together.

The late flight
Since the demand for child-seats is increasing, while the air companies keep a quota at eight children (aged 5 to 11 years) at each flight, the children are spread over a large number of flights. Most children will travel at reasonable times, but recently on a flight a boy – he was maybe 10 – entered the last flight along the coast. The flight landed about midnight, and happily a parent was waiting for him at the airport.

The issue is not only a national one. Children are also crossing borders.

The wrong flight
I was waiting for take-off on my flight from Berlin to Copenhagen. It was a Saturday morning in November 2004 as a problem caught my attention. The stewardesses were counting the passengers over and again. They had a mismatch of the numbers

on their list and the persons in the cabin. After a while we were asked through the loudspeaker if anyone on board rather should have been on the Stockholm-flight, waiting for take-off at the same time. From the very bottom of the aircraft a girl came forward. She could be about 10 years with the identity-folder around her neck indicating that she was in the wrong aircraft. Without knowing the circumstances my first reflection was that the little girl was travelling between a mother in Berlin and a father in Stockholm, or vice versa.

These scattered observations indicate that travelling alone may be necessary to fulfil children's need to see the father, but may also expose them to challenging situations. First of all a paradoxical feature of the mobile child is their immobility. They are driven in a private car, or seated in a public transportation. In most cases they are virtually tied to their seats by safety belts. Their 'power of movement', as Durkheim (1992: 148) describes as a condition of childhood, must be managed. Durkheim continues on his observations: »Do not ask it to come to rest; rather than remain idle it runs to no purpose at all; it is capable of everything except rest and inertia«. But to children moving between homes the primary task is not to move.

Most children will master the travelling. In most cases one parent will follow them to the departure and the other will be there to meet the child, but as described above this is not always the case. A parent may be absent at the arrival point due to neglect, but also due to reasons over which they have no control, such as to traffic problems or unexpected situations. The cases where things go wrong will be the exceptions. But the fear of such situations may be widespread. Also children without personal experience may have heard about this from other children. Travelling alone implies several tasks that the child must cope with if something goes wrong.

Public Discourse and Policy

As I am writing these lines – in my home by mid-December 2004 – I turn on the radio to get the news.[6] Children's travelling is a headline. Weekly, a representative from the national railway reported, some train ticket controller complains about difficult situations of children travelling alone. Children could be as young as four years, he recounted. As an example, we are told, a parent might follow a child into the train and jump off just as the train starts to move, leaving the child on its own. Other passengers, as well as train personnel, he continued, may try to prevent parents from leaving, but often without success. He assumed that parents sent their children alone due to lack of money and time. To the child the problems involved were manifold. Some children would fall asleep and forget to leave the train. Some would misunderstand where and how to leave. Some would leave without finding a parent waiting at the railway station. The railway now wanted to increase their efforts to dispel these problems.

Some time later, in spring 2005, media reportage indicates that a train-host(ess) was now employed to take responsibility of travelling children.

Stories surface in the media from time to time. In response to the situation the Norwegian Child Ombudsman has developed a set of guidelines.[7] A first glimpse at these guidelines remind us of the topography of Norway (described above). The Child Ombudsman informs about the age limits of children travelling alone by air, boat, bus, and train as well as combinations of several means of travelling. Parents are advised that even though the air company accept children to travel alone at age five, the Ombudsman finds this too young (without specifying an alternative age). Ferry and boat companies reject children's travelling alone if they are younger than 12 years, but some have their own arrangement of children's travels. Bus, the Ombudsman suggests, should only be for children of 8 years or older, while children travelling by train should be 10 years. If children need to combine different means they should be older, 12 years.

But children's need to be together with both parents is highly valued in the population and in public policy. During the 1990's several family policy measures were introduced to involve fathers in child care. Among these measures is the 'daddy quota' in which six weeks of the paid parental leave is reserved to the father. Efforts were also made to nurture a sustained relationship between children and their fathers after a parental break. Most significant is probably a change in the child allowance, which used to flow from the non-resident parent to the resident parent based upon his earnings. By 2003 the child allowance was made dependent on the visiting frequency. Since then fathers pay less when children visit more.

During the spring 2005 children's mobility between homes gained public attention along with increasing concern about child neglect and abuse. Children with two homes apparently have less protection than children in one home, it was claimed. When the parents have a high level of conflict, one parent's accusation is often neutralized by the other's. Typically the mother is accused of sabotaging visiting agreements (and nurturing Parental Alienation Syndome), while the fathers are accused of not fulfilling their parental duties. If visiting children are exposed to neglect or abuse, the child welfare authorities are obliged to interfere. However, child welfare officers hesitate to enter a struggle between parents. These children cannot turn to their mothers and neither can they turn to their fathers. They do, however, turn to the Child Ombudsman. Based on increasing communication from children the Ombudsman has declared that parents' statutory rights of time with children have turned out to be too strong. Children should not be forced to visit a parent who they do not want to see (Hjermann 2005). But what are the legitimate reasons for declining to commute between parents? Clearly, as the issue that provoked the Child Ombudsman to interfere, a risk of violence or sexual assault will meet broad agreement. This is also seen in the response by the Minister of Children and the Family, who declare that a change in the

Children's Act is needed. But will children's need to dispose more of their own time be met with agreement from the adult society? The position of the mobile children seems to be between a rock and a hard place. In order to be with their father many have to transgress the protected childhood space which adult society under other conditions allocate them. But it is justified in the best interest of the child.

Clash of Ideologies or Affirmative Structures?

Two developments in childhood mobility take place side by side, but they are seldom linked. Parents hesitate to leave children alone in outdoor public space. Also inside the home a 'protective industry' is gaining importance. Child seats are mandatory in cars, just as a helmet is expected on every child bicycling or down-hill skiing. Hazardous elements of the homes are removed. Increasing attention is given to the dangers of insecure staircases. Children's beds and hot ovens are secured. Protection of children is a yardstick of good parenting. In statistics this development is traced in the reduced number of children injured, in particular for traffic accidents. On the other hand children's commuting between homes arises from the growth in family dissolutions coupled with the ideology of children's need of time with the father. As a result an increasing share of children move between two parental homes, often alone and over long distances. Some of these children meet situations that modern parents (but not necessarily parents in former times) normally would evade. In other conditions many adults would interpret such situations as inadequate parenting. The case stories above illustrate this, may be most clearly in the wrong flight story. Despite the prevailing idea that children should be protected from outside danger, the standard for the good divorce is that children should travel between parental homes in order to spend time (and the more the better) with the father.

The rise in the number of children living in a single mother family attracts much attention in a symbolic warfare over parental justice. In public debates time is the symbol for a just sharing of children. Since time, unlike space, can be arithmetically divided in shares, a parental equation of just sharing can be calculated. Visiting agreements are sacred and part of a 'parental war'. There is wide acceptance of children's need of two parents, as reflected in the Convention of the Rights of the Child (Art. 9: 3). Typically children's voices do not enter the debates. It is taken for granted that the child's most important need is to keep in the most extended contact with the father, no matter the circumstances. What kind of circumstance is legitimate, from a child perspective, to avoid a scheduled week-end visit? Are children in this process enslaved in their parent's struggle of a 'just share'? In order to comply with their parents demands on their children's time, children's own needs have been referred to a very minor position

Children's spaces are expanded and children's homes are divided, but parent's time with children is no less precious than before. The focus of public debates is particularly directed to fathers, as the parent with the traditional more distant ties to children. Family life, as we have seen John Gillis argue (2003), used to be rooted in space while it is now shifted towards time. Similar changes in perceptions of family life are seen in other areas. Having a child used to be equated with marriage while the most important issue today has shifted to the needed father (Jensen 2003). An ill-functioning family is regarded as harmful and break-ups are justified by the best interest of the child (Moxnes 2003). However, 'the best interest of the child' is a slippery concept, ready to be defined by the present day 'discourse-rulers'. Nowadays children's need of spatial linkages to a home, a neighbourhood, and long-term friendships is secondary to time with the father. This can be traced in family policy that over recent years has lowered the economic costs of frequent visiting to non-resident fathers. While travel costs used to be covered by the non-resident parent, they are now shared between the parents. Presently claims on tax deduction for children's travel expenditures are forwarded. Furthermore, as already mentioned, child allowances are linked to visiting frequencies. Time is given a price, also for parents being together with their children.

Rising numbers of children commute between homes in order to fulfil their parents need for time with children. While this is understood within the discourse of 'the best interest of the child' it is notoriously difficult to determine what this interest is, and not the least what children's own needs would be, if they were asked. But we may ask whether mobile children may serve a purpose of a modern society? There are reasons to claim that the competence children may acquire in travelling is in accordance with the interests of future society. There is a correspondence between the flexibilization of the labour market and the commuting children.

One in four Norwegian children under 18 do not live with their father. An increasing share spend equal time in both homes and a substantial proportion may travel rather long distances by public means. Through commuting children do not only sustain their contact with both parents. Mobile children learn to navigate within a family network of relations rather than nurturing strong bonds to a home and a neighbourhood. To children, as Zygmunt Bauman (2001) suggests to adults, a permanent address of a locality, is replaced by the e-mail and mobile telephone number to keep in contact with friends (who also may be at the other parent's home). In accordance with this we may ask if childhood mobility fosters a 'flexibilisation' of life styles useful to modern societies. Bauman (2000) argues that the labour market in the 'new economy' needs people who are 'lighter on their feet'. Richard Sennett is making a similar case. In the capitalist economy »… instability meant to be normal« (1998: 31). Both state that detachment and superficial cooperativeness are better for the new economy than strong feelings of belonging and loyalty. Children take part in the modernization process of »… complex movement of people, goods, money and information« (Rapport and Dawson 1998: 7) through commuting between homes. The 'greedy' parenthood structures children's everyday life, their time use and their mobility. Just as homes are invaded by the flexible labour market, childhood is invaded by the time-shared parenthood. As parents become 'work nomads' (Jurczyc et al. 2004), children are turned into 'family nomads'. Childhood is, just as adulthood, characterized by increased mobility. But Sennett's message is that there is a mismatch between the individual life and the demands from the labour market. What may compose a labour market, may decompose a life, he warns us (1998: 43). Following this the 'liquid modernity' may nurture a competent child, but may it also decompose children's welfare?

»Are we living in an 'anti-child' society?«, Ulrich Beck and Elisabeth Beck-Gernsheim ask (1996: 102). The answer is no. Parent's struggle for a fair share of a child goes hand in hand with the elevated emotional value of children. »Children have become so central to adult identity«, John Gillis argues in the same line, »that the loss of a child is now considered the worst thing that can possibly happen.« (2003: 150). He is at the same time adding that »maintaining children as icons has been costly, particular to children themselves« (ibid.: 161). Children commuting between two parents' households seek to fulfil their parent's needs. Their problems in doing so are referred a very distant place in public debates and social science. Among the few studies on this subject, it is demonstrated how English children may feel that they are divided between their parents after divorce as were they a part of the sharing of properties. While there is a growing presumption that equal parenting is fair and moral, children would over time start questioning why they were the ones to carry the burden (Wade and Smart 2003). Hence, if the time-sharing is justified by the love of a child, to children the consequences may be 'anti-child'.

Children who commute between two homes may fulfil their parent's needs of emotional rootedness in a child, but depress children's social rootedness in space; in a home, a neighbourhood and community. We do not know if this is in children's best interest, but following Sennett and Bauman's argument of the flexible and liquid modernity, it may be in the best interest of a market society.

References

Alanen, L., H. Sauli and H. Strandell (2004): »Children and childhood in a welfare state: The case of Finland«. Jensen, A.-M. et al. (2004a): 143-210.
Bauman, Z. (2000): *Liquid Modernity*. Cambridge: Polity Press.
Bauman, Z. (2001): *Community. Seeking Safety in an Insecure World*. Cambridge: Polity Press.
Beham, M., H. Wintersberger, K. Wörister and U. Zartler (2004): »Childhood in Austria: Cash and Care, Time and Space, Children's Needs, and Public Policies«. Jensen et al. (2004a): 19-80.

Beck, U. and E. Beck-Gernsheim (1996): *The Normal Chaos of Love*. Oxford: Polity Press.

Beck, U. and E. Beck-Gernsheim (2002): *Individualization*. London: Sage Publications.

Blankenhorn, D. (1995): *Fatherless America. Confronting Our Most Urgent Social Problem*. New York: Basic Books.

Christensen, P., A. James and C. Jenks (2000): »Home and movement: children constructing 'family time'«. Holloway, S. and G. Valentine (eds): *Children's Geographies. Playing, Living, Learning*. London and New York: Routledge: 139-155.

Conti, C. and G.B. Sgritta (2004): »Childhood in Italy: a Family Affair«: Jensen, A.-M. et al. (2004a): 275-333.

Currie, C., C. Roberts, A. Morgan, R. Smith, W. Settertobulte, O. Samdal and V. Bernkow Rasmussen (2004): *Young People's Health in Context. Health Behaviour in School-Aged Children (HBSC) Study: International Report from the 2001/2002 Survey*. Health Policy for Children and Adolescents, No. 4, Geneva: WHO.

Devine, D., M. Nic Ghiolla Phádraig and J. Deegan (2004): »Time for Children – Time for Change? Children's rights and welfare in Ireland during a period of economic growth«. Jensen, A.-M. et al. (2004a): 211-274.

Durkheim, E. (1992): »Childhood«. C. Jenks (ed): *The Sociology of Childhood. Essential Reading*. London: Gregg Revivals: 146-150.

Gillis, J. (2003): »Childhood and family time: a changing historian relationship«. Jensen, A.-M. and L. McKee (eds): 149-164.

Hjermann, R. (2005): »Tvunget samvær« [Compulsory togetherness]. *Feature Cronicle, Aftenposten*. Oslo, 26. April.

James, A. (1998): »Home and the child«. Rapport, N. and A. Dawson (1998)(eds): *Migrants of Identity. Perceptions of Home in a World of Movement*. Oxford: Berg: 139-160.

Jensen, A.-M. (2003): »For the children's sake: symbolic power lost?« Jensen, A.-M. and L. McKee (eds): 134-148.

Jensen, A.-M. (2005): »Barn som bor med far bor også med mor« [Children living with their father are also living with the mother]. *Samfunnsspeilet* No. 2, Oslo: Statistics Norway.

Jensen, A.-M. and S.-E. Clausen (1997): *Barns familier. Samboerskap og foreldrebrudd etter 1970* [Children's Families. Consensual Unions and parental Break-Ups since 1970]. Norwegian Institute for Urban and Regional Research (NIBR): Report No. 21.

Jensen, A.-M. and L. McKee (eds)(2003): *Children and the Changing Family. Between Transformation and Negotiation*. London: Routledge Falmer.

Jensen, A.-M., A. Ben-Arieh, C. Conti, D. Kutsar, M. Nic Ghiolla Phádraig, H. Warming Nielsen (eds)(2004a): *Children's Welfare in Ageing Europe*, Vol. 1 and 2, Trondheim: Norwegian Centre for Child Research (NOSEB).

Jensen, A.-M., A.T. Kjørholt, J. Qvortrup and M. Sandbæk with V. Johansen and T. Lauritzen (2004b): »Childhood and Generation – Money, Time and Space«. Jensen, A.-M. et al. (2004a): 335-402.

Jensen, A.-M. and J. Qvortrup (2004): »Summary – A Childhood Mosaic. What Did We Learn?« Jensen, A.-M. et al. (2004a): 813-832.

Jurczyk, K., T. Olk and H. Zeiher (2004): »German Children's Welfare Between Economy and Ideology«. Jensen, A.-M. et al. (2004a): 703-770.

Kampmann, J. and H. Warming Nielsen (2004): »Socialized Childhood: Children's childhoods in Denmark«. Jensen, A.M. et al. (2004a): 649-702.

Moxnes, K. (2003): »Children coping with parental divorce«. Jensen, A.-M. and L. McKee (eds): 90-104.

Qvortrup, J. (1990): »Childhood as a Social Phenomenon – an Introduction to a Series of National Reports«. *EuroSocial Report* 36/1990, Vienna: European Centre.

Raboteg-Saric, Z. (2004): »Children's Welfare in the Context of Social and Economic Changes in Croatia«. Jensen, A.-M. et al. (2004a): 527-590.

Rapport, N. and A. Dawson (1998): *Migrants of Identity. Perceptions of Home in a World of Movement.* Oxford: Berg.

Sassen, S. (2003): »Global Cities and Survival Circuits«. Ehrenreich, B. and A. Russel Hochschild (eds): *Global Women. Nannies, Maids and Sex Workers in the New Economy.* London: Granta Publications: 254-275.

Sennett, R. (1998): *The Corrosion of Character. The Personal Consequences of Work in the New Capitalism.* New York: W.W. Norton & Company.

Sætre, A. H. (2004): *Undersøkelsen om samvær og bidrag 2002. Dokumentasjons- og tabellrapport.* [The Survey on Visiting Arrangements and Child Allowance in 2002. Documentation and table report]. Notat No. 26, Oslo: Statistics Norway.

Thomson, E. (2003): *Partnerships and Parenthood: A Comparative View of Cohabitation, Marriage and Childbearing,* CDE-Working Paper No. 18, University of Wisconsin-Madison: Center for Demography and Ecology.

Valentine, G. (1996): »Children should be seen and not heard: The production and transgression of adults' public space«. *Urban Geography,* Vol. 17, No. 3: 205-220.

Wade, A. and C. Smart (2003): »As fair as it can be?« Jensen, A.-M. and L. McKee (eds):105-119.

Zeiher, H. (2001): »Children's islands in space and time. The spatial differentiation of children's ways of shaping social life«. Du Bois-Reymond, M., H. Sünker, H. H. Krüger (eds), *Childhood in Europe. Approaches – Trends – Findings.* New York: Peter Lang: 139-160.

Notes

1. I thank Prof. David Morgan for commenting upon a previous draft and drawing this historical parallel.
2. Here selected among the countries participating in COST A19
3. COST A19, see http://cost.cordis.lu/src/home.cfm and http://www.svt.ntnu.no/noseb/costa19/
4. The response rate is 59 per cent, 55,4 among fathers and 62,8 among mothers.
5. Oral information given by air companies to PhD-candidate Tonje Lauritzen.
6. National broadcasting, channel 1, at 12.30 pm.
7. www.barneombudet.no

Immigration and the Enlargement of Children's Social Space in School

Dympna Devine

Introduction

In a globalising world migration patterns and the dynamics of social relations between ethnic groups are in a constant process of change. The global becomes local and the local is changed by the global. Representations of 'other' in concepts of national and ethnic identity are increasingly challenged[1]. While Ireland has never been ethnically homogenous, increasing and rapid immigration into Irish society as a result of unprecedented economic growth has taken place in the past ten years. While there have always been some minority ethnic groupings in Irish society, including indigenous Travellers, the vast majority of the population has traditionally been classified as white, settled and Catholic. Nonetheless, immigrant patterns in the past ten years reflect an increase in the proportion of the population who come from countries other than the traditional immigrant/returned emigrant base of the United Kingdom and the United States of America, to include in particular former eastern bloc European countries such as Poland, Lithuania, Latvia, Romania and Russia, as well as African (Nigeria and South Africa) and Asian countries (in particular China and Philippines). Figures from the most recent census of 2002 indicate that 6.3 per cent of the population classify themselves as non-Irish and it is likely, with on-going immigration especially from countries like Poland, that this figure will have increased somewhat in the census due to be taken in 2006. Contrary to popular misconception, a majority of those who come to Ireland do so legally on work permits, or by virtue of their membership of the EU, with only a minority coming to seek asylum[2].

The patterns indicate that immigration into Ireland of 'visible minorities' or members of identifiable minority ethnic groups is occurring within a situation of unprecedented population growth, and is particularly marked in the cities and surrounding commuter belts. Further, many of these immigrants are working in the lower paid service, domestic and catering sectors, giving rise to their predominance in low-cost public and private rental accommodation sectors. Their children can thus be expected to cluster in schools in these areas and this is also reflected in the CSO figures (2004). Immigration has resulted in schools and classrooms becoming more ethnically diverse spaces, hence spaces where there are also a growing number of children who are from religious and cultural traditions different to the norm.[3] Children no less than adults are embedded in the changing social landscape, their social world in school enlarged through engagement and interaction with others who are ethnically and culturally different. What is unique however to the experience of children is their confinement in the institutional space of the school – a space that is primarily controlled and defined by adults as they seek to normalise children in line with particular goals and values. Here Irish and immigrant children are confined together in classrooms, schoolhouses and school-yards. The fact that children's experience of confinement in the physical space of the school is now met by the enlargement of their social space through increasing diversity among the student group, creates challenges as well as opportunities for the construction of children's social identities, as well as for their responses toward those who are ethnically different.

Such change occurs within a domain primarily controlled by adults acting in line with the societal demands for schooling. The role of schooling in the production and reproduction of social identities (Arnot and Weiler 1987; Barton 1995; Connolly 1998) and the increasing focus European wide on education for and about citizenship cannot be divorced from concerns about social disintegration arising from mass migration (Bailey 2000; Osler and Starkey 2002). This chapter explores how, in a context of adult concerns for particular forms of schooling, children culturally work out their social space in school during a period of rapid and intensive immigration.

Drawing on research from two intensive studies of children and their schooling, it examines the interrelation between the parallel worlds of the classroom and the schoolyard, as children negotiate a path between adult and peer approval, grappling with concepts of difference/sameness, inclusion and exclusion in school. Key questions here relate to the message systems (Bernstein 1975/1996) regarding ethnic diversity imbued in teacher talk and how children incorporate such messages in light of their own interaction with their peers. The exercise of power is central to such processes. Discourses permeate practice, simultaneously challenging and/or reproducing ethnic stereotypes and racial prejudice, raising questions about the welfare of all children, but particularly those of minority ethnic status.

Theorising Space, Power and Intergenerational Dynamics in Children's School Lives

Schools are an important tool in the exercise of power in modern societies, socialising the young into the dominant mores and values of the society at large (Bourdieu and Passeron 1990; Bourdieu 1993; Bowles and Gintis 1976; Durkheim 1956; Parsons 1951). This has implications for both the experience and organisation of children's time and space in school. Schools are a key institutional backdrop to the experience of time and space in childhood, both mapped according to the specific demands and requirements of adult society and communicated through the curriculum, pedagogical and evaluative practices in schools (Devine 2003). This process of administrative surveillance and normalisation (Foucault 1979/1980) is evident in the responses of children, who when asked about their experience of school readily identified with 'real' learning as being that related to the world of adult work and school as a space where children are tightly regulated and controlled:

> Art, music and PE are the least important because they don't include brainwork … you can't get a job with those subjects. (5th class girl, Churchfield)[4]

> Sometimes it feels like a bit like being a robot…like as if the teacher is in the middle of the room with a great big remote control and you have to do everything she says or you will get into trouble. (2nd class girl, Churchfield)

However, drawing on Goffman's work (1961; 1971) in relation to front and back stage regions, agents also enjoy the capacity of reducing surveillance, hence control, through the complex differentiation of their activity/behaviour (deference and demeanour), into front and back stage regions. It is within back regions that individuals are afforded the opportunity to remove the »façade« arising from ascription to particular positions and /or roles within the front region (e.g. teacher or pupil). This is especially the case in situations where there is a distinct hierarchy in terms of subordination and control. For Anthony Giddens the capacity to usurp forms of control in this manner is indicative of the dialectic of control i.e. the mutual interdependence in all relations centred on power where outcomes deriving from social interaction are dependent on the doings of others:

> »These two axes of regionalisation (front and back regions) operate in a complex nexus of possible relations between meanings, norms and power. Back regions clearly often do form a significant resource which both the powerful and the less powerful can utilise reflexively to sustain psychological distancing between their own interpretations of social processes and those enjoined by official norms…the forms of

enclosure or disclosure which allow agents to deviate from or flout those norms are important features of the dialectic of control in situations involving surveillance«. (Giddens 1984: 126-127. See also 1976: 111; 1979: 92)

Applying this analysis to the area of children's interaction in school, children are not cultural dupes to be moulded unquestioningly into the 'adult' way of doing things. While they may be structured as 'other' in their relations with adults in school (Devine 2003: 127), children are also active agents with the capacity to reflect critically and constructively on their social experiences. Children and adults negotiate their relationships along a path of resistance/compliance dependent upon the 'locale' we are examining. Thus the classroom, conceptualized as a front region in which formal learning takes place, is one where typically relations will be along traditional adult/child, teacher/pupil hierarchical lines, with a high degree of compliance on the part of children as they conform to the demands of the formal curriculum, under the surveillance (Foucault 1979) of the teacher. In the schoolyard, or other backstage regions of school life (corridors, toilets, under the desk, behind copy books) children can engage in behaviour, which undermines the authoritative position of the teacher. And again the research literature is replete with examples of the pranks and escapades children get up to when out of view of their teachers (Davies 1991, Devine 2003, Opie 1994, Sluckin 1981). In these back stage regions, friendships are formed, fights are won and lost and games are produced and reproduced as children interact with one another on their own terms, regaining a measure of autonomy and control frequently absent in their more formal classroom life.

Child culture serves then as an important lens through which children mediate the message systems that are communicated in the formal learning space (front region) of school. This is an active process, with children, as reflective agents, positioning themselves and being positioned with respect to the dominant discourses and norms in their own and the adult world. For many children, a tension exists as they straddle both worlds, seeking approval and recognition from the teacher in the front region of the classroom while retaining status and recognition from peers in both the front and back regions of their school lives. This is accurately reflected in the comment of an older primary school boy below:

> You have to keep up your reputation…you can't be a goody goody either…like always telling and always getting your work right, asking questions, not breaking the rules. (5th class boy, Churchfield)

For our purposes, the social space of the school can be considered as an arena of struggle in which actors seek to impose particular definitions of the situation onto others (Bourdieu 2000). Such struggles are mediated by physical space (which space are we in now – e.g. classroom, staffroom, school yard, toilets?) as well as by underlying patterns of power and control that delineate behaviour into front and back stage positioning. As reflected in figure 1 below, such positioning can apply to both adults and children as they alter their role identities in line with the particular demands or configurations of power in the particular social context:

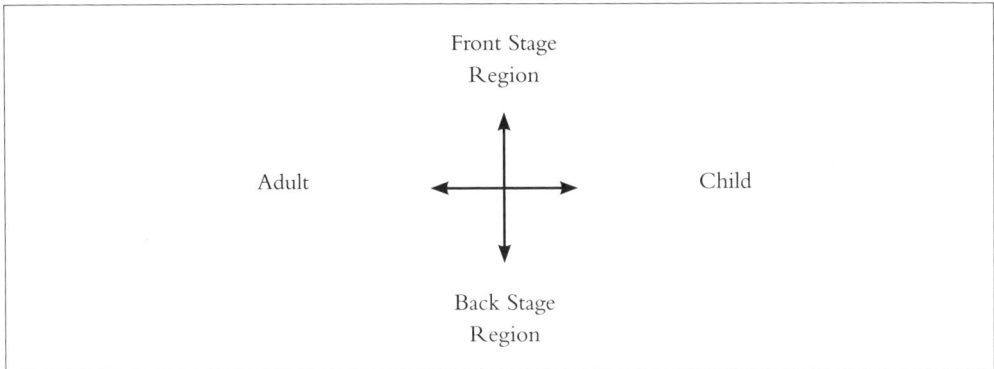

Figure 1. Spatial dynamics and social positioning

Much of children's social world – child culture – takes place out of view of the teacher and in the context of inter-generational relations, it can be defined as back stage behaviour, taking place at a level below the surface of teacher/adult surveillance/attention, something teachers are aware of but often unsure of its nature or composition. The contrasting experiences and dynamics of interaction/regulation over children's behaviour, depending upon which region they are positioned in is evident in the two quotations below, the first typifying the children's immersion in child culture, the second the front region of distinct adult control:

> Sometimes there does be a big crowd and everyone gathers around and the teacher does be saying: 'get away, get away' and the loser is hopped on…its' for fun…normally you see teacher doesn't catch them cos when the teacher comes over they shout 'sketch' and they all run away *and the teacher is trying to find out who did it and doesn't unless someone tells…mostly children say: 'oh I didn't see it'*. (5th class boy, Hillview)

> She's (teacher) watching your every move…every time you even look in your bag she's watching over you and if you want to get a head start over your homework she sees you. (5th class girl, Hillview)

The remainder of the chapter considers these spatial dynamics as important precursors to the experience of ethnicity in school. It explores how children's social interaction with peers is mediated by ethnic identity and the extent to which this interaction is informed by or contradicts the message systems they receive about ethnicity in the front stage region of the classroom. What is being argued is that within the formal learning space of the classroom, where children's activities are regulated via engagement with the curriculum (the front-region of adult/child relations), children encounter formal and informal messages about ethnic diversity and inclusion in a changing Ireland. In the back-stage regions, however, where child culture flourishes, children play out these message systems in their interaction with one another, which can be both inclusionary (conforming to teacher/school expectations and norms) and exclusionary (resisting the dominant message systems of the school/teacher) depending on the dynamics of power, control and status that underpins their relations with one another in their peer groups. Teachers as adults clearly have their own range of positions/dispositions depending on which locale they are in (e.g. classroom, staffroom etc). However our focus is upon the children's movement between the different locales and, reiterating the quotation from Giddens (1984: 126-127) above, how 'these two axes of regionalisation (front and back regions) operate in a complex nexus of possible relations between meanings, norms and power'.

Outline of Methodology

Two studies of children in Irish primary schools are the source of data utilised in this chapter. The first involved an ethnographic study of 133 children aged seven and eleven years in three co-educational primary schools over a period of one school year and was conducted in 1995/1996. Much of the theoretical work deriving from this study informs the writing of this chapter and is more substantively outlined in Devine (2003). A study of how childhood is structured in school, it explored the exercise of power between children and adults through the control of their time and space, life chances and social relations in school. A further study of children's experience was conducted in 2001-2002, with the explicit aim of exploring how children and their teachers were adapting to the changing ethnic profile of their schools. This study (Devine et al. 2002)[5] involved interviews with a selected sample of primary and second level students (311 in total) and fifty-two teachers. For the purposes of this chapter, data drawn from the primary sample only is utilised.

Table 1. Profile of the participating primary schools in the study 1995/1996[6]

School	Location	Social Class	Gender
Hillview	Suburban	Lower middle class	Co-Education
Parkway	Suburban	Working class	Co-Education
Churchfield	Suburban	Middle class	Co-Education

Table 2. Profile of the participating primary schools in the study 2001/2002[7]

School	Location	Gender	Social Class	Total Enrolm.	Minority Ethnic Enrolment	Minority Ethnic as % of Enrolm.
Oakleaf	Suburban	Co-Education	Working Class	300	73	24%
Newdale	Rural	Girls	Mixed social class	415	47	11%
Riverside	Suburban	Co-Education	Mixed social class	268	25	9%

Interviews were conducted with a selected sample of teachers and children in each of the studies, as well as with the school principals and/or vice principals. Children were organised for interviews on a friendship group basis, with no interview group larger than five children. Children in second (aged 8 and 9) and fourth/fifth class (aged 10 and 11) were selected with the total of children in each of the classes interviewed.[8] Observation of the children both in the classroom and in the schoolyard was also conducted. In the later study, the researchers also attended two general meetings of language support teachers (one for primary level teachers and one for second level teachers), giving an indication of some of the challenges that were being faced by teachers in schools other than those involved directly in the study. For the purposes of analysis, the remainder of the chapter is divided into two main areas: front stage adaptations to ethnic diversity and back stage adaptations to ethnic diversity.

Front Stage Adaptations to Ethnic Diversity

In Irish primary schools classroom spaces are very much under the control and 'ownership' of the class teacher (Devine 2003). It is the teacher who sets the tone for the class and chooses by and large how the classroom space is structured and organised.

The inclusion of children from a diversity of ethnic backgrounds provides a relatively[9] new challenge in the organisation of both time and space – a challenge that teachers in the study in general welcomed, albeit with some reservations. These latter revolved primarily around challenges to the existing sense of community and culture within the school, as well as catering to the diverse needs of the minority ethnic children themselves:

> Before they came we had a very clear community…whom we knew very well…we had an unspoken and unarticulated understanding about where they were coming from, their culture and their background…that made it very free and easy for us to deal with each other'. (Male principal, Oakleaf primary)

> Teachers have a lot of adjusting to do, they are finding it difficult. In a general class you'll have exceptionally good children, middle of the road children and weaker children. Then you get three who can't speak English. So you have four hard dimensions…you'd nearly need five strands of work'. (Female teacher, Riverside primary)

Nonetheless all of the teachers in the study spoke of the positive dimension of increasing ethnic diversity in school life and of the breadth of 'fresh air' the presence of many of these immigrant children brought to the school. Teachers were concerned that minority ethnic children would in general be included in the total life of the school and feel welcomed and valued there. In their talk, they mentioned the value of celebrating the diversity of cultures yet the importance of remaining sensitive to differences in context and background of the children:

> It's nice to come into the school and know immediately it has non-nationals – like a map of the world showing where all of our students come from…you know it's a multi-cultural school. (Female teacher, Oakleaf primary)

While teachers in their talk advocated the inclusion of all children in the life of the school, in practice they implemented a form of 'pragmatic multiculturalism' (Connolly 1998) – including the experiences of immigrant children where specific issues arose but in general minimising and rendering invisible the degree of difference that existed between the children. While there were some differences between teachers, observational data indicated very few, if any, references to cultural diversity either in the physical (e.g. notice board displays) or dialogical space (teacher talk) of the classrooms. This was in sharp contrast to the classroom spaces within which language learning support for immigrant children was provided, these spaces replete with references both physically in the décor and verbally in teacher talk, to the cultural and linquistic backgrounds of the immigrant children themselves[10]. While some teachers mentioned specific efforts they had made to incorporate intercultural methodologies in their teaching (through for example music and art work), by and large in all of the schools visited a targeted whole school focus on issues related to ethnic diversity and inclusion was absent. Indeed teachers were visibly uncomfortable talking about issues of culture and ethnic difference, stating their concerns that they would embarrass minority ethnic children by drawing attention to their specific cultural experiences in front of the class. While teachers encouraged children to be respectful and helpful in their interaction with one another, an emphasis on sameness over difference was seen as more important in promoting positive peer relations:

> You would be more conscious of what you would say and that the kids don't say things they shouldn't say. One day the kids saw a Chinese person and they were laughing and I said: 'no you can't, we have different cultures here and you can't laugh'. They all know to respect each other. (Male teacher, Oakleaf primary)

> I don't like any hatred towards other people as I can see how it affects the child. There is a lot of difference in my class but I can see past that, I see all the similarities. (Female teacher, Oakleaf primary)

Where there was evidence of racist behaviour, as in for example name-calling or the exclusion of children on the basis of their ethnic identity, teachers tended to speak about this in terms of bullying and the suppression of such behaviour in the school. While they were apprehensive about the onset of any racial conflict in schools, it was felt by and large that racism was not a problem in primary school children's interaction, and if identified would be dealt with authoritatively and as part of the overall disciplinary code and policy in the school.

By virtue of their authoritative position within the school and the resources that come with this (Giddens 1984), teachers in their talk demonstrate the importance they place on social inclusion in school, reflecting national and curricular policy in the area. Through the disciplinary and anti bullying policies in each of the schools, overt message systems were being communicated to the children regarding the importance of behaving in an inclusive manner and showing respect and tolerance to all children in school. However it could also be argued that the teachers' stated discomfort around issues of racism and cultural difference in itself communicates certain messages to the children. In this sense teachers also used their authoritative position to minimise the significance of racist incidents[11] and in their general inclinations to emphasise sameness over difference in their interactions with the children in their care. This was equally true of teachers with older second level students (Devine 2005) and so cannot simply be explained in terms of a paternalistic framework being drawn upon by teachers in the education of young children. Rather it signifies an uncertainty and insecurity among teachers themselves when confronted with issues of race and racism, something they often alluded to in the course of interviews (Devine et al 2004a). Within the front region of classroom life, a relative silence existed then in teacher talk and action around issues of ethnic diversity, such issues assigned to the language support teacher and perceived perhaps to be an area of interest for minority rather than majority ethnic children in the school. Issues when they did arise, either in relation to the curriculum or children's social interaction were dealt with on an individual basis rather than in a focused strategic manner, as part of an intercultural approach to the children's overall education.

From the children's perspective they had mixed views, some positive and some negative, on this enlargement of their social space in school. Observational data suggested that immigrant children on the whole merged into their classroom lives, participating in classroom activities, for the most part like their Irish peers[12]. Re-iterating the teachers' emphases on social inclusion, the children spoke of the importance of making new children feel welcome in school, in spite of differences in language and cultural background:

> Those refugees…they came in here and they didn't know no one. And *we had to make friends with them or the teacher told us to* … it was hard for us to get friendly with them cos they didn't know any English. (3rd class girls, Newdale primary)

There was also a clear sense in the talk of Irish children that children who came from abroad were interesting and could teach them new things, including information which could be used for their school work and projects:

> It's good having Maya in the class cos she's Egyptian and she's clever and we are doing a project now on countries so she is helping us. (5th class boy, Oakleaf primary)

> Interviewer: Do you think it is a good thing that there are lots of different people coming from lots of different countries?
> Child 1: Yes, you get to know about other countries, part of their religion, of their festivals and all.
> Child 2: Its kind of like fruits. If you only had a banana, you wouldn't know what kiwis and oranges tasted like. (5th class girls, Oakleaf primary)

Contrasts were drawn in this respect between children from differing minority ethnic groups, with Traveller children dismissed as being uninteresting as they had grown up in Ireland:

> Interviewer: I know there have been Travellers in and out of this town.
> Children (all) Yes.
> Child 1: I wouldn't make friends with them.
> Interviewer: You wouldn't, why not?
> Child 1: Because they probably won't make friends with you.
> Interviewer: So do you think it's easier for them to fit in here than the children from the other countries?
> Children (all): Easier for the children from the other countries.
> Child 2: Cos you are learning them English.
> Child 1: You don't know where they are from and ….
> Child 2: It would be more interesting…
> Child 3: Because Travellers they are from Ireland and we know everything about Ireland and all but if they came from like say India or Egypt we could learn all about their country.
> Interviewer: So you are more interested in the children from other countries because they have something to tell you?
> Children (all): Yeah. (3rd class girls, Newdale primary)

Some children commented however on the constraints imposed on their learning by virtue of the additional time spent by teachers with newly arrived immigrants into the classroom. Where time is itself a resource for learning, some immigrant children, by virtue of their specific learning needs, were perceived to reduce the time other children could spend with the class teacher:

> I like different people being in my school but I don't like them being in my class. It's very hard for the teacher because she has to teach another child from a different country instead of us. But if they had a different class for the people from a different country I'd love that cos then you could still play with them in the yard and the teacher can teach us without stopping. (5th class girl, Riverside primary)

Teachers also mentioned the issue of constraints on time as they felt their work was becoming increasingly intensified by the demands of greater diversity in their classrooms.

Within the front stage region of the classroom, ethnic diversity poses both challenges and opportunities for majority and minority ethnic children, as well as for adults (teachers) in the classroom setting. The enlargement of social space poses opportunities for the enrichment of learning, both academic and social as children come to know and learn about different cultures and ways of being. As Harriet Strandell notes in her chapter, the density of interchange brought by globalisation and shifting migration patterns challenges common sense understandings of culture, identity and place, and as we have seen, no less among children as among adults. This is especially important where the experience has been one of homogeneity and insularity, an experience traditionally noted with reference to Irish society (Devine et al 2004c). For teachers, utilising their authoritative position to maximum effect for the welfare of all children challenges them personally and professionally as they grapple with the reality of working with difference in a genuinely inclusive and tolerant way (Blair et al 2002, Devine 2005, Gitz-Johansen 2004, Sleeter 2004). The experience of time as a finite resource to be divided up between children adds a further challenge as decisions are made about where to invest the time that is available. And it is these decisions – the judgements teachers make about where and how to spend their time, and how to organise the learning space, that communicate to the children the norms and values which predominate in schools. What perhaps is most striking about experience within the front regions is the relative silence that exists around issues of race and ethnicity and the overriding emphasis on sameness over difference in the teachers' practice in the schools[13]. This is the subtext of teacher talk and behaviour, with overt rules and norms governing children's classroom interaction emphasising the need to be 'nice' to new children and welcoming of all irrespective of difference.

Back Stage Adaptations to Ethnic Diversity

When the lens begins to focus on the more hidden world of school – that located within the back regions, a more complex picture emerges and the salience of ethnicity to children's experience is identified. Research into children's social world draws attention to the nature of children's racialised attitudes and the degree to which these influence both the manner and extent of their interaction with one another in ethnically diverse classrooms (e.g. Connolly 1998, Devine with Kelly 2006, Holmes 1995, Troyna and Hatcher 1992, Van Ausdale and Feagan 2001). The meanings that children attach to their social relations with others can only be fully understood within the context of child culture. Such culture is characterised by both inclusionary and exclusionary elements underpinned by a series of rules and regulations clearly understood by children themselves. It is through these manoeuvres within friendships that children explore not only the dynamics of interpersonal relationships but also their own identities as they actively struggle for recognition, status and intimacy in the rough and tumble of their school lives (Adler and Adler 1998, Connolly 2004, Corsaro 2005, Deegan 1996, Devine 2003, Scott 2003, Thorne 1993, Troyna and Hatcher 1992). Children's interaction is also deeply embedded in power matrices that are reflected in the adult world. Dynamics of inclusion and exclusion are intertwined with concepts of normality and otherness, the latter framed in the context of the norms and expectations that structure social interaction within the society at large. With respect to ethnic identity, assertions of Irish identity may revolve around being white, Catholic and part of the settled community. Minority ethnic groups such as Travellers, Jews, or black Irish are often considered outside of this norm, with consequent implications for their status within Irish society as a whole. Children, no less than adults, draw on these discourses of difference, interpreting their interaction with others on the basis of their perceived normality or otherness with respect to dominant norms.

One way of considering the complexity of children's social world, especially in terms of specific social markers such as ethnicity[14] is through two interlinking dimensions related to inclusion/exclusion and sameness/difference. This is reflected in Figure 2 below:

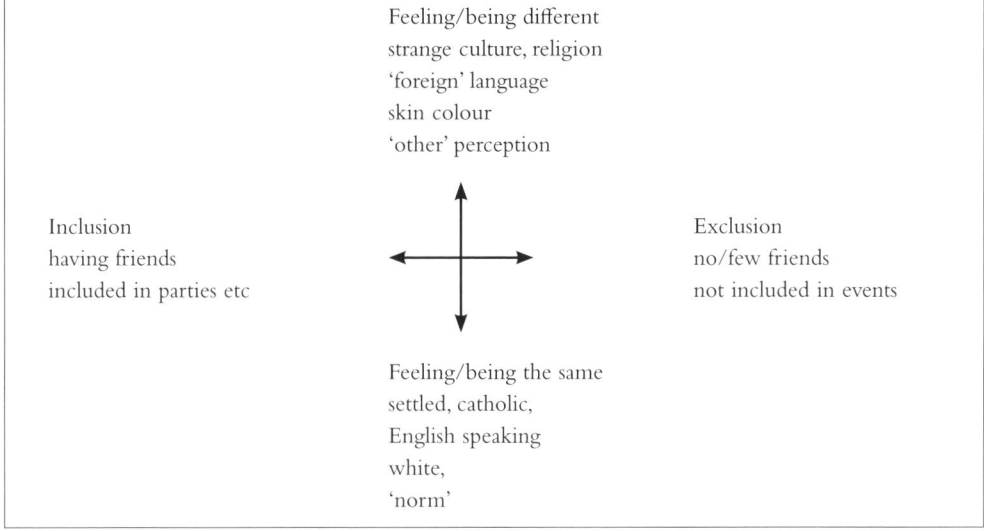

Figure 2. Dimensions of child social interaction and ethnicity in school

Children may be located in any one of the four quadrants as the dynamics of difference/sameness and inclusion/exclusion are played out in their interaction with one another. Being good at sport, sharing similar humour, not being favoured by teachers (teacher's pet) and sharing common interests were all identified in the children's talk as facets of the dynamic interplay between inclusion and exclusion in their friendship formations and encapsulated in the comment of one boy:

> Please people who are listening to this, pick up some sport or you get slagged. You have to be good at sport. (Minority ethnic boy, 5th class, Oakleaf primary)

Cutting across such patterns however are also those relating to difference/sameness, with children who are perceived as being different, often struggling to include themselves and be included in friendship groups.

One aspect of sameness and difference repeatedly focused on by the children was that of skin colour which in some instances was perceived as the basis for friendship formation. This particularly applied when a child was new to the school or classroom. In one interview for example, children spoke of the ease of a new child settling in if there were other 'coloured' children present:

> Child 1: Say one coloured person was in your class it would be really hard because it's just one coloured person. Say there's three coloured people in their class, cause they've got coloured people to play with them.
> Interviewer: But Anthony plays with all people.
> Child 2: Yeah but John and Luke only play with one person. *They like playing with their own colour.* (Majority ethnic girls, 2nd class, Oakleaf Primary)

Likewise for a Nigerian boy in Riverside Primary the sense of security in having another Nigerian boy present was spoken of in the context of sameness of colour, a marker of ethnic similarity:

> I felt so shy, everybody was different to me. There was a boy who was there, his name was… And he was a black boy as well, but now he left and I was the only one and I felt so shy. (5th class boy, Riverside Primary)

The sensitivity that children displayed towards issues around skin colour must be located within the general context of peer relations and the desire by children to 'fit in' and be the same as their peers. It must also be understood however within a broader cultural context, in which Irishness is firmly linked with certain traits (to include being white, settled, catholic etc.) and those outside of this norm clearly perceived as 'other'. Racist name-calling draws on discourses of difference or otherness and as such conveys the majority ethnic children's perceptions of what it is to be Irish and therefore the same:

> Interviewer: Why do people call names because of colour?
> Child 1: Maybe because they are Irish…I'm not talking about you now Rachel (Majority ethnic friend).
> Child: Maybe because they are white and we are brown, we lived in another religion. (Minority ethnic girl, 2nd class, Newdale primary)

> Child: I wouldn't like to be a Muslim in any school.
> Interviewer: Why?
> Child: I just don't want to get picked on by anybody. I wouldn't like to be a Protestant either. (Majority ethnic boy, 5th class, Oakleaf Primary)

It is also worth noting, however, that friendships are not simply based on factors such as colour and that sensitivity to differences related to colour and/or ethnicity can be eliminated when common bonds are formed. In practice this was reflected in the level of inter-ethnic interaction which was visible in the school yards during playtime, as well as observations of children's interaction in the classroom, and borne out by the following comments made by a friend of the Somali girl mentioned above:

> It's all about fitting in like. When I look at Nicola, I don't see a black person from somewhere else. I just see my friend. I don't notice the colour of you. (Majority ethnic girl, 5th class, Oakleaf primary)

Intergenerational dynamics, especially the authoritative resources teachers have by virtue of their adult status, cut across these dimensions of inclusion/exclusion and difference/sameness in the children's social interaction, but in a manner which is temporally and spatially defined. Teachers may for example invoke negative sanctions where children transgress behavioural norms in the front stage regions of school life or where children bring back stage behaviour to the front stage by 'telling' on one another. An interview with one group of children for example revealed how the principal 'nearly' suspended a child for engaging in racist name-calling:

> Child 1: Ava is called the black girl and Peter slags Antonio as well.
> Child 2: He nearly got suspended, he called her a nigger.
> Interviewer: Give me another name – say four eyes, will the principal nearly suspend them?
> Child 1: You get a report. You have five days and if he doesn't like your marks after that you get suspended. (Majority ethnic girls, 5th class, Riverside primary)

However teachers themselves spoke of their uncertainty around the incidence of racism in school and, reflecting the dialectic of control (Giddens 1984) in teacher/pupil relations, how impossible it is to surveil all of the children's behaviour, especially during break-times. For their part all children in the study were clearly able to recount incidences of name-calling that occurred out of ear-shot of the teacher, typified in the following excerpts from the data:

> Interviewer: Are there names that people are called that hurt the most?
> Child 1: Yeah, they call us the black people, chocolate boys.
> Interviewer: Is that 6th class boys?
> Child 1: yeah. And 5th class and second class too. (Minority ethnic boy, 2nd class, Oakleaf primary)

Child 1: There was a girl called Mary and she was called black blood and colourdy and spiky hair
Interviewer: Why would they call her those names?
Child 1: Because she has different skin. (Majority ethnic girl, 3rd class, Riverside primary)

While skin colour was an important defining feature of difference that in situations of conflict was used to exclude and denigrate those different to the 'norm', issues of lifestyle and culture also gave rise to exclusionary patterns in the children's interaction. Thus Traveller children were consistently spoken of in derogatory terms during the course of interviews and both they and muslim children recounted incidences of racial abuse they had experienced in school and on the way to school:

Child: A girl in my class called me a knacker and I went up and told the principal and he gave out to her. She threatened me. We are still getting it sorted out. (Traveller girl, 2nd class, Oakleaf primary)

Sometimes I hear a boy in my class say: I don't like these girls because they've a different language. (5th class Somali girl, Oakleaf primary)

It would be a mistake however to assume a linear relationship between the interlinking dynamics of difference/sameness and inclusion/exclusion in the children's social lives. Being the same does not automatically imply being included, just as being different does not automatically imply exclusion[15]. There were incidences of majority ethnic children defending their minority ethnic peers in the face of racial harassment and of minority ethnic children themselves excluding children from within their own ethnic grouping:

Child: They were calling Mary names like Chocolate and poo and all.
Child 2: Yeah, but we stand up for each other.
Interviewer: What did you say?
Child 2: We told them to leave her alone and stop bossing her around. And it's not fair cos if you were that colour you wouldn't like it if they were saying that to you.
Child 1: If I could get near them I'd try to beat them up if I could. (Majority ethnic girls 5th class, Riverside primary)

Me and Martha used to be friends because we are both muslims and everyone used to think we had loads of things in common. Since Anna came she took Martha away from me. They used to leave me out because I wear dresses and don't have a scarf, they just wouldn't let me in. (Minority ethnic 5th class girl, Oakleaf primary)[16]

The children's talk reveals their awareness of ethnic and cultural difference and how such difference can be exploited by them in their tussles for power, status and recognition among their peers. In all classrooms, some children were consistently named as engaging in racist name-calling more than others, although it was rarely labelled as such[17]. However even among children who denounced such behaviour, there was evidence of drawing on a racial frame of reference when minority ethnic children were deemed to be behaving in an unacceptable manner. In the following conversation, a minority ethnic girl who was excelling at school is labelled as being racist by her refusal to lend her rubber to a white child. The subtext however relates to this minority ethnic child breaching the norms of expected behaviour among her peers both in her exuberant confidence (thinking she is better than others) and in being able to compete on equal terms with 'Irish' children because she has acquired the Irish language with some proficiency:

> Child 1: There's a girl I sit beside called Ava.
> Child 2: And she's coloured....
> Child 2: She's racist, Ava's a racist.
> Child 1: If I say I need a loan of your rubber she says no.
> Interviewer: I heard you saying there that Ava was a racist, what did you mean by that?
> Child 2: She doesn't like white people.
> Child 3: She does get along with white people but sometimes she doesn't really like to be their friend.
> Child 2: She thinks she's all smart and all and great because she's from a different country. She knows her Irish the most. She thinks she's all popular. (Mixed gender majority ethnic group, Riverside primary)

Within the front region of child/adult relations there is an opportunity for minority ethnic children to shine, and this many, though by no means all of them did, much to the pleasure and surprise of their classroom teachers. However for those who do 'shine', this can be a double edged sword depending on their level and degree of integration with peers and the ultimate threat posed to the existing power and status matrices in the children's social world.

What the data highlights is the complex interweaving of ethnic identity with children's social positioning in school. Child culture is not uniform and is comprised of its own power matrices in which children will position themselves reflectively depending upon the context of interaction and the company of particular peers. Just as we can conceptualise child/adult relations in terms of spatial positioning, we can consider children's relations with one another in these terms also. Children's social world comprises its own back and front stage regions, in which children will position themselves differently with one another depending upon the allegiances which they have formed, the company of peers they are in and the degree of trust and friendship that exists between them. For minority ethnic children, especially when they are new to the school or classroom, negotiating a positive space for themselves in this complex social network is a major challenge, additional to the challenges facing them in the formal learning environment of the front stage region of the classroom.

Conclusions

This chapter set out to explore the dynamics of interaction between immigrant and Irish children in a context of adult control. How children (and teachers) cope with increasing and rapid migration of ethnic 'others' into the social space of the school raises important issues for children's welfare, in both a negative and positive sense. Clearly the enlargement of children's social space in this manner provides significant opportunities for them to draw upon a wider range of cultural resources in the construction of their social identities. Through newly formed friendships as well as increased opportunities for learning, children commented on the benefits of increasing ethnic diversity to their school lives. However it was also clear that the integration of migrant children into the social world of school is a complex task that challenges all those involved. Foregrounding the discussion in terms of the exercise of power between adults and children, the concept of space as a social dynamic was drawn upon to explore children's positioning with one another in inclusionary/exclusionary terms in school. For the purposes of analysis two spaces were presented as disparate – the front region of teacher/pupil interaction i.e. the formal learning environment, with the back region of child culture – each space governed by its own series of norms and regulations. In reality, children traverse both spaces in a complex interplay of appeals to both adult and peer norms. This process of adaptation and social positioning involves inclusionary and exclusionary elements which as we have seen draw on discourses of sameness and difference, with considerable implications for children's experience of belonging and adaptation to school.

What is most striking in terms of a welfare approach, is the absence of the creation of a discursive space for children that enables them to develop the skills required to deal with racial harassment and exclusion whenever and wherever it occurs. What takes place in the front region between teachers and pupils, cannot determine how children interact with one another in the back stage region – the relationship is not one of unilateral domination and control. It can however inform that interaction. As active beings, children reflexively monitor their behaviour (Giddens 1984) in the light of significant others. Creating a discursive space in the front region can enhance children's capacities for critical engagement with adults and one another upon issues of social justice and inclusion, challenging them to reflect upon their interpretations of the 'meanings, norms and power' (ibid.) that govern their social behaviour. In its absence children are left to work through their relations with 'others' drawing on the resources (cultural, emotional, economic, social) they bring themselves to school. For those who are positioned advantageously in this respect, grappling with the dynamics of power in children's social world, while challenging, need not threaten their experience of adaptation and belonging to school. However for children who are positioned at the margins, by virtue of their economic, cultural or social status, the challenge of negotiating their space among peers can be too great and result in isolation and alienation from the social life of the school. For most children, the discussion we had as part of the research process was the first time they had articulated or been asked to talk about their views on ethnic diversity, yet in their interactions with one another, ethnic identity was clearly one of a number of social indicators that could frame their positioning with peers. Further, the children were easily able to articulate racist comments and status differentials both between and within majority and minority ethnic groups that for the most part took place in the back stage regions of school life.

The paternalistic discourse which appears to inform teacher talk, coupled with their own stated discomfort around issues of racism, cultural diversity and schooling does little to equip children, both minority and majority ethnic with the resources they require to deal with racial harassment both inside and outside of school. This clearly has implications for the welfare of children and can be considered in terms of their right to equality of respect, recognition and esteem (Young 1990) irrespective of ethnic identity. Adults are imbued with the authoritative resources to equip children with these skills through the regulation of their time and space in school. To exercise such power authoritatively however requires knowledge and understanding of all the issues involved and a willingness to envision schools as important sites for cultural and social transformation, rather than as vehicles for social and cultural reproduction. Teachers in the study were working in a policy vacuum, struggling to come to terms with the changing social profile of their pupils and with the questions they themselves had about the changing nature of Irish society (Devine 2005). Because so much of the children's exclusionary behaviour takes place within the back stage of school life does not mean however that it should be ignored or rendered invisible in the process of schooling. If children's welfare is to be taken seriously, a discursive space where difference is discussed needs to be created, supported by a 'whole school' policy in which teachers and children are actively involved. Involving parents in the process, both minority and majority ethnic, is also crucial, given their own role in children's ethnic socialisation (Devine et al. 2004b, Spyrou 2002). Tackling the experiences of exclusion and absence of recognition in the front or back stage regions of their world can only be empowering for children, both minority and majority ethnic in their experience of time and space in school.

References

Adler, P.A. and P. Adler, (1998): *Peer Power: Preadolescent culture and identity.* New Brunswick, NJ: Rutgers University Press.
Arnot, M. and K. Weiler, (1993) (eds): *Feminism and Social Justice in Education,* London: Falmer Press.
Bailey, R. (2000): *Teaching Values and Citizenship Across the Curriculum.* London: KoganPage.
Connolly, P. (2004): *Boys and Schooling in the Early Years.* London: Routledge Falmer.
Corsaro, W. (2005): *The Sociology of Childhood.* London: Pine Forge Press.
Barton, L. (1995): *Making Difficulties: Research in the Construction of Special Educational Need.* London: Paul Chapman.
Bernstein, B. (1975): *Class, Codes and Control: Towards a Theory of Educational Transmission. Vol 3.* London: Routledge and Kegan Paul.
Bernstein, B. (1996): *Pedagogy, Symbolic Control and Identity: Theory, Research, Critique:* London: Taylor Francis.
Blair, M. (2002): »Effective school leadership: the multi-ethnic context«. *British Journal of Sociology of Education,* Vol. 23: 179-191.
Bowles, S. and H. Gintis (1976): *Schooling in Capitalist America.* New York: Basic Books.
Bourdieu, P. and J.C. Passeron (1990): *Reproduction in Education, Society and Culture.* London: Sage.
Bourdieu, P. (1993): *Sociology in Question.* London: Sage.
Bourdieu, P. (2000): *Pascalian Meditations:* Cambridge: Polity Press.
Central Statistics Office (CSO) (2004): *Usual Residence, Migration, Birthplace and Nationality.* http://www.cso.ie/census/Vol4_index.htm.
Connolly, P. (1998): *Racism, Gender Identities and Young Children:* London, Routledge.
Davies, B. (1991): »Friends and fights«. M. Woodhead and Light, P. (eds): *Growing Up in a Changing Society.* London: Routledge: 134-156.
Deegan, J. (1996): *Children's Friendships in Culturally Diverse Classrooms.* London: Falmer.
Devine, D. (2002): »Children's citizenship and the structuring of adult/child relations in school«. *Childhood,* Vol. 9: 303-321.
Devine, D. (2003): *Children, Power and Schooling – How Childhood is structured in the primary school.* Trentham Books: Stoke-on-Trent.
Devine, D. (2005): »Welcome to the Celtic Tiger? – Teacher responses to immigration.
and increasing ethnic diversity in Irish schools«. *International Studies in Sociology of Education.* Vol. 15: 49-71.
Devine, D., M. Kenny with E. MacNeela (2002): *Ethnicity and Schooling: A Study of Ethnic Diversity in a Selected Sample of Primary and Post-Primary Schools.* Dublin: School of Education and LifeLong Learning, University College Dublin.
Devine, D., M. Kenny with E. MacNeela (2004a): »Experiencing racism in the primary school: children's perspectives«. J. Deegan, Devine, D. and Lodge, A. (eds): *Primary Voices – Contemporary Issues in Primary Schooling.* Dublin: Institute of Public Administration: 183-205.
Devine, D., A. Lodge and J. Deegan (2004b): »Activating subordinate voice: Curriculum, contestation and consultation in the primary school«: J. Deegan, Devine, D. and Lodge, A. (eds): *Primary*

Voices – Contemporary Issues in Primary Schooling. Dublin: Institute of Public Administration: 245-262.

Devine, D. with M. Kelly (2006 forthcoming): »I just don't want to get picked on by anybody«: Dynamics of Inclusion and Exclusion in a Newly Multi-Ethnic Irish Primary School«. *Children and Society.*

Devine, D., M. Nic Ghiolla Phadraig and J. Deegan (2004c): »Time for children – time for change? Children's rights and welfare during a period of economic growth in Ireland«. A.-M. Jensen, Ben Arieh, A., Conti, C., Kutsar, D., Nic Ghiolla Phadraig, M. and Warming Nielsen, H. (eds): *Children's Welfare in Ageing Europe. Vol. 1*: Trondheim: Norwegian Centre for Child Research: 211-274.

Durkheim, E: (1956): *Education and Society.* New York: Free Press. (first published 1922).

Foucault, M. (1979): *Discipline and Punish: the Birth of the Prison.* New York: Random House.

Foucault, M. (1980): *Michel Foucault: Power Knowledge.* Hertfordshire: Harvester Wheatsheaf.

Giddens, A. (1976): *New Rules of Sociological Method: A Positive Critique of Interpretative Sociologies*. London. Hutchinson: 1976.

Giddens, A. (1979): *Central Problems in Social Theory: Action, Structure and Contradiction in Social Analysis.* London: MacMillan.

Giddens, A. (1984): *The Constitution of Society: Outline of a Theory of Structuration.* Cambridge: Polity Press.

Gitz-Johansen, T. (2004): »The incompetent child: representations of ethnic minority children«. H. Brembeck, Johansson, B. and Kampmann, J. (eds): *Beyond the Competent Child.* Roskilde: Roskilde University Press: 199-229.

Goffman, E. (1961): *Asylums. Essays on the Social Situation of Mental Patients and other Inmates.* Middlesex: Penguin Books.

Goffman, E. (1971): *The Presentation of Self in Everyday Life.* Middlesex: Penguin Books.

Holmes, R. (1995): *How Young Children Perceive Race.* London: Sage.

Lortie, D. (1975): *The School Teacher.* Chicago: Chicago University Press.

Opie, I. (1994): *The Little People in the Playground.* Oxford: Oxford University Press.

Osler, A. and H. Starkey (2002): »Education for citizenship: mainstreaming the fight against racism?« *European Journal of Education*: Vol. 27: 143-159.

Parsons, T. (1951): *The Social System.* London: Routledge.

Scott, J. (2003): »In girls, out girls and always black: African-American girls' friendships«. *Sociological Studies of Childhood and Youth*, Vol. 9: 179-207.

Sluckin, A. (1981): *Growing Up in the Playground.* London: Routledge and Kegan Paul.

Sleeter, C. (2004): »How white teachers construct race«. G. Ladson-Billings and Gillborn, D. (2004): *The Routledge Falmer Reader in Multicultural Education.* London: Routledge Falmer: 163-179.

Spyrou, S: (2002): »Images of 'the other': 'the Turk' in Greek Cypriot children's imaginations«. *Race, Ethnicity and Education*, Vol. 5: 255-272.

Thorne, B. (1993): *Gender Play: Girls and Boys in School.* Buckingham: Open University Press.

Troyna, B. and R. Hatcher (1992): *Racism in Children's Lives – A Study of Mainly-White Primary Schools.* London, Routledge.

Van Ausdale, D. and J. Feagan (2001): *The First R: how Children Learn Race and Racism.* Lanham, MD: Rowman and Littlefield.

Young, I. M. (1990): *Justice and the Politics of Difference.* Princeton, NJ: Princeton University Press.

Note

1. See Harriet Strandell's chapter in this book for more detailed commentary.
2. Applications for asylum have dropped considerably following changes to the citizenship laws in 2002.
3. A system of state funded denominational schooling predominates in Ireland with a majority of children at primary level attending Roman Catholic schools (Devine et al. 2004). With increasing immigration, however, such schools while denominational in ethos and character are being challenged by an influx of students from a diverse range of religious and cultural backgrounds.
4. All quotations here are taken from Devine (2003)
5. The author would like to acknowledge the contribution of Mairin Kenny and Eileen Mac-Neela to the collection of some of the data for the second study listed. The author accepts sole responsibility for the ideas expressed in this chapter and for the analysis of the data itself.
6. Reflecting the changing context of Irish society, ethnicity was not identified as a category for analysis in the earlier study and in the classrooms studied, there were no minority ethnic children present.
7. Newdale primary level was co-educational up to first class and single sex girls from second to sixth. The classes presenting for interview were all girl classes.
8. Interviewing all of the children in each targeted class was important in revealing the overall patterns of friendship within each of the classes, through socio-metric analyses.
9. I use the term relatively here as Irish classrooms have always had some ethnic diversity although not to the extent that there is now.
10. In this sense these classrooms, which were only used by the language support teachers with a rotation of immigrant children were in themselves part of the backstage regions of the school – out of full view and visibility of most children in the school –a space within which immigrant children were instructed in the English language within a context which drew on their distinct cultural resources and experiences.
11. What is being argued here is not that teachers were insensitive to racial abuse where it occurred but rather that their refusal to name it as such, preferring instead to interpret racist behaviour in the general context of bullying indicates an unwillingness to tackle and confront openly hostility that arises on ethnic grounds.
12. An exception in this study related to some Roma children whose patterns of attendance and participation in school life was viewed by the teacher as erratic and unpredictable.
13. The conservative nature of the teaching profession has often been alluded to in the educational literature (Lortie 1975). This may explain the relative reluctance on the part of teachers to confront issues of power and status directly and critically in their classrooms when it occurs.
14. Others include social class, gender, age, dis/ability and sexuality.

15 Indeed the research indicated how being different, by being new to the class, can ensure initial inclusion in female peer groups (Devine with Kelly 2006).
16 We can still see the dynamics of inclusion/exclusion and difference/sameness at play here except in this instance the exclusion and difference occurs within a minority ethnic grouping – as one of the children expresses her faith and culture differently to the other two and is thereby excluded from their friendship.
17 As recounted elsewhere (Devine et al 2004a) while majority ethnic children in the study were aware of racism and had some understanding of what racism entailed, their understanding was limited, and very much located in their day to day experience. This often yielded contradictory and confusing responses that the children were uncomfortable expressing. For their part, minority ethnic children had a deeper understanding of racial abuse that was rooted in the reality of their daily lives and many viewed such abuse as an unavoidable fact of life.

Flexibilisation of Time and Space

Flexible Places for Flexible Children? Discourses on New Kindergarten Architecture

Anne Trine Kjørholt and Vebjørg Tingstad

Introduction

Day-care centres or kindergartens, called 'barnehager'[1] in Norway, are important social spaces for children's lives in modern welfare societies. The increasing tendency to place children in formal institutional care like kindergartens, can be seen as a feature of modern child life shaping children's identities and spaces of action through particular cultural understandings of the child and 'the good childhood' within a specific historical and cultural context. Kindergartens are also spaces for children's constructions of their own childhoods in accordance with, or in opposition to, dominant discourses. The particular social and cultural space of a kindergarten represents and produces images of childhood and what it means to be a child, as well as particular notions of learning, knowledge and care. *Time* and *place* are important dimensions of the social space that is constituted. Teachers and staff in kindergartens – as well as children – are active participants in constructing time and space through every day social practices. However, these social practices are to a certain extent inscribed in discourses outside the walls of the institution. The organisation and structuring of time and place of and within the kindergarten thus to a certain degree reflect dominant political discourses on welfare and subjectivity in society.

The aim of this chapter is to reveal how constructions of children, as well as organisation of time and place, are changing in the light of ideological changes in the Norwegian welfare state and kindergarten policy from the mid 1990s. Hence we want to argue that there is a relation between neo-liberal discourses on rights and consumerism on the one hand, and new trends in which the kindergarten is constructed and designed physically as appropriate and flexible places for children, on the other. A core issue is to discuss how discourses on flexibility are represented in the construction of *place* and hence how this new construction of place relates to changing discourses on children as subjects. Pertinent questions to address is *if* and, in case, *how* notions of children as subjects and active social participants in kindergartens are affected and changed through these discourses that are market-oriented in the way that they borrow statements from the consumerism vocabularies. We want to argue that there are three different but closely intertwined discourses with major influence in the constitution of kindergarten as a space for children as subjects: 1. The universal discourses on children as social participants or fellow citizens as manifested in the UN Convention on the Rights of the Child, 2. The market oriented discourses on flexibility, individual choice and consumer orientation in Norwegian kindergarten policy, and 3. Cultural discourses on children as subjects and the 'good childhood' in Norway. According to the anthropologists Chris Shore and Susan Wright, who use the concept of discourse to analyse the field of policy, discourses are: »[…] configurations of ideas which provide the threads from which ideologies are woven« (Shore and Wright 1997:18). Discourse can be used to shed light on how a certain text is culturally constructed in a particular time in history – aimed at serving certain interests – representing a specific 'regime of truth' that is often taken for granted (Foucault 1972; Kaarhus 1992). The term 'text' does not only refer to written and spoken texts, but includes materiality and social practices as well.

An important task is to explore discourses on 'children as participants' by questioning and discussing constructions of children and childhood that seem to be taken for granted, and which in certain contexts seem to have attained a hegemonic position in recent years. Central questions to be addressed are: How are children constructed as the 'active and participant child', 'the natural child', 'the flexible child', and 'the autonomous child' within kindergarten policy in contemporary Norway? We want to underline that the discussion in this chapter is not anchored in empirical ethnographic data of children as social participants in kindergartens. Rather, it represents an attempt to prospect and bring to the fore possible implications of the political discourses. It is important to underscore that our ambition with the discussion is to be tentative and exploring, rather than being conclusive.

The chapter is structured in the following way: First we will present contemporary political discourses on flexibility and user orientation based on state political kindergarten documents. This is followed by a short outline of cultural notions of childhood related to 'free' time and space structures, in order to illustrate the interconnection between the historically and the 'new' market-oriented discourses. A written report from a 'development study' on flexibility related to the physical place in the 'new kindergarten building' conducted by five Norwegian municipalities will be described and discussed as a case representing the political discourses.

Flexibility and User Adjustment as Key Terms in Kindergarten Policy

In order to understand the new discourses on children related to flexibility, participation rights and individual autonomy, it is important to analyse contemporary political discourses related to kindergarten. Compared to other European countries, the number of kindergartens in Norway up until the 1990s has been remarkably low. In 1970 only 3 per cent of Norwegian children below school age were provided with a place in kindergarten. The slow increase in the development of institutional care for children in the period from 1950 to the late 1980s is related to discourses on (good) childhood and children's place(s) in Norwegian society. This discourse will be elaborated in the next section. During the 1990s the development of kindergartens expanded dramatically up to today's rate of 72 per cent (SSB 2005). Due to a rapid increase in female employment the Norwegian welfare state was forced to take a considerably stronger interest in kindergarten in recent years, both in relation to its expansion and to its content (Korsvold 1997).

Kindergarten policies in modern welfare society are characterised by inherent ambiguities and contradictions; such as the relation between play, care and learning, which are seldom brought to bear as ideological and culture specific perceptions. In recent years discourses on flexibility and user orientation are connected to the labour market as well as to the field of kindergarten policy in Norway. *User adjustment* and the notion of *choice* and *flexibility* as key values have gained great influence in developments and reforms of kindergarten in Norway during the last ten years. Discourses on flexibility are also reflected in recent changes in architectural style of the kindergarten building. These changes in the physical design illustrate how these institutions in particular ways seem to be embedded in discourses on flexibility and individual choice related to the labour market. Flexibility is a key term in the new discourses both in kindergarten policy and related to the new design of the building.

That the concepts flexibility and user adjustment have been of prime importance in the development of the kindergarten policy is mirrored in different state political documents. The Norwegian Government has stated as an explicit goal »to develop a kindergarten that is diverse, flexible, and user friendly« (Ministry of Children and Family Affairs, BFD 1999). The same statements are clearly expressed also in 'The Developmental Program for the Kindergarten Sector' initiated by the same ministry in the period 1995-1997 in 50 Norwegian municipalities (BFD 1998), and Quality for the Kindergarten Sector (Kvistad 2003). An important question can be formulated as follows: What does it mean »to run a kindergarten in regard with the users' needs?« Although children are in fact mentioned in the political documents (Næs and Mordal 1997), it is first and foremost parents who are regarded as the users of kindergartens.

According to the Developmental program (BFD 1998), user orientation means that parents are allowed to decide how long they want their children to be in the kindergarten daily based on their needs and wishes. It is the users' interests that are going to be at the core of how the kindergarten is to be developed and designed.

In a political document from the Government in 2000 it is stated that user orientation and flexibility must not affect the quality of the pedagogical approach provided for children in the kindergarten. But the concept of quality as such is hardly discussed nor problematised and defined (BFD 1999). A national three-year programme for quality in kindergartens that was initiated in 2001 also has user orientation as an explicit goal. Critical voices questioning the quality from children's perspectives in this program, have been raised (Sandve 2001). Some of these state political documents and programs, as for instance the Developmental programme (BFD 1998), have the reduction of public costs related to kindergartens as an explicit goal. During the reforms of the 1990s and the expansion of kindergartens, earlier national and fixed standards according to the regulation of permitted number of children per teacher were changed and laid open for 'flexible interpretations'. The result of this is reduced cost for the municipalities, but also that one kindergarten teacher has to take care of a larger group of children. Another fixed rule that has been changed in the same period is laws regulating the physical size of the kindergarten building according to the number of children attending the kindergarten. Earlier standards in this area are now also open to more 'flexible interpretations' that in practice mean less physical space per child. Local initiatives, based on state political directives are exploring how the architectural style of the kindergartens can be made more flexible and user friendly. Such changes, under the umbrella of user adjustment and flexibility, highlight the need to critically explore discourses on flexibility, user orientation and choice, in order to get knowledge about how they affect children. Critical voices have described this ideology as characterised by a weaker role of the state, connecting welfare to the individual and the individuals' possibilities to make their own choices with regard to services and goods in the welfare societies (Kjørholt, Rantalaiho and Tingstad 2004). According to neo-liberal trends in the welfare state, citizenship does not seem to be connected to solidarity, security and welfare in a community, but turned into questions about the subject's individual 'free choice' and self-realisation (Edwards 2000).

An important issue to discuss in this chapter is if and, how, notions of children as subjects and active social participants are affected and changed through the new market-oriented discourses described above. These issues are related to a significant question concerning political discourses on flexibility and user adjustment: What is the problem that 'flexibility' is introduced as an answer to? (Kjørholt, Rantalaiho and Tingstad 2004). This is closely connected to the political decision in the Norwegian Parliament in Spring 2003, aimed at guaranteeing all children below school age a place in a kindergarten and, not least, a place for a lower cost for parents than the previous norm, by implementing a so-called maximum price and obligatory siblings-reductions. Public documents and debates about this decision mainly deal with questions pertaining to the cost for the municipalities (ibid.). The new situation is firmly related to an aim of reducing the costs of kindergarten services per child, especially amongst the youngest children (0-3 years).

This huge expansion of kindergartens causes considerable challenges for the local authorities in the municipalities, particularly in the largest cities, where the growth in the number of kindergartens is supposed to be the most extensive in the years to come. When a new building is to be established or an old one is going to be changed or refurbished, some local authorities handle these challenges by looking at how the present utilization of the buildings may be reorganised in order to satisfy new demands. Another solution to solve the problem of cost is to establish so called 'nature kindergartens'. This elucidation reveals the connection between discourses of a 'good childhood' in Norway and political discourses on flexibility and user adjustment. Before presenting the development project related to the new kindergarten building, we will therefore give an outline of these intertwined discourses.

Reconstructing 'Free Space' and 'Natural Childhood' within Institutional Structures

Former as well as contemporary notions of 'a good childhood' in Norway are connected to the right to move freely in the physical landscape and to children's possibilities to structure time according to their own needs. Autonomy, freedom and play with peers in the close neighbourhood, and in particular in natural settings are favoured (Gullestad 1997; Nilsen 2000; Kjørholt 2001). Childhood and nature are seen as closely intertwined. The cultural meaning of 'free play' practiced among peers is highly emphasised, and even more so when taking place outdoors, preferably in nature settings. The concept of 'children's own culture' referring to play and peer-cultural activities initiated by children themselves is part of these notions. Contemporary childhood has been characterised as institutionalised, controlled by adults, and embodied with a high degree of organisation of time and space (Kjørholt, Korsvold and Telhaug 1990; Aasen and Haugaløkken 1994; Kjørholt 1994; Korsvold 1998).

Cultural notions of a 'good' natural childhood have been contested by the development of trends such as controlled space and time structures and increased expansion of formal institutions for children below school age. Since the beginning of the 1990s there has been a growing public concern about the increasing organisation and structuring of children's time and space in everyday life. A 'natural childhood', where children can move freely and decide what to do together with other children is seen as threatened, and state political authorities such as Art Council Norway and various ministries have initiated projects to counteract this development and stimulate children's own culture (Kjørholt 2001). The resistance towards the increased 'institutionalisation' of childhood was also reflected in the intense and heated political debate about primary school reform in 1997, lowering the age of entrance to school from 7 to 6 years. In order to get this reform adopted, the curriculum was changed and 'free play' and physical activities like going for a walk or playing in the forest were highly emphasised, in particular for the youngest children (6-9 years) in the primary school.

Following this school reform, the number of *lavvos* in primary schools has increased extensively. A lavvo is a traditional tent connected to the indigenous people – sámi – geographically belonging mainly to the northern part of Sweden, Finland and Norway. A lavvo has a particular form with an outlet at the top that makes it possible to build a fire to make it warm. It is common to use the lavvo as an outdoor place for different curriculum oriented activities during the day. The lavvo can be seen as an important cultural sign, reflecting notions of a 'natural childhood' and children as an indigenous tribe practising 'their own culture' freely, even within highly organised time and space structures. Childhood in Norway has been described as a metaphor for nature, and the meaning of nature is significant in cultural values (Gullestad 1989,1997; Stephens 1995).

The use of lavvos is a minor but still vivid example which illustrates that discourses emphasising the value of moving freely in natural settings have been gaining momentum since the 1990s. Similarly important is a particular increasingly popular type of kindergarten in recent years, the so called *naturbarnehager* – 'kindergartens out in the nature'. These kindergartens are often placed in the forest where children spend most of the day outdoors, climbing trees, playing, eating and so on. 'Nature kindergartens' usually lack physical buildings of the same standard as ordinary institutions; consequently these arrangements are much cheaper. Discourses valuing nature-kindergartens as preferable places for children are increasingly powerful. The number of such kindergartens has increased at the same time as the municipalities have come under increasing political pressure from the state authorities to offer a place in a kindergarten to all children below school age. In kindergartens it is also common to have a lavvo. We want to argue that these 'traditional' notions of a good childhood, emphasising, freedom, individuality, and 'free play' in natural settings, may reinforce and be reinforced by market oriented discourses on consumer orientation, flexibility and individual choice. Cultural and historical notions of a 'natural childhood' related to freedom of time and space is thereby revitalised and intertwined with contemporary discourses on freedom, individual choice and rights to participation.

Flexible Time and Flexible Place; the Prospect of 'the New Kindergarten'

We will now continue with a presentation of written texts related to a 'development study' on the physical environment of 'the new kindergarten'. In 2003, seven of the largest 'cities' in Norway funded a project involving architects and local planners of new kindergartens aimed at contributing to new knowledge and competence on how to design and arrange the kindergarten building to fit new demands of flexibility and user adjustment. The project was initiated by the so-called 'Large City Network' consisting of staff members from the public administration of the municipalities responsible for the development of new kindergartens in these cities, which are ranging from 50 000 to 500 000 inhabitants. A central issue was also to adapt to what was conceptualised as 'new knowledge' of the modern child. The 'new knowledge' referred to prominent discourses in policy and research conceptualising children's competence and autonomy from an early age, rejecting earlier discourses on the developing and vulnerable child. The 'modern child' is asserted individual freedom of choice and rights to influence their every day lives.

Based on their particular insights and experiences with flexible organisation of time and place in different 'developmental projects' (a practice where a barnehage initiates and carries out new pedagogical principles), the principals of kindergartens in the cities were invited by the 'Large City Network' to take part in the project by presenting their experiences of the 'new kindergarten building'. Earlier local projects have aimed at discussing new ways of organising the buildings in order to:

> »improve the quality by promoting more openness, more effective use of the localities, and to promote active participation and freedom of choice for children as well as adults to choose activities according to their own interests« (Storbysamarbeidet i barnehagesektoren 2003:26).

These aims are further elaborated by the following quotations from the principals:

> »The pedagogical intentions are to give children freedom to choose what they [the children] want to do, with few and clear rules« (Storbysamarbeidet i barnehagesektoren 2003:48). »An important working principle is that children themselves can choose the kind of activities most of the day and have enough time to become deeply involved in the play« (Storbysamarbeidet i barnehagesektoren 2003:49). »Children choose all the time what to do and with whom they want to be, and whether to be outside or inside« (Storbysamarbeidet i barnehagesektoren 2003:50).

As we can see, all the quotations reveal how individual freedom of choice is underlined as an important aim and value embedded in the changes in the structuring of time and place. Flexible places are connected to the aim of giving children increased freedom of choice. Children are further constructed as a collective group with a common interest: the right to practice play together. This complies with discourses emphasising children's right to be released from adult control. As outlined earlier in this chapter the construction of 'the tribal child' – as a group with a common authentic culture has been prevalent in child policy as well as within research in Denmark and Norway since the 1990s (Kjørholt 2001, 2004; Kampmann 2003). From the 1990s the concept 'children's own culture' representing a particular understanding of childhood has had an increasingly powerful position in the discursive field among researchers and various professional groups in Denmark and Norway (ibid.). Actors in the field present the position as representing a shift from a focus on the *developing child* to the *competent child,* from *pedagogy* to *culture,* presented as dichotomous and opposite positions. The anthropologist Eva Gulløv asserts that contemporary discourses connected to day care in Denmark are characterised by » moral assumptions and understandings concerning individual autonomy, social coherence and conceptions of children and childhood« (Gulløv 2003: 24). The emphasis on the individual child's possibilities to make their own choice and decisions is significant.

From Unit to Base: What is the Difference?

Traditionally, kindergartens have been divided in separate sections or units, which have been organised for a particular and fixed group of children and adults. Kindergartens vary in size, from one unit up to eight units (normally 2-5) with a fixed group of children. Every unit has its own defined playing area which usually consists of a large playing room, a smaller one where it also is possible to rest or sleep, and finally, there is often a room for cooking and a wardrobe where every child has its own shelf and peg for clothes, shoes and other personal belongings. A unit also has a separate entrance. The playing room is usually designed in the same way in all the units.

The point of departure for the Large City Network project was that this way of organising the use of rooms and buildings does not permit the flexibility required in terms of in door space and adult resource persons. To obtain the sufficient level of flexibility, the network started to discuss the present relation between the number of children and adults and how one may obtain a maximum utilisation of the building. A simple logic is, for instance, that a norm where 35 children share six adults in a flexible building is better than the previous norm, where 18 children share three adults in a unit meant for them only. Thus, an alternative to the traditional model is to include parts of the area defined for a particular and fixed group in a common playing area defined for all the children in the kindergarten. The area, which remains for a particular group is called 'base area' and is smaller than the previous unit. What defines a base seems to vary a lot, from just a fixed and permanent table to a more extensive area like a traditional unit. The area defined for common use may be organised as workshops for various activities or as a large room which can be used for large gatherings, physical education, performances, celebrations etc. A consequence of a situation where more space is given to joint groups is that less space is reserved for particular child groups. Figure 1 illustrates how the indoor localities are organised and structured in these two different ways, which are based upon quite different pedagogical principles and practices.

One argument for the new model is that it is supposed to enable the staff to be more flexible in their organisation of children in different and flexible groups in order to promote increased freedom of choice for individual children. The staff will then be able to give children a broader range of different activities to choose between, along with increased possibilities for 'free play' and the practice of 'children's own culture'. Furthermore, children will have increased possibilities to make their own decisions according to the choice of activity and playmates during the day. The shift from fixed sections to a more open landscape that can be used differently by various groups of children and adults implies a new kind of flexibility relative to modern organisational structures (Fendler 2001). The new organisation of physical place is related to changes in the organisation of time, from fixed time with a more detailed timetable and structure of activities during the day according to time, to a less structured program, intended to give more space to children's choices. From a liberal point of view it has been argued that this new kind of organisation of the educational landscape promotes flexibility that provides an essential sort of freedom, liberation, or release from regulation. However, on the other side it has been asserted that this argument is connoted with particular notions of freedom that should be criticised (ibid.). Educational practices that may appear to be exercises of freedom may, on closer examination, turn out to be repetitions and reiterations of the status quo Fendler argues. In this respect, flexibility is not necessarily equivalent to freedom and self-determination within an extended social space, opening for a variety of different subject positions and social actions to be taken. Rather it may also, if not problematised, hide unintended power relations that have been described as new forms of governmentality, delimiting in some instances the space for freedom and self-determination (Rose 1999; Hultqvist and Dahlberg 2001).

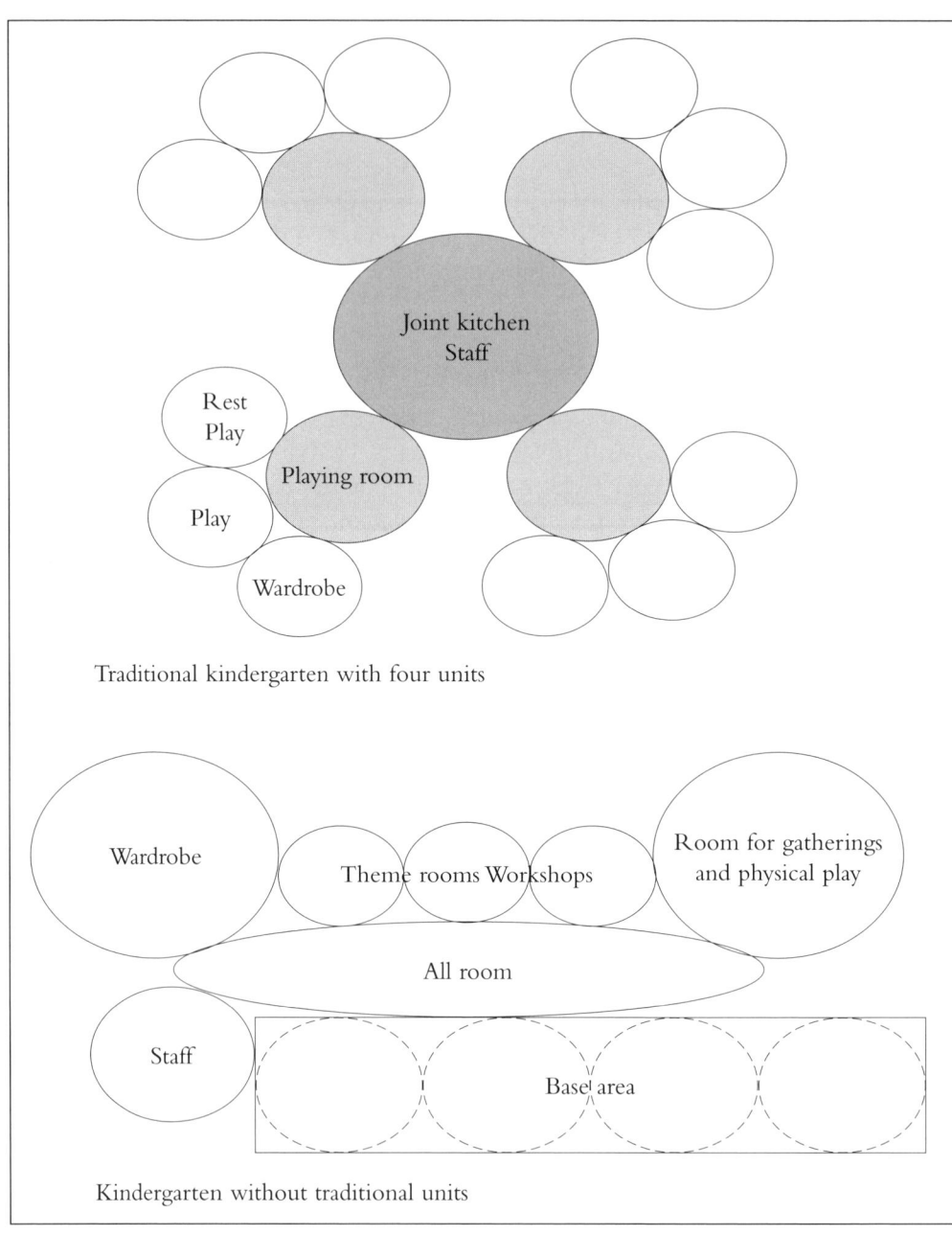

Figure 1. Kindergarten with four sections or units and 'The New Kindergarten' organised without units

Source: Storbysamarbeidet i barnehagesektoren 2003: 25 (The project report was given financial support from the Ministry of Child and Family Affairs, and is published both in print and on the web site www.etablerebarnehage.no).

From Development and Needs to Rights and Interests

A pertinent question is if this case study, revealing new ways of thinking related to the construction of kindergarten as a 'flexible place' indicates a break with former developmental oriented discourses on children as subjects in need of care from adult caretakers in day care centres. In some ways, we will assert that the new construction of flexible time and flexible place seen in the 'new kindergarten building', challenges former discourses and pedagogical practices of the traditional kindergarten. The traditional ways of structuring time and place in fixed groups and sections are inscribed in discourses emphasising toddlers' (and older kindergarten children) needs of stability, close emotional relations to a limited number of caretakers and stable small groups of children. Within these pedagogical discourses the construction of the physical place is based, as we have already seen, on the division of the physical place in particular separate territories or units. One kindergarten can have one unit, but in cities they normally consist of two to seven units. Children are gathered in smaller groups (eight to nine children below age three and 16 to 18 children four to six years olds) inhabiting their own territory and having their own staff.

The discourse of the 'new kindergarten building' is characterised by promoting flexibility in various ways. In addition, we may ask if the new discourses represent a *destabilisation* of pedagogical assumptions rooted in dialogue-pedagogical theory and practice, which in recent decades have informed and influenced traditional pedagogical thinking and practice and kindergarten policy to a large extent. Aiming to link the theoretical base for the pedagogical program in the kindergarten, influenced by Jean Piaget and Erik H. Eriksson, the dominating concepts in the Nordic kindergarten context in the 1970s were 'interaction' and 'dialogue pedagogy' (SOU 1972; Socialstyrelsen 1975). Dialogue pedagogy was emphasised as a 'way to relate' vis-à-vis children, claiming adults to develop their reflexivity and capacity to understand their own ways of receiving, interpreting and giving information, i.e. being sensitive according to information children give simply by their 'being'. Dialogue with small children thus presupposes »supervision of the children by respecting the child as a human being capable by her/himself of discovering, acting and learning. In this process children need help from adults who share emotions, knowledge and experiences, but who also decide some boundaries. Dialogue with children presupposes that the adult is able to listen to children; if not, he will talk *to* children instead of in dialogue *with* them« (Socialstyrelsen 1975: 51, our translation).

The new situation encourages new practices, allowing larger groups of children below three years to attend the kindergarten, and more flexible groups of children, than was the case earlier. The institutions present a choice to the parents characterised by more flexible solutions and increased user adjustment. Flexible places are connected to flexible time and user adjustment. This means that parents have increased freedom daily and weekly to choose when and for how long children will spend their time in the kindergarten. This increased freedom of choice for parents implies that the time for children's daily and weekly stay varies more than before. Former practices delimited the number of children's shared 'places', permitting only two children to share one full time place. This kind of practice was legitimated for pedagogical reasons, namely the children's need for stability and small stable group size. Today this rationale has changed and it is possible to adjust children's time in the kindergarten to parent's working life and the time that is suitable for the parents. Thus children's needs, such as small groups, emotional trust and the feeling of safety, the value of few and stable relations for children, a peaceful space for resting and sleeping etc, which was emphasised as crucial for children's development and well-being (The Ministry for Consumption and Administration, FAD 1976), is no longer a part of the discourse today. A consequence is 'flexible child-groups', implying that children can choose where to be and what to do. The physical and social presuppositions for children's construction of social relations, friendship and play within the kindergarten have thereby changed. In this respect, the new discourses on the flexible kindergarten building encourage new constructions of time and place for children as social participants reflecting new demands of flexible working life and 'flexible identities'.

If we compare the new and former discourses on children, physical place and pedagogical thinking in kindergarten, changes in the terms by which children and a 'good' childhood is described and conceptualised are apparent. In traditional pedagogical thinking in kindergarten children were conceptualised mainly in terms of *development*. In Norway, developmental psychologists like Jean Piaget and Erik H. Eriksson had a significant influence on pedagogical thinking and practice. However, while critiques of developmentalist discourse rightly point to the construction of children as vulnerable and human 'becomings' more than 'beings', this pedagogical tradition has also been described as child-centred, emphasising children's own perspectives and opportunities to active exploration of their environment in order to learn and develop as creative beings. For instance, through her extensive literary work, the Norwegian psychologist Åse Gruda Skard challenged traditional views on the relation between children and adults. She emphasised the adult responsibility for having knowledge about children and adapting the methods of upbringing to the basis of this knowledge (Tingstad 2003). Skard's vision was conceptualised by the term of 'democratic upbringing'. She related this concept not only to privacy, but also to a question of democracy. Goals for upbringing were, from Skard's point of view, to establish childhood as valuable in its own capacity and to arrange the environmental conditions in such ways that children are given opportunities to express themselves and develop their creative abilities (Skard 1973).

The following terms were central in these discourses: *needs, vulnerability, closeness, emotional relations, emotional support, care, trust, 'feeling safe', growth, creativity, belonging, dependency, caring and supportive adults, caring environment, borders, structure, rituals, routines, stability, fixed and permanent groups, fixed and predictable daily routines.* In order to learn and develop into mature human beings, a fulfilment of basic needs was seen as crucial. Children's basic needs were seen as the need to be loved and cared for in a stable and stimulating environment by supportive and emotionally close adults. The professionals' knowledge about the individual child's personality and characteristics were seen as vital in order to give the 'proper' emotional and cognitive support, and to create the best possible learning environment. Children's 'free play' and relations to other children were emphasised. However, a structured and stable environment, both according to organisation of time and place, as well as according to adults and children were seen as crucial for children's ability to learn, grow and develop, cognitively, emotionally and socially. 'Feeling safe' was seen as connected to belonging to a stable community of children and of caring adults. A prescribed organisation and structure of time and place were highly emphasised, seen as necessary tools to contribute to cognitive and emotional predictability. Repetition of daily activities and routines and ritualistic *assemblies* were seen as contributing to make the world and every day life more understandable. Children's needs for clear 'boundaries' and rules in everyday life were a popular and ongoing theme.

In particular, children below three years were seen as being in need of close emotional support and care from (as few as possible) adult caretakers. The Swedish book 'Eight babies start in day care' (Sjöblom 1974) is based on an empirical study where a researcher extensively observed the development of eight babies during one year from the time they started in different Swedish day care institutions in the early 1970s. The conclusion of this book, used widely as a reference in the education of preschool teachers in Nordic countries, was that it was highly important for babies and toddlers to be in a stable and emotionally caring environment, in a small group with permanent and few, stable, staff members. It was regarded as particularly important when the children started in the kindergarten that one main caretaker developed the 'feeling of safety' in the new day care environment.

It is interesting to notice that in the new discourses on children and a 'good' childhood related to kindergarten, a lot of these terms which were so central in the former discourses, are not now referred to so frequently. We do not have the empirical evidence to conclude about the appearance or disappearance and the detailed distribution of these terms in relation to new terms, but it is beyond question that new terms have taken a more central place, leaving the other ones to a more marginal position in the discourse. However, at a time in history, children and childhood are always constituted by different and often competing discourses. The former discourses are therefore still contributing in some ways to constitute kindergarten as a proper place for children in contemporary society. However, today's central terms in the discourses on children and kindergarten seem to be *rights, participation, the competent child, autonomy, freedom, individual choice, flexibility* and *children's own culture*. The conceptualisation of relations between children and the professional adults in the former discourses, discussed in terms of care, dependency and belonging, seem to be replaced by notions of autonomy and control. In the new discourse, children's rights to being freed from adult control, both individually and collectively are a crucial issue. Autonomy, freedom and individual choice seem to be key terms. 'Flexible places' and 'flexible time' are tools to realise children's possibilities to decide on their own in the everyday life in the kindergarten. Children's 'needs' for stable emotional relations in order to learn and feel comfortable in every day life, fixed places and belonging to a permanent and stable community of children, are being contested. In sum, we can say previous understandings related to development and basic needs are being challenged. Children are no more seen – or at least not to the same degree – as dependent upon adult care. Adults' main responsibility towards children seems to be to constitute kindergarten as a flexible space for children's active participation and autonomy, individually and collectively, providing them with a maximum freedom of control from adults. Accordingly, children are themselves to an increasingly degree given the responsibility for their own learning and well being in the everyday life. The notion 'responsibility for one's own leaning', which is an often a repeated key term in discourses related to aims and methods in curricula in primary schools in Norway, clearly illustrates this. This tendency is also to a large extent seen in day care centres, after school clubs and primary schools in Denmark (See Warming Nielsen's and Kampmann's chapter). As Hanne Warming Nielsen and Jan Kampmann argue, this reveals an expectation to establish a form of 'self-governance' and self-control, linked to notions of how children in a reflexive and democratic welfare state are expected to behave.

Governing the Child through Freedom and Self-Determination

However, the case study of the 'new kindergarten building' also reveals that there seem to be certain paradoxes and challenges connected to the construction of kindergarten as a flexible place. One obvious paradox is that connected to the relation between flexibility, freedom, self-determination and governing in day-to day practices. The discourse about flexibility and user adjustment implies that children are free to choose what to do and where to play to a larger extent than previously, and that this is more to preferable than previous regulations in fixed groups in specific places. It implies that children should be allowed to use the building without adult limitations and that children can choose and use workshops, playrooms and outdoor space as they want. However, practical solutions which are introduced to cope with more children and younger children still seem to imply a high level of regulation. Some of the staff members report that they prefer some children to be outside during the day because this gives more peace and quiet space inside. A form of regulation often referred to is 'the principle of sluicing' which means that in early mornings and late afternoons, half of the base area is closed in order to enable the staff to fully know and control what is going on and make the tidying easy. The paradox is that in order to obtain the aim of increased individual choice, flexibility and self-determination for children, the staff members feel obliged to organise strictly. As referred to in a study of Norwegian leisure time clubs, there seems to be a strong correlation between a high number of children present in a limited physical area and a high degree of adult control and structure (BFD/KUF 1996).

Another challenge, which arises from the pedagogical practice of closing half of the base in the morning and in the afternoon, is related to the question of how to establish and maintain high quality in the contact and the flow of information between staff and parents. Wardrobes have traditionally been used as the place for the daily and informal encounters between the 'home' and the 'kindergarten'. Close cooperation between parents and staff has been a crucial part of the pedagogical mandate in Norwegian kindergartens, regulated by the law of 1975. Staff members judge the wardrobes in the 'new buildings' to be too small to ensure close communication and cooperation between parents and staff. Some parents argue that the changes of 'the new kindergarten building', implying a greater 'flow' of different children and staff present in a particular physical area as a result of the 'developmental project', prevents stability and continuity that is necessary to establish a close cooperation among people. Some parents argue that they miss the close contact between parents and staff, which they had when there were smaller units.

It might be seen as a paradox that pedagogical innovation emerges, not as a process within the institution, on the basis of personal skills, interests and resources or related to new theoretical knowledge, but rather as a consequence of a political decision to extensively increase the number of kindergartens in a short period of time. The point of departure for the 'developing projects' in the local kindergartens in recent years was in this respect based on increasing expectations from the authorities to cope with larger groups of children and younger children within the existing buildings. One of the principals, cited in the report from the Large City Network, said that after the 'barnehage' received more and more children, the need for more and smaller rooms for children's play increased. »Tidying and cleaning are easier as half of the base is closed in the end of the day, and »when staff-members are ill, organising as a base is less vulnerable and the need of substitutes is reduced«. As these statements show, the *political* (more and younger children), the *economical* (cope with new challenges without more costs) and the *practical* (internal organising) rationale represent the structural conditions, from which new kinds of pedagogical discourses emerge. Some children perceive an open architecture very challenging, and staff report that they often feel best when being together with smaller groups of children over a period of time without interruptions. Such kinds of evaluation are mentioned, however, as marginal phenomena in the report. A sigh from one of the children after a trip »Oh, if we could have been that few children every day!« is added, not as a substantial problem or incitement for a further discussion about the number of children on a 'normal' day, but rather as an individual and marginalised comment.

From a cultural analytical perspective Eva Gulløv argues that the discussion of what is the best place for children reveals ambivalences and paradoxes reflecting a more profound cultural uncertainty about the role of children, citizenship and the welfare system in society.

> »While an important stated goal of day-care practice is to teach children to make decisions for them selves, their choices are restricted by the fact that they cannot place themselves, nor do they have any influence on adult ideas of what is a proper childhood. Children are controlled and protected, but at the same time regarded as self-managing individuals, a paradox that points to an unsolved conflict regarding children's social position« (Gulløv 2003:24).

One may ask how the new trends, which 'celebrate' flexibility and user adjustment, represent a change of former political practices and norms. Norwegian kindergartens have been regulated by common and fixed standards. Flexible use of the physical environment may suffer from a risk of becoming the opposite of flexibility for the children who live their daily life in the kindergarten. On the other hand, we might argue that contemporary discourses on individualization and self-determination in modern societies may create new forms of solidarities, cooperation and communities among children in kindergarten. The changing discourses may result in an increasing individualization of children's lives in the kindergarten, emphasising individual choice and self-determination.

We should further ask: to what degree are the individual child's right to be autonomous and decide for him/herself promoted by professional practices? We may argue that the discourses open up for new positions and constructions of identities that increase children's possibilities to influence their everyday lives in new forms of communities and 'solidarities' among children. These issues have to be an object for further empirical investigations. Today, we do not know in which ways contemporary changes from this former organisation of physical place to new constructions of the kindergarten building affect children's play, friendship and social relationships with adults and children. It is crucial to underscore the importance of studying these changes from a childhood perspective, which is so absent from the political plans. Empirical studies with an ethnographic approach are necessary to get insight into these questions and issues.

From Fixed Standards to Flexible Interpretations

Flexible places are connected to flexible time and user adjustment. As already stated, parents have increased freedom to choose for how long time and what time they are planning to use the kindergarten 'service'. This means, for example, that the time for children's daily and weekly stay varies more than before. While the former practices have delimited the number of children's shared 'places', it is now possible to adjust children's time in barnehager to parent's working life and the time that is suitable for the parents. Thus parental wishes and the demands of the labour market have replaced earlier assumptions of the value of few and stable relations for children. A consequence of this flexibility is 'flexible child groups', implying that friends do not necessarily meet every day, or every week. The physical and social conditions for children's construction of social relations, friendship and play within the kindergarten have thereby altered compared to earlier times. The 'new kindergarten building' represents a new and different space for children as social participants, reflecting new demands of flexible working life, 'flexible identities' and blurring boundaries between work and family (see Karin Jurczyk's and Andreas Lange's chapter). In constructing flexible places for children's every day life the 'new kindergarten building' thus challenges discourses of traditional kindergarten pedagogy which emphasised toddlers' (and older kindergarten children's) needs of stability, close emotional relations to a limited number of caretakers and a stable small group of children.

Conceptualising changes as 'developmental features' may establish and maintain a discursive practice, in which changes are constructed as having only positive connotations and as a linear process. Anthony Giddens (1990) argues against an evolutionistic approach, where 'history' can be told in terms of a 'story line', which imposes an orderly picture upon the jumble of human happenings. Displacing the evolutionary narrative and arguing for a 'discontinuist' interpretation of modern social development, Giddens understands social change as a series of break stages, in which societies are re-organised according to totally new principles.

Self-Determination and Well-Being in Kindergarten: a Childhood Perspective

As we have outlined, the theoretical starting point for this chapter is that political discourses on flexibility and user adjustment constitute a social space for children as social participants within the kindergarten. We have argued that these discourses are closely intertwined with global discourses on children's rights to participation. In other words: the social space is not only constituted by children and pedagogical actors in the kindergarten; as we have seen, it also reflects discourses outside the field of children and professional care. The concepts flexibility, user adjustment and quality have hardly been problematised in political documents and public debate, and fundamental questions have not been addressed about how these discourses affect children. A pertinent question to be addressed is if there is a potential conflict between parents' qua workers interests on the one hand, and children's interests and needs on the other (Kjørholt 1998; Bjørngaard and Mordal 1998; Sandve 2001). The presented case study on the 'new kindergarten building' reveals that notions of how a proper kindergarten should be designed as a physical place is changing in accordance with neo-liberal discourses on flexibility and user orientation.

We have argued that contemporary assessments of the flexible kindergarten represents a discursive break with former discourses, which focused on 'children's needs' rather than 'the users' wishes and expectations'. Thus we are witnessing a destabilisation of former taken for granted assumptions and pedagogical hierarchies about what should be included in the discourse of a proper day care facility. However, it is important to underline that different discourses initiated at different times in history work together, representing continuity in notions of children as well as in the social practices that are established. In order to evaluate how the new market oriented discourses affect children, and whether they mainly represent continuity or change, a more in depth and detailed analysis of discursive texts and social practices in kindergarten is necessary. Nevertheless, the new design of kindergartens as 'flexible places' connected to a tentative shift from need and developmentally oriented discourses, to discourses about rights promoting children's rights to individual choice and self-determination, raises questions related to the consequences for children's welfare. Welfare is often discussed in relation to a macro perspective in terms of provision and access to resources (Esping Andersen 2000). However, welfare has also been analysed by relating to individual needs with the terms 'Having, Loving and Being' (Allardt 1976). According to Erik Allardt 'having' refers to access to resources and 'loving' to social integration, friendship and community, while 'being' refers to self-realisation and human efficacy. A strong interrelatedness between the three terms is emphasised (Allardt 1989). Researchers using Allardt's concept as a starting point have also added a cultural dimension, arguing that welfare and well-being is related to people's own experiences and perceptions of a 'good life' (Bakke 2004). However, a 'needs approach' to well-being is not unproblematic since children's needs always are developed within and dependent on a particular social context. Cultural analyses focussing on children's perceptions of and preferences in every day life in kindergarten represent a useful point of departure for generating knowledge of how the described contemporary discourses on flexibility, freedom and user orientation affect children's well-being. The relationship and tension between the construction of modern identities of autonomy and individual choice on the one hand, and collective responsibilities and belonging to communities on the other, represent a core issue for further investigation of children's well-being in kindergartens.

References

Aasen, P. and O. Haugaløkken (eds) (1994): *Bærekraftig pedagogikk: pedagogiske og utdanningspolitiske utfordringer i velferdsstaten*. Oslo: AdNotam Gyldendal.

Allardt, E. (1976): »Dimensions of welfare in a comparative Scandinavian study«, *Acta Sociologica*, Vol. 19: 227-240.

Allardt, E. (1989): *An Updated Indicator System: Having, Loving, Being*. Working Papers 48, University of Helsinki: Department of Sociology.

Bakke, M. (2004): »The cultural welfare: parliamentary debates about culture during the creation of the Norwegian welfare society«. Paper at the 3rd *International Conference on Cultural Policy Research*. 25-28 August, HEC, Montreal, Canada.

BFD (1998): Utviklingsprogrammet for barnehagesektoren *1995-1997*. Report Q-0962.

BFD (1999): Barnehage til beste for barn og foreldre. *Stortingsmelding* nr. 27.

BFD/KUF (1996): »Skolefritidsordninger for 6-åringer og barn i 1.-3. klasse. Resultater fra en undersøkelse i 28 skolefritidsordninger våren 1996«. *Report* F-4028.

Bjørngaard, J. H. and T. L. Mordal (1998): »Økt brukertilpasning i barnehagen?« *Report* nr. 2. Oslo: Statens institutt for forbruksforskning.

Edwards, T. (2000): *Contradictions of Consumption*. Buckingham: Open University Press.

Esping-Andersen, G. (2000): »Social indicators and welfare monitoring«. *Social Policy and Development Programme*, Paper Nr 2, United Nations Research Institute for Social Development UNRISD.

FAD (1976): *Lov om barnehager*. m.v.

Fendler, L. (2001): »Educating flexible souls: the construction of subjectivity through developmentality and interaction«. Hultqvist, K. and G. Dahlberg (eds): *Governing the Child in the New Millennium*. New York: Routledge Falmer: 119-142.

Foucault, M. (1972): *The Archaeology of Knowledge*. London: Routledge.

Giddens, A. (1990): *The Consequences of Modernity*. Oxford: Polity Press.

Gullestad, M. (1989): *Kultur og hverdagsliv. På sporet av det moderne Norge*. Oslo: Universitetsforlaget.

Gullestad, M. (1997): »A passion for boundaries. Reflections on connections between the everyday lives of children and discourses on the nation in contemporary Norway«, *Childhood*, Vol. 4: 19-43.

Gulløv, E. (2003): »Creating a natural place for children: an ethnographic study of Danish kindergartens«. Olwig, K. F and E. Gulløv (eds): *Children's Places. Cross-Cultural Perspectives*. London: Routledge: 23-38.

Hultqvist, K. and G. Dahlberg (2001): »Governing the Child in the New Millennium. Introduction«. Hultqvist, K. and G. Dahlberg (eds) *Governing the Child in the New Millennium*. New York: Routledge Falmer: 1-14.

Kaarhus, R. (1992): »Diskurs som analytisk begrep«, *Norsk antropologisk tidsskrift*, Vol. 3: 105-117.

Kampmann, J. (2003): »Udviklingen af et børnekulturelt pædagogisk blikk«. B. J. Tufte, J. Kampmann and M. Hassel (eds): *Børnekultur – et begreb i bevægelse*. Denmark: Akademisk Forlag: 86-97.

Kjørholt, A. T. (1994): »Institusjonalisering av barns liv – en barndom på avveier«? Aasen, P. and

O. Haugaløkken (eds): *Bærekraftig pedagogikk: pedagogiske og utdanningspolitiske utfordringer i velferdsstaten*. Oslo: AdNotam Gyldendal: 115-136.

Kjørholt, A.T. (1998): »Barnehagen som arena for endringsprosesser i det moderne samfunnet. Barns rettigheter og perspektiver; retorikk og realiteter. Den offentlige og private barndommen. Retorikk, realiteter, idealer«. *Report*. Trondheim: Queen Maud's College, 1: 20-33.

Kjørholt, A.T. (2001): »The Participating Child – A Vital Pillar in this Century«? *Nordisk pedagogikk, Vol*. 21: 65-81.

Kjørholt, A.T. (2004): *Childhood as a Social and Symbolic Space. Discourses on Children as Social Participants in Society*. PhD thesis. Trondheim: Norwegian University of Science and Technology.

Kjørholt, A.T., T. Korsvold and A. Telhaug (1990): Pedagogisk tilbud til 4-7 åringer i et komparativt perspektiv. Trondheim: Norsk senter for barneforskning. *Report* No. 18.

Kjørholt, A.T., M. Rantalaiho and V. Tingstad (2004): 'Barnehager' as spaces for children as social participants. Discourses on flexibility, user-orientation and individual choice in contemporary Norway«. Paper at the *seminar »The modern child and the flexible labour market«*, 14-15 May, Norwegian University of Science and Technology, Norwegian Centre for Child Research.

Korsvold, T. (1997): *Profesjonalisert barndom. Statlige intensjoner og kvinnelig praksis på barnehagens arena 1945-1990*. PhD thesis, Trondheim: Norwegian University of Science and Technology.

Korsvold, T. (1998): *For alle barn!: barnehagens framvekst i velferdsstaten*. Oslo: Abstrakt Forlag.

Kvistad, K. (2003): *Underveis – alltid?* Trondheim: Queen Maud's College, *Report* 1.

Nilsen, R. D. (2000): *Livet i barnehagen. En etnografisk studie av sosialiseringsprosessen*. PhD thesis. Trondheim: Norwegian University of Science and Technology.

Næs, T. I. and T. L. Mordal (1997*)*: *Barns trivsel i barnehagen*. Report No. 13. Oslo: Statens institutt for forbruksforskning.

Rose, N. (1999): *Power of Freedom. Reframing political thought*. Cambridge: Cambridge University Press.

Sandve, A.M. (2001): *Kvalitet i barnehagen – for hvem? Om barns plass i kvalitetsdiskursen: kritisk analyse av styringsdokumenter på 90-tallet*. MA-thesis Oslo: Oslo University College.

Shore, C. and S. Wright (1997): »Policy: a new field of anthropology«. Shore, C and S. Wright (eds): *Anthropology of Policy. Critical Perspectives on Governance and Power*. London: Routledge: 3-39.

Sjöblom, K. (1974): *Åtta spädbarn börjar på daghem: en undersökning av barnens behov, anpassning och utveckling på olika daghem*. Stockholm: Wahlström and Widstrand.

Skard. Å. G. (ed) (1973): *Barn – kultur – samfunn*. Oslo: Cappelen.

Socialstyrelsen (1975): *Vår förskola. En introduktion till förskolans pedagogiska arbete*. Stockholm: Liber Förlag.

SOU 1972:26: *Förskolan,* del 1 och 2. Barnstugeutredningen. Stockholm: Liber Förlag.

SSB (2005): *Barn og unge*, Barnehagestatistikk. www.ssb.no.

Stephens, S. (ed) (1995): *Children and the Politics of Culture*. Princeton: Princeton University Press.

Storbysamarbeidet i barnehagesektoren (2003): *Utforming av barnehager. På leting etter barneperspektiv*. Report www.etablerebarnehage.no.

Tingstad, V. (2003): *Children's Chat on the Net. A Study of Social Encounters in Two Norwegian Chat Rooms*. PhD thesis, Trondheim: Norwegian University of Science and Technology.

Notes

1. The term 'barnehage' or 'kindergarten' refers to institutional care for children aged 1-6, lead by an educated preschool teacher. 'Barnehager' are today administered nationally by the Ministry for Education and Research.

Children in command of time and space?

Hanne Warming Nielsen and Jan Kampmann

An Everyday Narrative

»Shit! Where has the day gone«, she thinks, as so many times before. She had planned to collect Emma, the youngest, early today, but now it will be at least half past four before she gets to the kindergarten. Fortunately, she has not – wise from past experience – promised anything.

Actually, she is rather privileged, that she has both an interesting and stimulating job, lovely children, and flexi time into the bargain. That gives her the chance to get to work a little later so that the children do not have to be pulled out of bed at an unearthly hour in the mornings – or the chance to collect them early, and then just take some work home and do it in the evening. The drawback is just that you easily become stressed. At least she does, but maybe she is just not good enough at saying no: no to new work tasks, no to going on a course, no to doing things with the children, no to being on the parents' committee for the kindergarten. But that is also because this is what she wants herself. These are things she chooses and gives high priority to and which help to give her life meaning and substance.

On the way home in the car, she curses herself. If she had left an hour earlier, she would have avoided the rush-hour queue on the motorway. Now the car was crawling along and it would take at least twice as long to get home. She puts on the radio where the speaker is introducing the results from the latest PISA study: »Danish children read badly« is the headline. It catches her attention, and she listens with interest and a little concern. Various politicians talk about their ideas for a solution. The Minister of Social Affairs says that we are already well on the way with the new teaching plans in day-care institutions, but that we must also look at primary schools again. An obligatory kindergarten class must be introduced, more tests of the pupils, more state control and more lessons in subjects such as Danish and arithmetic for example. She wonders vaguely how this will link up with the school's work with »the many intelligences«, but her thoughts are interrupted when the speaker reports that the Danish Union of Teachers had pointed out that tests and control alone are not enough, that there are problems with outdated textbooks and high average class size. This leads her thoughts to the eldest child, Line, who is in second grade. It seems to be a rather restless class – »with 28 small individualists«, as the class teacher had said at the last parents' meeting. A few times, she had stayed for the first lesson and had watched the teaching. Once she had also been with them on a trip. In that way, flexi time is a privilege, because it gives the chance to participate in the children's life. She believes it is important to show an interest and involvement in their schooling.

At the kindergarten, Emma rushes to meet her: »Mommy, can't Sofia come home with us? We've agreed to sleep together«. She looks up at her with expectant eyes. »That about sleeping will have to be another day, but Sofia may come home for a while if it's all right with her parents«, she answers. She would have greatly preferred to have complied with her wish, both to please the girls, but also because she thinks it is important to support the children's friendships – but today it just will not do. She has a meeting early tomorrow morning, and should preferably manage to prepare beforehand – so everything just has to work out this evening and early tomorrow. She hopes that her husband can take the children tomorrow, but she cannot count on it, before she hears about his appointments.

»Sofia«, she says: »Do you think it's all right with your parents? Who is going to collect you?« Sofia's parents are divorced. They have a mutual arrangement with Sofia's mother that the girls can always just go home with each other. They do not live so far apart. With Sofia's father, it is a little more complicated because he lives 30 km away. »It's Daddy« says Sofia and points at the weekend bag that is packed for a few days with her father. »Shall I find his phone number for you?« asks the teacher. She is already on the way to the office to find the card with the phone number. »Yes, please« she says and follows her. Sofia's father does not answer. She leaves a message on his answering machine, but he is probably already on the way.

The teacher asks if she has seen the notice about next week's feature week on healthy food. They will all together in their room talk about healthy and unhealthy food and different food cultures. Then the children from all the rooms have to choose a group where they will work with the subject in different ways. Some will perform a play, others will make an exhibition with »food from different countries«, and still others will prepare food themselves. It will all culminate with a party where parents, brothers and sisters, and grandparents are invited to see the play and exhibition as well as getting some tasty snacks. As a matter of fact, the teachers in the kindergarten have become really good at that sort of thing. But it is also something that they have talked a lot about in the parents' committee, that it is important both to make space for children's free play and friendships and to stimulate their learning and development.

The teacher says that by and large Emma has had a good day, but that she had been unhappy that morning after her father had left because she did not have toys with her. »Ah … that is typical of him, not to remember that it is toy day«, she thinks, annoyed. The teacher says that as a consolation Emma had been allowed to sit on her lap during the circle when the other children had displayed their toys, but that they also had said to her that she must try to remember it herself – that it was not just something that her father and mother should remember.

On the way home in the car, Emma sings a song that she has learned in the kindergarten. The trip home in the car is their private little cosy time together. Line goes home by herself from the after-school club. She has been allowed to do that since she went into second grade. It was with a little knot in her stomach that she allowed her – but Line had argued that her other class mates were allowed, and that you have to learn it at some stage. Fortunately there is only one busy street that she has to cross and there are traffic lights – and they have trained intensively. Today she has actually gone from the after-school club over to music lessons, which are held in another part of the school and from there, home. It is actually marvellous that Line has become so independent, she thinks proudly. At the same time, it has also helped a little that they did not have to arrange to collect her in the after-school club, to go with her over to music and then under an hour later, collect her to bring her home. That is how it was last year, three times a week! Because she also goes to dancing and handball. The little one only goes to dancing.

Suddenly Emma stops in the middle of the song. »Mommy, where do we actually live?« She does not really understand the question: »Why are you asking that? – you know well!« »No, no, I mean what is the name of our road and the number, and our town and phone number. We are going to talk about it again next time in the circle – I don't think I can ever learn it, and Sofia knows it already, both at her mother's and father's – I am just so bad«. She sounds despairing. »Of course you're not. It's just a question of practice«. Maybe she should have rehearsed it with her earlier, she thinks. They agree to practice until she knows it.

On the way home, they have to go to the supermarket. They try to shop for a week at a time, but there is always something they have forgotten. At home, the older girl has just got home. She is sitting in her room with the television on and is watching Barracuda – a children's programme on the only national TV channel without ads. And even there, there are indirect advertisements in the form of whole cartoons that are about a special toy. Emma rushes into her older sister. After putting the things in place, she begins preparing the food. The little one comes out to her, takes a stool and crawls up on the kitchen counter: »Will I help you?« Together they wash, cut and arrange lettuce, cucumber, tomatoes, maize, peas, peppers and bean sprouts on a dish. Then the only thing left is to fry the meat and heat the pitta bread. Pitta bread is one of her favourites, because it is a good way also to get »some vegetables« into the children who otherwise would rather have meat. But she tries to get them to understand that they also have to choose some »vegetables«, »that you become what you eat«, as they said that time in Line's kindergarten. They have often made fun of it with »Will I become a carrot now« Line can sometimes ask for example with a big grin, but there is no doubt that they have got the point.

The phone rings. It is the husband. He will be half an hour late because there was a meeting with a customer that dragged on. »Ok« she says. She was prepared for the possibility that it could happen. It sometimes does and that was precisely why she had decided to wait to fry the meat and heat the bread until he arrived. They give high priority to eating together, all of them, even though, of course, it cannot always happen.

Line comes out to the kitchen. »Mommy, I have these notes home with me. They are like a sort of lesson, I think, – something we have to talk to our mothers and fathers about«. She looks at the notes. One of them says there will soon be school-home conversations, and that the children this year – in contrast to last year – will be with them. They are being asked to prepare for it with a preparation sheet. On the sheet of paper there are questions: What am I good at? What should I make a greater effort with? What would I like to have help with? What will I make an extra effort to be better at? After that there are a lot of subjects, such as for example: reading, being quiet and listening, cooperation, remembering to put up my hand, keeping my school things in order, remembering to do homework, being a good pal, saying in a nice way if my schoolmates make me unhappy or angry, consoling my partner etc. »I want to do homework too« says Emma. She finds one of the task books that they have bought for her and then all three of them sit around the dining table in the kitchen and do homework.

At half past six, the husband comes in the door. After giving them a hug, he sits down and joins in the discussion on the preparation sheet. »I'm hungry« says Emma »aren't we going to eat soon« »Yes«, she gets up and begins to clear the papers to set the table. The husband starts frying the meat and heating the bread. Soon after that they are gathered around the meal. The children are quite quickly finished, after which they get up and go into the room. They have agreed to practice grand prix. Over in Line's after-school club, they are going to have a children's melody grand prix like the Eurovision song contest and Line is taking part with a couple of girls from the class. She wants to practice and Emma is allowed to be stand-in for the friends.

She and her husband have taken out their appointment books and plan the next days. Fortunately, the husband can start work later tomorrow so he can take the children to school – and she can get to her meeting. On the other hand, he will have to drive directly from work to football. So the principle of the evening meal together is gone, but there is just nothing to do about it. It is often a big jigsaw puzzle to get everything to work out: children, work and leisure interests – both the children's and their own. But mostly it works out in one way or another, with a willingness to compromise. Some times they have to get a baby-sitter – a young girl they know whom the girls like and who likes to earn a little extra. The worst is when the children – not to mention when it is themselves, her and her husband – are sick, so all the planning collapses. Then they cannot even draw on the young girl because she goes to school herself. They try to have their social life with friends and family at the weekends. On week days, it is simply too stressful.

When they have cleared the table, she sits at the computer to prepare for the meeting next day. She likes her work but just now, she is tired. Emma coughed and coughed last night and it affected her night's sleep. Line comes in to ask if she will play a game. She answers a little irritated: »not right now, I'm sitting working,« and immediately regrets it. »I'm sorry I snapped. I'm just a bit tired. When I'm finished with this, I'd like to«. She hurries to finish so they can play a game before bedtime, but during the game her thoughts all the time go back to the work that she had not completely finished. »Mommy! You are not answering, are you asleep? – Or can't you be bothered playing after all?« Line asks annoyed. Emma crawls up on her father's lap and snuggles down. She looks tired. Now it is a question of pulling herself together and being more attentive for the last rounds of the game. She gets a guilty conscience from being mentally preoccupied when she is together with the children. That is one of the drawbacks of having an interesting and stimulating job.

At the children's bedtime, she and her husband look at each other: You or me? They usually read a goodnight story for them and sometimes they also sing a song and then they stay there until Emma falls asleep. They tuck them into the double bed, because that is cosiest, and they do not have to tuck in twice. Then when they go to bed themselves, they carry them into their rooms. On the one hand she would like to tuck them in because it is so pleasant and cosy. On the other hand, she is quite certain that she would fall asleep. And that means she would miss adult time with her husband and the chance to look at the papers for tomorrow just one last time. »I would really like to see this«, says the husband. She nods ok, and says to the girls: »So, now it is bedtime« »Ah … not yet«, Line protests: »When exactly may I stay up later? The others over in school can decide themselves when they go to bed.« »I don't really believe they can. And besides I don't care. You're going to bed now – otherwise you're tired and sleepy in the morning when we waken you and you have to go to school.« »No, honestly, I'll get up« »It's no use. You're going to bed now. Out and brush your teeth!« The girls go out and brush their teeth. Line with a single grunt, but luckily she does not seem to be really sulky.

The Everyday Narrative – a Fictional Construction Based on Facts

This introductory story is a fabricated story, which should serve as an exemplary singling out of central aspects and themes in what we with a single term will call children's everyday life (in the narrative told through the mother's thoughts and interactions with the children). Line, Emma, their parents, friends and teachers are fictional persons, however the production of the story about their interactions and thoughts are based on empirical research on the everyday life of Danish children. This construction of a fictional story based upon empirical research is what we address by the term »a fictional construction based on facts«. The empirical data, upon which we have based this fictional construction, include qualitative, ethnographic data, as well as quantitative data. Some of the data derived from our own research, whereas others originate from empirical work of other researchers[1]. The everyday narrative is an attempt to summarize various research findings regarding Danish children's everyday life in a figurative form, and thus to have a presentation form in which many dimensions and elements in children's everyday life are made visible. Some are afterwards thematised and conceptualised, while others just help to maintain the complexity and the conflicts in children's everyday life, without the chance to pursue them theoretically in this context.

The inspiration for the everyday narrative has come from the Danish psychologist Nikolaj Lunøe, who back in 1979 wrote a long article about children's everyday life, where, correspondingly, he started with an everyday narrative which he afterwards used to launch more thematic analyses (Lunøe 1979). The key idea was to make the narrative serve as a thought provoking illustration of the dialectic between macro societal structures and everyday life. Correspondingly, in this chapter we want to use the everyday narrative as the launching pad for a more thematic discussion of some everyday phenomena, which we will argue do not occur just in this story but seem to apply more broadly to Danish children's everyday life. We do so by reference to empirical studies, and by arguing that these everyday phenomena relate to broader societal and cultural changing processes.

At the same time as there are clear parallels to Lunøe's article, we find it interesting, how the specific narrative in many ways is very different today from that of 25 years ago. The everyday life of families and children in 1979 and 2005 seem on the one hand to have quite a number of common features, for example the splitting up of life arenas in time, space and age; on the other hand there are correspondingly quite a lot of types of everyday life events and phenomena that are completely different today. The aim of the chapter is not to give an overview of these changes[2], but rather a deeper discussion of some of these changes from the perspective of governmentality, social integration, marginalisation and social exclusion, and further to discuss the theoretical challenges regarding grasping the changes of childhood. Thus we will discuss how changes in time structure, and in discourses about children and parenthood, change the social spaces of children's life arenas towards on the one hand increased autonomy; on the other hand increased demands and new, maybe narrowed, normalizations norms. The aim of the discussion is to thematise these changes as ambivalent: simultaneously promising and worrying, and to link the changes to broader changes in the welfare society.

Children's Everyday Life as the Pivotal Point

This perspective of ambivalence in everyday life changes is quite different to Lunøe's more unambiguous critical perspective. However, while we find it important to apply an everyday life perspective, and have chosen the everyday narrative as the way of communicating it, it is not only in order to create a historical contrast to Lunøe's contribution. Danish – and at least generally also Nordic – childhood research has, within recent years, to a large extent been oriented towards working with an everyday life perspective, but we would like, through our narrative and the subsequent analyses, to bring a broader understanding of the everyday life concept into play, when compared to the tendencies within Danish childhood research to operate with a narrower everyday life concept and perspective.

Danish childhood research with its focus on an everyday life perspective has to a large extent been inspired by the phenomenologically inspired everyday life concept such as that, for example, formulated by Alfred Schütz (1973; 1982)[3]. Schutz ties the everyday life perspective to an interest in understanding – in this case children's – own experience and meaning dimensions, their life worlds, and not least in focusing on their own active involvement in these meaning making processes. Within childhood research this ambition has been expressed through the interest in establishing a child perspective, where it is the child's approach to, and understanding of, the ordinary and common-sense everyday actions and thoughts that have been in focus (Kampmann 1998; Lewis and Lindsay 2000; Milner and Carolin 1999). This has also been reflected in a widespread tendency to favour micro-sociological studies, where method development and testing have been occupied with investigating how the research can gain an insight into children's own experiences, and also how they can therefore be seen as actors, who contribute to ongoing meaning constructions, actions, etc.[4]

Ethnographic and anthropological inspired studies have subsequently dominated Danish qualitative-based childhood research during the past 10-15 years. We have also, in our own work, contributed to this (cf. Andersen and Kampmann 1988; 1996; Nielsen 2001; Warming 2003b; 2005a; 2005b) and consider the continuation of such work to be an important challenge for childhood research into the future. However, at the same time, it is our intention in this chapter to argue that the everyday life concept's strength and potential does not only lie in its utilization of the subjective experience and actor dimensions, but that it also has a material and structural dimension, which at least in the Danish context has not been nearly so prominent.

With inspiration from Henri Lefebvre (1992; 2000; 2002), amongst others, the everyday life concept can also be seen to be a more macro-sociologically sensitive concept, which builds on a particular understanding of how societal development establishes particular conditions for the shaping of everyday life. From this perspective, it is not only the children's experience of and approach to daily routines that is interesting, but equally how such everyday routinizations are the result of particular societal change processes. The societalization[5] of childhood can be seen as important aspects in what Lefebvre would generally call the bureaucratization of consumption. As we have seen in the everyday narrative, and as we will refer back to in the following analyses, the increasing extent of children's institutionalization, both quantitatively and qualitatively, is an important dimension.

A central intention with this chapter is therefore to maintain childhood research's productive use of the everyday life concept as an important point of departure. With its potential for opening for both a micro-sociological 'meaning perspective' and a macro-sociological 'structure perspective', it is able to establish a fruitful challenge to the tendency within Danish childhood research to focus too narrowly on interactionism. Thus in the last part of the chapter we – by illustrations from the everyday narrative – will thematise how societal changes, conceptualised in macro terms as changes from modernity to late or reflexive modernity (Beck et al. 1994; Bauman 2001) flexible time and time bind (Hochschild 1997), individualization (Beck and Beck-Gernsheim 1990; 2002) and institutionalisation (Beck and Beck-Gernsheim 2002; Frønes 1994), are reflected and (re)-produced in children's everyday life at a micro sociological level, and consider how this may simultaneously produce democratisation, social inclusion and marginalisation.

The Impact of Parents' Flexible and Stimulating Work on Children's Time and Space

In the everyday narrative, Emma's mother is late, in spite of the fact that she had planned to collect Emma early, and does not arrive at the institution until just before closing time. She was absorbed in her work and had not noticed the time. Later in the story, we hear how she and her husband coordinate their appointments with a view to planning the following days.

Like so many others in 'reflexive modernity' (Beck et al. 1994; Bauman 2001), both Emma's mother and father have flexible, stimulating jobs with responsibility. This way of working has both a direct and an indirect impact on the children's everyday life. On the one hand, it gives the parents the possibility of an everyday togetherness with the children with a less rigid time structure than if they both had jobs with fixed working hours. On the other hand, flexibility does not just take family life into consideration, but also the perhaps unpredictable duration and timing of work tasks at many different times of the day and the week[6]. That is why Emma is collected late, even though her mother had planned to collect her early. So the children, like the parents, have to learn to be flexible about time. The difference is just that while the parents have insight into and influence on the tasks that control their time, even though to varying degrees, this applies to a much lesser extent or not at all to the children.

The children's lack of insight into and influence on the flexible time is primarily in evidence to the extent that the flexibility stems from and is adapted to the parents' job. However this is not exclusively the case. In the story we hear how the flexible job enables the children's mother to see the first lesson in school occasionally, to go on trips, collect the children early or take them to the institution late, possibly conforming to the children's needs and wishes. And we hear how, from the school's side, the parents' participation in the daily life of the school and in special events is regarded as positive, that it is interpreted as »a way of showing an interest« in the children's schooling. Today, some people have flexible working hours in the sense that they have great influence on what times and during what periods of the day and week they work. This is the case for Emma and Line's mother, and the story illustrates how this gives her the chance »to show an interest in Line's schooling«. However, others do not have the same possibility, either because they have fixed working hours, or because their working hours are variable, but not in a way where they can administer the hours themselves. In this way the experience of flexible working hours differs among different children, and to some extent is mediated by social class. Thus some children regularly experience that their parents »show an interest« and »choose« to participate in the children's everyday life, while other children's parents do not have the possibility for such an involvement[7]. Together flexible working hours and the encouragement of parent's participation in the daily life of the school changes the social space of the school from being a pure pupil – teacher space to a space of teachers, pupils with participating parents and pupils with parents who do not participate to the same extent.

Even though the mother leaves her work later than planned, she feels it necessary to take work home with her. By this, the story illustrates how the stimulating and flexible job, affects the children's life in this manner. At first it does so because it is part of the reason that she says no to Emma's friend Sofia going home with them to sleep. Then it is evident when she becomes irritated when Line asks her to play a game, and again when she is preoccupied during the game. What should have been so good, the flexible job, which should make it possible to adapt work to family life, also proves to be a barrier to being positively mentally present when together with the children. The flexible work can be said to colonize family life, not only with regard to time, but also with regard to rationality and mentality. Thus it changes the quality of the social space of the family.

The flexible time structure constitutes a radical change in relation to the relatively rigid time and space structure of industrial society, which – for the children – has both positive and negative consequences regarding the parents' physical and mental availability. Thus it has consequences both for the children whose parents have flexible working hours and for the children whose parents do not have them. Time – as a structuring category – is something that is chosen and a result of priorities, rather than of compulsion and necessity as, in industrial society. At the same time, the children themselves have a relatively limited influence on the time structure of everyday life.

The Need for Temporal Coordination, Spatial Movement and Coherence in Daily Life

In the everyday narrative, both children spend many hours of the day in 'children-specialised institutions' (Frønes 1994). In the case of Emma, it is the kindergarten, while for Line it is divided between schooling and the after-school club. In addition, both children go to leisure time activities with children of their own age – Emma once a week; Line three times a week[8]. This is probably something they want themselves, but the parents also support it, because such activities are regarded as broadening and stimulating for the children[9].

Children's everyday life in reflexive modernity is characterised by a splitting up of life areas in time, space and age and this gives a number of boundaries and dividing lines: some that lock children out, for example from working life; and dividing lines and boundaries between the child's own different life arenas, for example between home and day-care institution, between school, after-school club, leisure activities and home, and between the child's two homes if the parents are divorced. The boundaries and dividing lines between the child's own different life arenas require coordination, communication, organisation and the ability to readjust[10] (Engelbert 1994). This is illustrated in the everyday narrative when Emma and Sofia want to continue their time together after the time in the kindergarten. In the everyday narrative we hear about how the continued togetherness needs coordination with Emma's mother and Sofia's father and that it is made difficult because Sofia's father, on account of the divorce from Sofia's mother, lives relatively far from the kindergarten. This spatial distance is why the time together is postponed until the weekend[11]. It is moved in time because of spatial distance caused by new family patterns, and thus constitutes another example of new demands on children's time flexibility.

The children's own organising and communication about their time together may have been going on for a long time before the arrival of Emma's mother. It is not just the adults who coordinate their appointments, but the children themselves too, and to do it successfully implies an insight into the time-space structure of the day, for example when I will be collected, who will collect me, what I will do and where will I go, when I am collected etc. (Nielsen 2001) – or in the case of Emma's sister: Am I going to music lessons, dancing, handball or directly home to day after the after school club, and at what time. Organisation, communication and coordination of time and space thus constitute central pivotal axes in children's everyday life, and thereby central demands on their handling of this everyday life.

These tendencies in childhood, however, are not just characterised by a splitting up of life arenas, but also by an opposing tendency in the form of efforts to create a wholeness and coherence in children's life, as well as the breaking down of boundaries and dividing lines[12]. The cooperation between the teacher and Emma's mother on supporting the girls' wish to play together can be seen as an effort for wholeness and coherence and the same is true of Sofia's father's 'compensation suggestion' about talking together at the weekend. Likewise, the party for parents, brothers and sisters and grandparents as well as the mother's occasional participation in school lessons and trips and the openness of the school to these forms of participation, illustrates such an effort towards breaking down of some spatial boundaries and dividing lines, which were more 'watertight' just 25 years ago. In this connection, the idea of 'the child's book' can also be mentioned, which follows the child from crèche/day care, through kindergarten to school, where there are 'narratives' in words and pictures about the child's life, both at home and in the institutions. Examples of such ideas, initiatives and efforts are numerous. At the same time, they are also institutionalised in legislation in the form of demands for cooperation between the day-care institution, school and home[13].

Demands on Self-Governance

The many hours that children spend in 'children-specialised' institutions can be regarded as a professionalized pedagogisation of children's lives in that the staff of the institutions are especially trained for the job. This assumes a quite special form, which in the following we will thematise as institutionalised individualisation (Beck and Beck-Gernsheim 2002; Sünker 1995; Kampmann 2004).

As illustrated in the story about Emma and Line, daily life in day-care institutions and schools is characterised by the fact that adult norms do not just revolve around the children acquiring cultural techniques such as reading, writing and arithmetic, but in addition work is done more and more systematically on the children's acquisition of personal competencies. In this, there is an increased societal expectation that the progress of the individual child's personality development and thereby the individualisation process is linked to and takes place in the official institution system. The starting point for considerations about activity and learning, as early as in the day-care institution, seems increasingly to be the individual child, the separate individual, explicitly formulated in the pedagogical formula: »In our institution, our point of departure is the individual child«. In Danish pedagogical practice, this does not seem to be just an ideological figure, but also seems to be a real expression for intended pedagogical forms of practice where work is done on the development of the individual child's ability and will to be participatory in her/his own learning processes in daily life. It can be said that this development tendency establishes a basis for a new form of normalisation practice, where individualisation and focus on the individual child is not only a setting free and an expansion of the single individual's action space, but also constitutes the foundation for demands made on the child, with accompanying assessment and evaluation criteria. The child and the pupil are expected to take on responsibility for the management of time and space: for their own learning and individualisation to such an extent that it constitutes an essential element in the basis for what is increasingly regarded as *expected*, as *desirable*, and as *attainable*, or in the short form: what can be regarded as *normal* in relation to the individual child's development and daily performance. There is in this a special form of expectation that the individual child should be able to 'control itself' – to establish a form of 'self-governance' – and with that, in many ways, of its own initiative and on its own accord be rational, sensible and by and large 'un-childlike' (Fendler 2001; Kampmann 2004). In the everyday narrative, Emma acts in accordance with this when she imposes on herself and her mother the start of rehearsing to learn her address so she can be better at the next circle time. She does it off her own bat – it is not something the teachers have asked her to do.

In the Danish context, expectations of children, as in the example, will often be in the form of demands and requirements that are not very explicit, but rather can be understood in the light of Basil Bernstein's concept of an *invisible pedagogy* (Bernstein 1996). The demand is thus not just that the individual child is expected to control itself, but in addition it is expected to control itself without seemingly being explicitly told to do so (Nielsen 2001). In other words, the child, as part of the normalisation demand, must be able to 'break the code', to get the feeling itself that this is what is expected. The optimal in the new form of normalisation practice would be that the individual child on its own initiative makes the choices of activities, action forms and manners that are expected by the adults, but without the adults saying this explicitly, and so it is felt by the individual child that the choices are precisely in accordance with what he/she wanted to do and felt inclined to be involved with.

The Idea of the Competent Child

These reflections have set the foundation for understanding an essential dimension in the concept that in a Danish context has been very widespread for the past 10 years: 'the competent child' (Juul 1995; Brembeck et al. 2004). The widespread projection of the competent child can be seen as an idealised expression for a certain idea about how children in a particular Danish welfare-state, reflexive, and democratically oriented social and cultural context, are expected to be able to act. The competent child has thus primarily signal value, in that it signals a new childhood ideal, a new idea of normality that is more a value standard than necessarily a descriptive category, which on the basis of scientific material captures how 'the Danish child' is in 'reality'. It captures some common approaches to and ideal notions about what 'the Danish child' *should* be.

A certain degree of compulsiveness enters into this, in that increasingly a common discourse has developed across a broad spectrum including politicians, pedagogical experts, professionals and parents, that children *are* competent. Conversely this means that those who in various ways are deemed to be incompetent, now constitute a problem, because in a manner of speaking they become subnormal – below the expected standard. In the everyday narrative, the fact of Emma's forgetting the toy day is thematised first with regard to Emma, and later with regard to the mother, as being less than the expected standard. In Emma's case her performance is probably the exception rather than the rule, while for other children, the situation may be reversed. Throughout the day and the week, there are innumerable risks of failing and being »below the expected standard«.

Coincident with children becoming increasingly respected as 'beings' and not just 'becomings' (James and Prout 1990; James, Jenks and Prout 1998), as individuals with rights, who must be listened to and be party to decisions, (influenced by the UN Convention on the Rights of the Child, understandings created by the new childhood sociology, from the most recent ten to fifteen years' pedagogical initiatives, and from a growing 'culture of negotiation' in the family), there is also an opposite movement, which can be described as making ever greater demands on children at an ever earlier time of their life. Rather than speaking about the liberation of children and childhood, one can at least critically pose the question of whether there is not equally an expanded version of a pedagogically reflected seizure of childhood.

Pedagogicalisation of Children's Everyday Life in the Family

We have already suggested with the above that the new understandings of and approaches to children, the pedagogically reflected seizure of childhood, are not restricted to the 'children-specialised' institutions, but also include family life. In recent times, the concept of parenthood has embraced the idea that with a knowledge-based, goal-directed effort one can ensure one's children's happiness and development – together with a great emotional investment. Through TV docu-soaps about family life and child rearing, along with the presentation of a growing number of scientific studies, popular science books and to a more limited extent lectures and parent courses, parents have been increasingly implanted with a readiness and obligation to be pedagogical with their children. The parents' eye on the child is not primarily characterised by attention to good manners, as it was previously, but rather to development, stimulation and self control. To put it bluntly, it can be said that parents no longer read goodnight stories just for the sake of togetherness, but also to stimulate the child linguistically, and they do not involve the children in food preparation because they are happy to have the children's help, but also to stimulate development of their fine-motor skills and their experience of the change of food from raw material to dinner. Thus not only work, but also school seems to colonize family life, changing rationalities and roles in the social space of the family.

With the equation of parenting with that of a pedagogical relation to the child, the meeting between teacher and parent becomes more a meeting between parties who agree with each other, as illustrated in the collaboration between the mother and the teacher about supporting the children's wish regarding continuation of their play together at home. This is in contrast to the picture drawn in Lunøe's article from 1979 where the teacher and the mother do not understand each other's approach to the child at all, and where it is the teacher who is the child expert. Today, both parents and teacher are, in a sense, child experts with a certain common frame of reference, even though the teacher is specially trained for pedagogical work. However, this inequality is equalized in reflexive modernity by the fact that the general level of education has risen, so that the parents will often have had a longer educational background than the teacher.

The pedagogisation of children's everyday life in the family can be understood in continuation of an increased societal attention to children as society's most important resource, combined with an increasing number of 'child experts', who ceaselessly produce studies about how one can optimise and invest in this resource in the best possible way. Nearly every single week, there are new results from studies. In the everyday narrative, it is the PISA study, which time after time has caused uncertainty and fear (cf. The Ministry of Education 2004; Olsen 2005). This fear is expressed partly by politicians who worry about how Denmark will compete successfully in the future globalised market, where the most important resource is knowledge in the absence of being able to compete with cheap labour. Fear is also partly expressed by parents who worry about how their child will manage in uncertain economic times. Other studies indicate a connection between a proper breakfast and children's learning ability, daily reading aloud and language competence, art subjects' stimulation and learning, lack of physical activity, obesity and lifestyle illnesses etc. From a control perspective, it is about investing rationally in children, so that in the future they can constitute a well-qualified, fit and healthy labour force. In this connection, the parents as well as the children themselves are perceived as central partners, and it is considered 'below the expected standard' and thereby a social problem, if parents and children do not actively play their roles (Bloch et al. 2003; Brembeck et al. 2004).

Responsibility for Own Learning and Development

These developments, where parents become responsible parents in a particular manner, along side increasing responsibilities being given to children, can be seen as part of broader societal and cultural changing processes, which can also be connected with changes in the administrative principles of the welfare state. Among other things these principles are based on »a wide-ranging activation and mobilisation of people with a view to increasing their own efforts to improve their quality of life, health and potentiality.« (Mortensen 2004: 122).

In the everyday narrative, Emma thinks that she »is just so bad«, because she does not yet know her address and phone number and she makes an arrangement with her mother about practising until she knows it. Later Line comes home with a conversation sheet where she has to think about her own skills in subjects, her application and her social competences. What these events illustrate are the greater demands on children to take responsibility for their own learning and development.

In recent years developments in the pedagogical field in general and in this connection within the field of day-care institutions in particular, can be perceived as an ever stronger movement towards precisely making the learner, and here the individual child, responsible for its own learning. The intention of placing responsibility for their own learning on pupils was deliberately developed as a pedagogical system in relation to pupils' learning in a school context, also called AFEL (Responsibility for Own Learning) (Bjørgen 1994). There are thus clear trends towards a stronger focus on what could be called 'imposed self-governance'[14]. But it is increasingly a term that also accords with the pedagogical basic principle in Danish kindergarten pedagogy – yes, even the pedagogical work in day nurseries.

Children are expected to an ever greater extent not just to take responsibility for their own learning, but strictly speaking also to take responsibility for themselves as such, for the improvement of their quality of life, their health and potentiality. That is why the conversation sheet, which Line in the everyday narrative has taken home from school, contains not just issues concerning subject achievements, but also questions about being »a good pal«, about »saying in a nice way if my schoolmates have made me unhappy or angry« etc. Even subject formation has thus been put on the curriculum agenda, responsibility for own learning does not only include the responsibility to learn numbers and letters, animals and plants, but just as much the responsibility to learn to reflect on and create one's own management of time and space, through learning.

When one applies this to the types of demands that are made on the children in day-care institutions' practice, one can speak of the expectation of the self-monitoring and watching-over child, which really contains two different types of self-governing dimensions. On the one hand the demand for self-monitoring and watching-over signals that the child is expected to watch out for itself, to take care of itself, to be careful to manage the types of conflicts, challenges etc. that can threaten its »good conduct in the world« or its welfare, for instance understood as its mental well-being, its health, its social inclusion etc. Work is done intensively with this daily by inviting and involving the children from a very young age in managing time and space through making choices that concern their well-being, which is expressed in constant opportunities for, but also demands on, the children to find out whether they want – and whether they think they will prefer – one activity or another. Thus it is no accident in the everyday narrative that the children have to *choose* an activity in the kindergarten feature week, that they are not just allocated to groups. One should not be beguiled into thinking that this is just an expression of total liberty, the adults' abdication of their responsibility, lack of upbringing, laissez-faire, or whatever else it has been called. On the contrary, substantial demands are placed on the children so they cannot avoid taking a position, making the choice and with that the development of choice competence and responsibility for choosing. To choose, and to experience and evaluate the consequences of one's choice are an important part of the learning both in the kindergarten, as exemplified by the feature week, where the children choose different activities, and in school. If the children try to escape or do not do it well enough, they will gradually at a younger and younger age be confronted with: »You can do it well, just try to concentrate, pull yourself together, try now to really feel, etc.« The children are met daily by requests to reflect consciously on how they can take personal responsibility for the care of themselves and for their own well-being. This is continually emphasised in the form of daily recurrent reflections on life practices, but of course in such a way that it appears to be the children's own active choice. In relation to health, it is expressed in recurrent talk about what is eaten, what is healthy, what it does to us. The knowledge of even the youngest children about healthy food, health, the body as a health project etc. is very extensive, and the expectation that on their own initiative they will manage their everyday actions in accordance with this is also quite widespread, even among the youngest children.

One can also point to the demands made on the children to take personal responsibility for their social relationships. While children's play has always been prioritised because of the opportunities it provides for children's social development, in recent years it has become even more embedded in institutional daily life precisely because it provides children with these skills in dealing with choice and rejection. The emphasis has also been placed on children practising the competence to solve their own conflicts. In connection with this, both within the framework of the day-care institution and the school, it has become increasingly widespread to involve conflict-solving systems, such as 'step-by-step' (Elgin 1995), as a means to practise the children's own conflict preparedness. The quite widespread focus on and also quite far-reaching expectations of the children's will and ability to take care of their own conflict situations indicate that there are both pedagogically and administratively established definite registration systems governing children's social behaviour.

On the other hand, the request for self-monitoring and watching-over suggests something more than being simply aware of oneself and taking care of one self, in that there is also a clear demand that the child observes itself, inspects itself. In particular, it is demanded that the results of this self- observation – or introspection – become known publicly. Thus it seems to be a quite widespread pedagogical phenomenon to use the pedagogical tool which Foucault would call 'confession'. There is persistent work on even the youngest children acquiring awareness of their inner thoughts and feelings, which are then expected to be put into words, and explicated in the public space in the form of confessions and announcements. A crucial pedagogical element in this from an adult perspective is that it is crucial that this is done without the children being burdened with guilt. But it can easily be part of the confessional process to assume guilt, to collectivise guilt among the children, to forgive and reconcile oneself with oneself and with each other.

One can say in continuation of the request to be able and willing to observe oneself that in an almost pure form it seems to be a restoration of that form of upbringing and socialisation norm, where it is the process rather than the result that is the object of intervention. This resonates with what was spoken of in the 1960s and 1970s as a typically middle-class upbringing code. Here, too, Bernstein's concept of invisible pedagogy can be employed. But at the same time, it is important to highlight the new element in this practice, in that the driving force of the intervention is expected to be the children themselves. By the introduction of pedagogical tools such as 'my suitcase', 'leaving traces', 'the Child's book', 'step-by-step', the use of log books and portfolios, this process of self observation and confessional is enacted. Through these devices, children outline the reasons for their choices and rejections, their evaluation of their own and others' efforts and management of time and space, their admissions of lack of discipline and motivation, their sympathies and antipathies, their emotional and bodily feelings in connection with conflicts, school work, achievement problems etc. Taken together they comprise the different confessional practices, whether it is orally in the circle, for a single teacher and perhaps one other child, in the small work group in the school, in class after break in dealing with a conflict in the school yard, or it is written in the logbook and portfolio, as the child is constantly encouraged to write down its thoughts on quite wide-ranging subjects and themes.

New Ambivalences and Differences between Children

In this chapter we have tried to single out some trends where, by using the everyday life perspective and with a distinct focus on the societalisation of childhood (Sünker 1993; Kampmann 2004), we particularly single out conditions that help to create seemingly homogenizing conditions for children in a Danish context. From one perspective, one could point at a general trend to strengthen children's democratic rights and their right and opportunity to participate in many types of everyday life contexts.

However, it is important to emphasise that even though it can be a question of types of organising everyday life, which affect more and more children at an earlier and earlier age, this does not imply that it necessarily creates a more equal or uniform childhood for Danish children. There are trends that clearly can be said to have had a greater impact in for example urbanised areas than in other parts of the country and with that contribute to new types of differentiations in geographically determined different childhoods. Furthermore, it is precisely a case of organisations and structures of daily life, which also within limited geographic areas will create new differentiations, linked to the individual children and their family's social background, ethnic and culturally related conditions, and to new conditions for constituting and managing gender. Put in another way, it is important to study more closely in what way breaks and changes in children's everyday life, and processes linked to increased institutionalisation and individualisation, contribute to new forms of inclusion, but also exclusion. In continuation of the section on new forms of normality requirements, attention can thus be drawn to the possible consequences for new types of exclusion mechanisms. We must consider what are the implications for the children – and families – who do not on their own initiative act in accordance with the expectations of responsibility, participation and commitment in learning processes. The institutional life as described in this chapter exposes such children and families in such a way as to legitimize administrative interventions and regulations, without it necessarily being made explicit what the real demands were that those in question did not act in accordance with.

Perspectives and Challenges for Researching Children's Everyday Life

A focus on children's changed everyday life conditions therefore draws attention to the conflicting changes in modern childhood: on the one hand seemingly greater opportunities for autonomous governing of time and space in the form of assigned democratic rights, increased participation and responsibility, on the other hand new excluding and marginalising forms of practice, that have been studied only to a limited degree in recent childhood research.

Our ambition with the everyday life concept is to establish an analytical grasp which on the one hand provides insight into children's everyday meaning production, negotiating processes and positioning, and which on the other hand simultaneously maintains the focus on societal-based organizing and structuring of that everyday life, thus facilitating possibilities for understanding the actual discussions on childhood from different perspectives. It is therefore relevant to discuss the far-reaching changes to children's everyday life, which create the conditions for very different types of differentiation processes. On the one hand, the recent tendency to be open for children's involvement and increasing participation, in relation to their institutionalized everyday life as well as in their everyday life in general, establishes increased possibilities for children as social actors to create new forms of differentiation, based on integration through diversity, as well as the increasingly public administration of children's everyday life. On the other hand, the related new types of normalizing claims establish other forms of differentiation, which to a much larger extent contribute to the reproduction of differences, which in a partly different guise maintain and legitimize different forms of marginalization and exclusion.

The everyday life concept, and by this the specific focus on children's access to and governance of time and space, highlights how homogenized tendencies are situated in a more and more globalised context so that we can speak about *the* modern childhood, in singular form. On the other hand it is also essential to talk about plural childhood*s*, because *both* the impact of structured and organized societalisation of childhood, *and* the concrete child's active and productive approach to and own administration of these conditions of everyday life, occur in and are influenced by specific local contexts. We therefore see it as a continuous challenge to childhood research to insist on the everyday life concept's and everyday life perspective's particular contribution to maintaining the complexity and dichotomies of the single child's, group of children's, and childhood's concrete contextualisation and active involvement in time and space. This also implies that it is important that childhood research, rather than being either singularly optimistic or pessimistic about recent developments on behalf of children, should maintain these ambivalences, as we have tried to explore in this chapter.

References

Agervig-Carstensen, T. (2001): »Børns hverdagsliv i tid og rum«. Nyström, L. and M. Lundström (eds): *Barn i stan? Om barns tillgång till stadsbygden*. Karlskrona: Boverket: 105-126.
Andersen, D and A. Hestbæk (1999): *Ansvar og værdier i Børnefamilier*. Working Paper. København: Socialforskningsinstituttet.
Andersen, P.Ø. and J. Kampmann (1988): *Vuggestuen – hverdag og utopi*. København: Munksgaard.
Andersen, P.Ø. and J. Kampmann (1996): *Børns legekultur*. København: Gyldendal.
Bauman, Z. (2001): *The Individualized Society*. Cambridge: Polity Press.
Beck, U. and E. Beck-Gernsheim (1990): *Das ganz normale Chaos der Liebe*. Frankfurt am Main: Suhrkamp.
Beck, U. and E. Beck-Gernsheim (2002): *Individualization*. London: Sage Publications.
Beck, U., A. Giddens and S. Lash (1994): *Reflexive Modernization: Politics, Tradition and Aesthetics in the Modern Social Order*. Cambridge: Polity Press.
Bernstein, B. (1996): *Pedagogy, Symbolic Control and Identity. Theory, Research, Critique*. London: Taylor & Francis.
Bjørgen, I. (1994): *Ansvar for egen læring:'den profesjonelle elev og student'*. Trondheim: Tapir.
Bloch, M. et al. (eds) (2003): *Governing Children, Families and Education. Restructuring the Welfare State*. Basingstoke: Palgrave.
Bonke, J. (2000): *Børns tidsanvendelse*. Working paper. København: Socialforskningsinstituttet.
Bonke, J. (2002): *Tid og velfærd*. København: Socialforskningsinstituttet.
Brembeck, B., B. Johansson and J. Kampmann (eds) (2004): *Beyond the Competent Child. Exploring Contemporary Childhoods in the Nordic WelfareSsocieties*. Frederiksberg: Roskilde University Press.
Carstensen, T.A. (2001): »Børns transportvaner – trafikstrukturer og børns selvstændige mobilitet«. *Trafikdage på Aalborg Universitet*. The Council of transportation and Aalborg University, The Traffic Group: 153-161.
Christoffersen, M.N. (2003): *Risikofaktorer i barndommen og social arv – særlig med henblik på mishandling og vanrøgt*. Working Paper 1, Vidensopsamlingen om social arv 2003. København. Socialforskningsinstituttet.
Csonka, A. (1999): *Det fleksible arbejde*. København: Socialforskningsinstituttet.
Dean, M. (1999): *Governmentality. Power and Rule in Modern Society*. London: Sage Publications.
Douglas, J. (ed) (1970): *Understanding Everyday Life*. Chicago: Aldine.
Douglas, J. et al. (1980): *Introduction to the Sociologies of Everyday Life*. Boston: Allyn & Bacon.
Elgin, S. (1995): *You Can't Say that to me: Stopping the Pain of Verbal Abuse: an 8-step Program*. New York: John Wiley.
Engelbert, A. (1994): »Worlds of Childhood: Differentiated but Different. Implications for Social Policy«. Qvortrup, J. et al. (eds): *Childhood Matters. Social Theory, Practice and Politics*. Aldershot et al.: Avebury: 285-298.
Fendler, L. (2001): »Educating flexible souls: The construction of subjectivity through developmentality and interaction«. Hultqvist, K. and G. Dahlberg (eds): *Governing the Child in the New Millennium*. London: Routledge Falmer: 119-142.

Fotel, T. and T.U. Thomsen (2004): »The surveillance of children's mobility«. *Surveillance & Society*, Vol. 1: 535-554.

Foucault, M. (1991): »Governmentality«. Burchell, G. et al. (eds): *The Foucault Effect. Studies in Governmentality*. Chicago, University of Chicago Press.

Frønes, I. (1994): *De ligeværdige. Om socialisering og de jævnaldrendes betydning*. København: Forlaget Børn og Unge.

Hochschild, A.R. (1997): *The Time Bind: When Home Becomes Work and Work Becomes Home*. New York: Metropolitan Books.

Holm, U. and J. Lau (1998): *Helhed og sammenhæng i børns liv. Projekt læring, Slangerup Kommune*. Copenhagen: The Danish University of Education.

Holt, H. (2003): »Indflydelse på egen arbejdstid som løsning på tilpasning mellem arbejdsliv og familieliv«, *Tidsskrift for arbejdsliv*, Vol 5, No. 3: 23-46.

James, A. and A. Prout (eds) (1990): *Constructing and Reconstructing Childhood*. London: Falmer Press.

James, A., C. Jenks and A. Prout (1998): *Theorizing childhood*. Cambridge: Polity Press.

Jensen, S.U. and C. H. Hummer (2002): *Sikre skoleveje. En undersøgelse af børns trafiksikkerhed og transportvaner*. Lyngby: The Danish Transport Research Institute.

Juul, J. (1995): *Dit kompetente barn. På vej mod et nyt værdigrundlag for familien*. København: Schønberg.

Kampmann, J. (1998): *Børneperspektiv og børn som informanter*. Copenhagen: Børnerådet.

Kampmann, J. (2004): »Societalization of childhood: new opportunities? New Demands?« Brembeck, B. et al. (eds) (2004): *Beyond the Competent Child. Exploring Contemporary Childhoods in the Nordic Welfare Societies*. Frederiksberg: Roskilde University Press.

Kampmann, J. and H.W. Nielsen (2004): »Socialized Childhood: Children's Childhoods in Denmark«. A-M., Ben Arieh, A., Conti, C., Kutsar, D., Nic Ghiolla Phadraig, M. and Nielsen, H.W. (eds): *Children's Welfare in Ageing Europe. Vol. 2*: Trondheim: Norwegian Centre for Child Research: 649-702.

Lau, J. and L. Nielsen (1999): *Helhed og sammenhæng i børns liv. Forslag til samarbejdsrelationer og pædagogiske planer*. Copenhagen: Danish University of Educational Research.

Law on Social Service. Copenhagen: The Danish Ministry on Social Affairs.

Lefebvre, H. (1992): *Critique of Everyday Life*. Vol. I. London: Verso.

Lefebvre, H. (2000): *Everyday Life in the Modern World*. London. Athlone.

Lefebvre, H. (2002): *Critique of Everyday Life*. Vol. II. London Verso.

Lewis, A. and G. Lindsay (2000): *Researching Children's Perspective*. Buckingham: Open University Press.

Lunøe, N. (1979): »Ulvetime – kritik af det kapitalistiske hverdagsliv«, *Udkast* 7.

Milner, P. and B. Carolin (1999): *Time to Listen to Children*. London: Routledge.

Ministry of Education (2004): *Danske PISA-resultater skaber behov for øget indsats*. Press release Dec. 6, 2004. www.uvm.dk/nyheder/pisa2003.

Ministry of Social Affairs (2000): *Early Childhood Education and Care Policy in Denmark*. Background Report. OECD Thematic Review of Early Childhood Education and Care Policy. Copenhagen: The Ministry of Social Affairs.

Mortensen, N. (2004): *Det paradoksale samfund*. København: Hans Reitzels Forlag.

Nielsen, H. W. (2001): *Børn i medvind og modvind. En relationel analyse af børns livtag med livet i det refleksivt moderne.* Roskilde: Roskilde University.

Olsen, L. (2005): »Skoledebatten overser social polarisering«, *Ugebrevet A4* 4: 8-10.

Ottosen, M. H. (2004): *Samvær og børns trivsel.* Copenhagen, Socialforskningsinstituttet.

Raymond, C. and I.S. Larsen (2002): *Børns oplevelse af forlænget skoledag.* København: BUPL.

Reksten, P. M. and S.S. Jørgesen (1996): *Fremtidens børneinstitution. Fra pasning til udvikling.* Copenhagen: Mandag Morgen Strategisk Forum.

Schütz, A. (1972): *Hverdagslivets sociologi.* København: Reitzel.

Schütz, A. (1982): *Life Forms and Meaning Structure.* London: Routledge & Kegan Paul.

Sünker, H. (1993): »Childhood as a social phenomenon: societalization, individualization, institutionalization«. J. Qvortrup (ed): *Childhood as a Social Phenomenon: Lessons from an International Project.* Wien: European Centre for Social Welfare Policy and Research/Sydjysk Universitetscenter: 91-104.

Sünker, H. (1995): »Childhood between individualization and institutionalization«. Neubauer, G. and K. Hurrelmann (eds): *Individualization in Childhood and Adolescence.* Berlin: Walter de Gruyter: 37-52.

Thomsen, T.U. (2005): »Parent's construction of traffic safety. Children's independent mobility at risk?«. Thomsen, T.U. et.al. (eds): *Social perspectives on mobility.* Series on Transport and Society. Ashgate: Aldershot: 11-28.

Warming, H. (2002): *Det er lidt svært, men jeg må jo sige min mening.* København: Frydenlund.

Warming, H. (2003a): »Literature review on listening to young children: views and experiences of childcare, education and services for families«. Clark, A. et al. (eds): *Exploring the Field of Listening to and Consulting with Young Children.* Research Report 445, Department for education and skills, Thomas Coram Research Unit: 62-80.

Warming, H. (2003b): 'Børn er da også en slags mennesker'. *Socialpolitiske værdier.* Copenhagen: The Ministry of Social Affairs: 64-79.

Warming, H. (2005a): »Participant observations: A way to learn about children's perspectives«. A. Clark, A. et al. (eds): *Beyond listening. Children's perspectives on early childhood services.* Bristol: Polity Press: 51-70.

Warming, H. (2005b): »Erkendelse gennem oplevelse: Når indlevelse ikke er mulig«. Mik-Meyer, N. and M. Järvinen (eds): *Kvalitative metoder i et interaktionistisk perspektiv.* København: Hans Reitzels Forlag: 145-168.

Notes

1 It is meaningless to refer to all these different research projects and publications. Later in this chapter, however, in the more theoretical discussion of some of the themes from the object picture we make references to the empirical studies we draw upon.
2 We have presented such an overview in Kampmann and Nielsen (2004).
3 It is though important to stress, that the inspiration has not only come from Schutz, but refers

4   to a broader work on everyday life sociologies, which especially were established in the USA from the 60'es and onwards (cf. Douglas 1970; Douglas et al. 1980).
4   A review of such studies can be found in Warming (2003a).
5   The concept of societalization is translated from the German concept Vergesellschaftung, referring to the increasing inscription of modern childhood in an administrative logic with particular consequences for the organizing and structuring of children's everyday life, as well as childhood's increased inscription as a particular 'segment' in relation to the market, and the formalisation of children's rights in accordance with the UN Convention on the Rights of the Child (Sünker 1993; 1995).
6   In a Danish context this has been pointed to by Helle Holt (2003). Further we have found it, and how it affects the children's everyday life, in qualitative interviews with parents and children about their everyday life and observation studies of children's everyday life in a day care institution. These interviews and observations were carried out in a project about children's everyday life in a day care institution (Nielsen 2001), and in a project about supervision of children and parent in relation to divorce (Warming 2002).
7   Helle Holt (2003) has pointed to how different kinds of flexibility give different possibilities of combining work and family life in a satisfying way, and Agi Csonka (1999) found that the flexible work (meaning the engaging work with a high degree of selfmangement of time and space) is most widespread among the higher educated, and quite rarely among the low educated.
8   80 per cent of all Danish children aged 0,5 to 9 years are enrolled in a day care institution (Ministry of Social Affairs 2000:25). The average preschool child spends around 37 hours per week in the day care institution (Reksten and Jørgensen 1996). Regarding organized leisure time activities Bonke (2000; 2002) found that some children are very active and others rather inactive; school children are more likely than preschool children to spend time on organized leisure activities, thus 85 per cent of all school children are active.
9   This is what the children themselves and their parents say in qualitative interviews about their everyday life. These interviews and observations were carried out in a project about children's everyday life in a day care institution (Nielsen 2001), and in a project about supervision of children and parents in relation to divorce (Warming 2002). Regarding children aged 10 to15, Dines Andersen and Anne-Dorthe Hestbæk (1999: 81) found that 86 per cent decide themselves about participation in organized leisure time activities.
10 This is reflected in interviews with children and parents about children's everyday mobility (Fotel and Thomsen 2004; Thomsen 2005; Carstensen 2001; Jensen and Hummer 2002) and in a study about children's everyday environment (Agervig-Carstensen 2001), and further in observation studies of children's interactions in a daycare institution (Nielsen 2001).
11 Mogens Christoffersen (2003: 111) estimates, that around one third of all children will experience divorce of their parents (or separation if parents are not married). A growing number of children visit the parent whom they do not live together with; thus 79 per cent of the children with parents living apart visit »the other parent« every second week or more often (Ottosen 2004). Further a growing number of children live half the time with their mother and half the time with their father (ibid). In qualitative interviews children and parents talk

about how this demands a lot of coordinating, flexibility and sometimes also negatively impacts on children's ability to take part in social activities with peers (Warming 2002).
12 This is reflected in (reports about) different pedagogical initiatives (Holm and Lau 1998; Lau and Nielsen 1999; Raymond and Larsen 2002), as well as in qualitative interviews with parents and pedagogues and observation of the every day life in a daycare institution (Nielsen 2001).
13 Law on Social Service.
14 We are inspired by Foucault's governmentality perspective (Foucault 1991; Dean 1999).

Blurring Boundaries of Family and Work – Challenges for Children

Karin Jurczyk and Andreas Lange

Introduction

During the processes of modernisation in Western Europe, childhood was constructed as separate from the sphere of work. The exclusive places of children were considered to be the institutions of family, school and some selected and protected leisure areas (Honig 1999). Although the separation of family and waged work as shaped in the male breadwinner model never reflected the realities of families and children completely, the ideology of the privacy of the family and childhood was undeniably strong. Nowadays, we are facing important changes in the structures, ideologies and constructions of the triangle of the family, working life and childhood. Work-family issues are becoming prominent topics for debate as in similar historical periods of flux, such as when the first waves of mothers were entering the paid labour force. That resulted in a moral uproar as well as in intense discussions of the impact of mothers' work on children's everyday life, their socialisation and development – a discussion which was especially value-laden in Germany and dominated by anxieties about elements which could be lost that were considered the 'core' of society (Schütze 1986; Sommerkorn 1988; Kuller 2004).

This chapter refers mostly to Germany, because here recent changes of the work-family interface are very obvious, and we are faced with a situation of complex and contradictory transformations. The German case stands for countries like Austria, Italy and Ireland as well, in which the privacy of the family and childhood has been, until now, extremely highly valued and supported by rather conservative family policies (Jurczyk et al. 2004; Klaus et al. 2005: 20) that give more or less support to the male breadwinner model (Hofäcker 2004: 277). For a long time, it was taken for granted that a child 'belongs' to its family, and in the family private motherly care was seen as the main prerequisite of children's welfare. Nowadays this very close connection is dissolving. The main reason for the recent changes in the gendered patterns of privacy, family and childhood is the transformation of waged work within a service economy, with downsizing, an increase of contract and short-term employment, the partial feminisation of the labour market and the rise of telecommuting. A crucial element of these transformations in the forms and processes of production is the partial substitution of the standardised 'normal', male-oriented working day by flexible work schedules. We will be focusing on these transformations because they have the greatest impact – as a resource and as a restriction – on the everyday lives of children and their families: the number of hours parents work, which hours they work, whether they work weekends, the extent of flexibility in their working hours and last but not least the extent of work-related travel (Crouter and McHale 2005).

By assuming that children's welfare is shaped by their everyday lives, its times and spaces (Jensen and Qvortrup 2004), which depend on the times and spaces of opportunities for care as well as on parental working times and their interdependencies, we do not imply any deterministic connections. As an overarching theoretical frame for interpreting the situation of children in '24/7 society' we rely on a subject oriented approach (Voß and Pongratz 1997) as it is used in general social science and in childhood studies (Corsaro 2005). Seen through this theoretical lens, structures – such as working and school times – have to be acquired by the individual, and have to be seen as embedded in the complex settings of the living conditions of families as well as in the mutually influenced interaction of the persons concerned. Within these settings, they are reworked and get specific meanings and shapes (Projektgruppe Alltägliche Lebensführung 1995). But on a more differentiated level, not all families and not all children have the same capacity to redefine structures and not all families have options as to how they can structure work and family life. In other words, first, 'agency' is a relational concept and children's and families' capacity for agency depends on their social, cultural and economic capital. Second, there is evidence in studies conducted in the field of the sociology of childhood that children's agency differs according to systems and domains: their agency is relatively strong in the fields of media and consumption and they contribute to 'doing time' in families, but their agency to influence their parents working time patterns is much more limited.

So trying to grasp the recent transformations in society, we will focus on the erosion of Fordist patterns of gendered work and family life, its times and its spaces. Childhood is touched by this development in many aspects, partially becoming both more *and* less autonomous from families, partially becoming more institutionalised (Zeiher 2005: 78ff.). Parts of childcare that were formerly done mainly by parents, in particular mothers, are now being delegated to institutions such as day-care centres. In this chapter, it is one particular aspect of recent social transformation which we will focus on: the transition to more *flexible and individualised working hours*, which raises the question if and how this process is changing the times and spaces of children. Viewing this as a crucial dimension of children's welfare, we will try to assess the risks and opportunities of modernisation processes in connection with children.

Blurring Temporal, Spatial and Social Boundaries of Work in Late Modernity

Western societies are experiencing a transformation in their forms of working, living and consumption. Well known labels for this transformation are 'late modernity', 'risk society', 'network society', 'post-modern society', 'post-Fordism', 'reflexive modernization' (Beck et al. 1996; Stehr 2003; for a critical review see Kübler 2005). To describe recent social changes we will employ the more concrete term 'blurring boundaries' ('Entgrenzung'), which is closely linked to the idea of post-Fordism as the erosion of the gendered spheres of work and family (Bertram 2000; Hausen 2000) and its consequences in terms of 'fighting for time' (Epstein and Kalleberg 2004). We suggest that boundaries and structures that were established during the first process of modernisation in the last hundred to two hundred years are eroding and becoming increasingly fluid. This is happening to the boundaries between the private and the public, the family and work, working, learning and leisure time activities, and stages of the life course such as childhood and adolescence, adulthood and old age – many more examples could be added. The erosion of boundaries does not mean that these structures are vanishing – it means the blurring of boundaries. This process implies that new but less clearly defined structures are emerging; perhaps more subtle boundaries, existing in addition to and not excluding fixed boundaries and powerful predominant superstructures. This corresponds to processes of 'individualisation' and 'subjectivation', understood as loading new burdens of responsibility for one's own life onto the individual as well as opening up new opportunities for moulding it. The openness, inconsistency, insecurity and contingency of post-Fordist societies was summed up by Zygmunt Bauman (2000) in the illustrative term of 'fluid' or 'liquid' society.

As far as working life is concerned, the following developments point to these patterns:

(1) Economic turbulence and the fast ups and downs of economic cycles cause many people to experience increasing economic insecurity in their everyday lives and during the life course. Because of downsizing and rationalisation as well as the trend toward contract and short-term employment, workers can no longer assume that their employment will be permanent. Much like during the periods of early capitalism, employment

today depends primarily on how long employers need their employees. The unemployment rate has risen dramatically to more than 10 per cent and is much higher in eastern Germany than in the western 'Länder'. The phases of the life course that used to be organised consecutively – vocation training work, family (for women), retirement – are becoming increasingly intertwined. One outcome of this new discontinuity of the life course are feelings of anxiety and stress that accompany everyday life for more and more men and women. The fear of unemployment rose from 10 per cent in the year 2000 to more than 15 per cent in 2004 (Mansel and Heitmeyer 2005).

(2) In many areas, work restructuring and higher economic insecurity go hand in hand with work intensification. Not only is the pace of doing one's work in many sectors and professions increasing, the mentally and emotionally demanding structures of work in a service and knowledge society are taking their toll as well. These new forms of intensification have a Janus face: On the one hand, work is becoming extremely demanding and energy consuming, with people feeling increasingly stressed and exhausted and experiencing psychologically caused health problems (Ehrenberg 2004). On the other hand, a larger part of the post-modern work force is expressing an intense need for satisfying, interesting work. The things people do in their work and on the job are an important element of their identity. The complex debate on this 'subjectivation of work' points out the many advantages and disadvantages of this process (Krömmelbein 2004; Lohr 2003).

(3) The places where paid work is carried out are no longer exclusively bound to where companies are located; work places are not only offices any more. This blurring of boundaries in terms of space is connected to increasing temporal flexibility and supported by the intensified use of new information and communication technologies. Work can be brought home, and travelling while working is becoming increasingly commonplace, accompanied by working tools such as the ubiquitous laptop with Internet access and the mobile phone. Mobility is on the rise, and the distances between different work places and between the work place and living space are growing. Studies on mobility and the family (Schneider et al. 2002) as well as on 'mobility pioneers' (Bonß and Kesselring 1999) show the increasing tendency toward daily or weekly commuting caused by long distances between home and work.

(4) Changing gender roles and pluralising family structures are both the cause and the result of blurring boundaries. More mothers are entering the labour market, and fathers are taking some modest steps toward more participation in their families (Döge and Volz 2004; Matzner 2004; Walter 2002). That most women reject being confined to the exclusive 'housewife and mother' role for longer periods of their lives is shown by the increasing employment rate of mothers in West Germany from 35 per cent

in 1961 to 62 per cent in 2004 (Cornelißen 2005). But in connection with mothers' employment and day care systems in Germany, there are pronounced differences between East and West that always need to be taken into account. Although nowadays the employment rate of mothers is converging, for East Germany this means a strong decrease and for West Germany an increase, with a corresponding decrease and increase of day-care facilities (Jurczyk et al. 2004). However, this increase of women's employment in West Germany is exclusively in the form of part-time work, even as full-time work, which used to be the norm for mothers with small children in East Germany before reunification is declining (Dressel 2005; Bothfeld et al. 2005). Therefore the West German male breadwinner model and the dual full-time worker model of East Germany are both exhibiting a tendency towards coming together in a modernised breadwinner model with a full-time working father and a part-time working mother.

(5) Our argument focuses on pointing out how the increasing flexibility of working times is significant for blurring boundaries. The tendency towards a '24/7 society', a term introduced into social scientific discourse by the American sociologist Harriet Presser (2003), underlines how times of production are distributed more and more continuously over the day and the course of the week. A representative survey shows that in 1999 only 15 per cent of the dependently employed in Germany were still working according to so-called 'standard working hours' (cf. Groß and Munz 2000), compared to 27 per cent some ten years ago (cf. Groß et al. 1987). The remaining 85 per cent put in (Bauer et al. 2004):
- regular shift and night work (16 per cent),
- weekend work (13 per cent on Sundays, 32 per cent on Saturdays),
- regular overtime (54 per cent),
- part-time work (24 per cent, of which 87 per cent are women),
- variable distribution of daily working time by 'flexitime' (50 per cent – 18 per cent regulated by the company, 32 per cent self-regulated),
- working time account schemes (41 per cent), e.g. block leisure time and sabbaticals.

Parallel to this process of *normalising flexibility* (and in spite of the promise of shortened working time which was given with increasing flexibility), the actual time worked is rising again, especially in working time arrangements with less control by the employer such as self-managed working time. For some years, the average real working hours per week have exceeded the working hours fixed by contract by 2.5 hours. This recent increase differs according to qualification and gender: while more than half (52 per cent) of the highly qualified are working more than 40 hours per week, only a fifth (19 per cent) of the lower qualified work such long hours. On average, men work for longer than 40 hours and women for less than 35 hours. Therefore it is no surprise that the working time preferences of (mostly male) full-time workers are for a reduction by more than four hours a week. Their interests in flexibility point to a crucial difference between accepted and not accepted flexibility: work on Saturdays and Sundays is especially unpopular (Bauer et al. 2004).

Taking a closer look at parental working time arrangements and what parents expect from family responsive companies, recent studies underline and specify these results (Bundesministerium 2004): besides rejecting work on weekends, mostly on Sundays, parents struggle most of all with unpredictability and short-term changes of working hours. Perceived deficits in day-care facilities exacerbate such time constraints for parents: about 60 per cent of parents would like to have institutional care for their children from their second birthday on, but there are places for only 10 per cent (Bien and Riedel 2006). The lack of day-care facilities is one of the main reasons why parents, e.g. mothers themselves prefer part-time work, flexitime, working time accounts and telecommuting under certain conditions as a way of reconciling work and family responsibilities.

In sum, these tendencies toward blurring boundaries are generating a new type of worker. Nowadays, we can observe a qualitative shift: the old fashioned employee, working in a standardised employment relationship is being phased out and being replaced by the 'entreployee' ('Arbeitskraftunternehmer'), the worker as a manager of him- or herself (Voß and Pongratz 1998). This worker can no longer take for granted fixed and stable time schedules and working spaces, continuous career patterns and stable jobs with benefits. To work at flexible times is becoming the norm. The clear divide between working days and holidays, working time and leisure time is becoming a thing of the past. The 'entreployee' is not only becoming more flexible in time, but in space and in job and status stability throughout the life course as well. The consequences of these processes for family life, parenthood and patterns of childhood are still largely a 'black box', which we will now turn to in the following section.

Parents 'Doing Family' under the Conditions of Blurring Boundaries

Researchers seem to agree on the ambivalent character of this transformation as a combination of opportunities and risks for children and their families. Studies about 'the conduct of everyday life' in Germany in the 1990s (Jurczyk and Rerrich 1993; Projektgruppe Alltägliche Lebensführung 1995) have shown that blurring boundaries have led to the organisation of daily life becoming a challenge with a constant demand for renegotiating the work-life equilibrium. Concerning time, we can observe that time structures of families, jobs, schools etc. no longer fit together and time conflicts are growing. Besides time shortages and acceleration, there is more need for time management. The erosion of external time structures reinforces the necessity of creating the time structure of working and living by each person, or to put it simply: what society no longer provides has to be made up by the individual. All the different activities the individual is involved in that take place at changing times and at various locations have to be managed flexibly in time and space. One has to find the right moment and time period as well as the right speed for each activity and everything has to mesh with upcoming activities and coordinate with the activities of others (such as colleagues, friends, children etc.). A high level of skill is necessary to manage to do this, pointing more often in the direction of 'getting the right feeling for time' ('kairos') than in the direction of strict and linear strategy ('chronos'). An active 'doing time' is becoming more important than reactive moves in defined, rigid time structures. It is easy to imagine that new challenges resulting from job flexibility are exacerbated if people live together with others and even more if both parents work flexible hours. The counterpart of employment, the family, is touched in many ways by these blurring boundaries, some of which will be described here.

The tendency towards economic insecurity delays the entry into paid employment. This has become a very long process with the effect of postponing parenthood and encouraging childlessness among highly educated men and women. Feelings of insecurity and the unpredictability of living conditions and economic status are not only a barrier to having children, they are also a burden in everyday life with children. Today parents cannot give their children advice about the right career pattern to follow for their future professions since they cannot predict the demand for the qualifications and jobs of fifteen years from today. Furthermore, many children experience their parents' unemployment and this has a strong impact on children's lives. New research from the German Children's Panel shows that parents try their best to buffer the negative effects of unemployment and that children seem to be a stabilizing factor for their unemployed parents by structuring everyday life and being a source of positive emotions (Strehmel 2005). On the other hand, there are clear debilitating effects of poverty on children's school careers and educational and vocational aspirations.

The tendency towards the intensification of work means that parents tend to blur the emotional and mental barriers between work and family life as they are constantly influenced by new and demanding requirements of work. They are bringing stress home, even if they leave their work behind at their work place. Spillover phenomena are a burden for both parents and children: exhausted parents try to be attentive to their children's needs while feeling guilty for not being a good enough father or mother, sometimes combined with feeling guilty for enjoying a satisfying job. And last but not least, children have to balance their needs with regard to what they feel their parents need.

The tendency of blurring spatial boundaries results in a number of changes for parents and their families. Commuting can lead to weekend relationships and weekend parenthood, as can forms of living apart together. The multilocality of work (as well as the multilocality of families as the result of divorce, which is not the focus of this chapter) is connected to a rising need for mutual information and organisation. Lots of time has to be spent on the road. If work is brought home, the economic and rational logic of the marketplace is transferred to private space that was traditionally dedicated to care work and recreation by structural differentiation in the historical process of industrialisation. Instead of the established spatial separation between family and professional work, today it is becoming more necessary to separate different activities that are taking place in the same location oneself. Flexibility in time and space results in interpenetrating phases and places of work and private life. Living that way there are new difficult decisions to be made: am I supposed to be working or is this free time for me? More and more people 'work' in their leisure time, by reading journals, writing memos for the job, programming, building networks for their next job and chasing the next order. Parents have to combine all this with raising their children, juggling the parallel but contradictory logic of activities. New forms of telebusinesses are, on the one hand, potentially new opportunities of combining work, care work and time for children. On the other hand, there are intense ambivalences and problems of 'boundary maintenance work' being reported by mothers and fathers working at home as well as difficulties remaining integrated in the firm.

All these aspects are intertwined with the tendency towards changing gender roles, mostly to be seen in rising rates of female employment. Although mothers in Germany are not all following the same path (the largest group of them (50 to 60 per cent) currently follows a model combining part-time work and the family, about 20 per cent are home-centred and the other 20 per cent work-centred (Bertram et al. 2005: 26)), the problems of reconciling family and work in everyday life are widespread. Mothers' everyday lives are hindered by family hostile work places and infrastructures that still have traditional home-centred mothers and the Fordist pattern of the traditional division of labour between men and women in the public and the private spheres as their reference point. Resulting from this there is a specific time lag between different structural developments in the modernisation process of West Germany: the entry of large numbers of women into the work force has not yet been accompanied by adequate child care (Bundesministerium 2005). The number of places and the opening times of day-care centres do not meet the needs of parents and do not make allowances for their flexible working times (Stöbe-Blossey 2004). The resulting 'care crisis' in (West) Germany causes daily balancing acts, especially for mothers, which are not compensated by the slowly rising involvement of fathers in families.

All the trends mentioned above seem to contribute to the widespread experience of time squeeze in Western European families, which is influenced negatively *and* positively by the tendency towards temporal flexibility. A huge proportion of parents recognise they are under pressure, although, as time diary data show, they do not spend less time with their children than parents did ten or twenty years ago (Statistisches Bundesamt 2004). Parents' time squeeze is not unique to Germany, it can be found in many highly developed countries (Milkie et al. 2004). Its emotional effects result from the combination of the following factors, which show that time squeeze encompasses much more than the quantitative problem of too little time for too many activities:

- Being under stress in varied and demanding work environments, which derive from the economic imperatives of velocity, efficiency and service orientation;
- The challenges of multitasking and fast changes between different activities;
- The different and contradictory time logic and demands of family and job related activities;
- The lack of self-determination on the topic, duration, temporal position and velocity of job related activities;
- Role conflicts between being good mothers (Blair-Loy 2003) or fathers on the one hand and responding to job interests and constraints on the other;
- The striving of parents today, especially in the middle classes (Büchner et al. 1998; Lareau 2003; Pasquale 1998) to give their children a foundation for their current und future success in an uncertain world. The phenomenon of 'soccer moms' is but one element of this sort of time stress, which is experienced by a large segment of parents today (Arendell 2001).

In line with the development that Murray Melbin (1987) has described as the colonialisation of the night, more and more families have to cope with a broad variety of working time arrangements covering days and nights, the work week and the weekend. In the flexible 24/7-economy (Presser 2003) families are facing new problems trying to organise family life including adequate care settings. Their ambivalences will be the focus of the next sections.

The Ambivalences of More Flexibility for Family Time and Care

The ways in which parents coordinate everyday life with their children and childcare (which includes physical and emotional care, socialisation and education) and their own work commitments are often ignored. What they do to balance work and family tends to be taken for granted. Because the Fordist division of labour between women-centred family and male-oriented professional life is not in place any more, it has to be looked at anew. Within this context, it is an open question whether the flexibility of parents' working times complicate or support their time needs and those of their children, including the effects on the so-called care crisis. To discuss a possible ambivalent impact on children's time we first have to understand the phenomenon of time in families. Which temporal demands result from the specific quality of family life and care work and what do families need time for?

Family is a relational system and doing relationships needs time: this is true for the family as a whole as well as for the family subsystems of the couple, the siblings, parent-child relationships and the circle of relatives. Therefore common time and co-presence is a core element of the family, although there is no way to make a general statement about the number of hours which must be shared to constitute a family. Virtual contact, based on the phone and email, may support families, but is not a total substitute for co-presence, because families are bound to physicality and to physical touching. The complementary need is time on one's own, both for adults and growing children.

As for care work, the 'object' of care – work with human beings – produces specific demands. Family care for children as well as for sick and elderly people is based on the meeting of physical and emotional needs and embedded in a private context of exclusive personal relations. As such these are, on the one hand, unforeseeable and permanently changing. Specific demands for care may differ from day to day, because they are flexible themselves and change in intensity, possibly needing quick reactions. Sudden illnesses of children or the elderly, the unforeseeable need for support in critical periods of school or adolescence and last but not least the rigid institutionalised care system require flexible structures, e.g. of working time. On the other hand successful care depends on self-determined rituals, rules and rhythms of the people concerned in order to make being together possible at all. How to care for children or the elderly is not something one can decide anew every day. It commits the carer to reliable and stable arrangements, because the relationship includes the dependency of the other person. Therefore the logic of care time does not follow the rational logic of efficiency, oriented to accelerated productivity in time sequences that are fixed in advance. Caring for people does not follow a logical purpose, a time schedule or a program that can be made more efficient (Ostner 1978), although in the empirical reality of everyday life the different strands of emotional care come up against the organisational aspects of care, which often leads to problems and discontent. As the latest Federal Report on Families pointed out (Bundesministerium 2006), the answer to these specific requirements of care is that families need both – reliability and flexibility. As far as work schedules are concerned, from the perspective of parents they have to be flexible in a self-determined way as well as allowing regularity and planning. From the perspective of children, work schedules need to allow reliable time together, but flexible parents' time should also offer self-determined time on their own.

Since the conduct of everyday life as a family means the coordination of multiple time structures and the 'doing time' of several people which makes synchronisation necessary no matter what the circumstances are, it is obvious that problems of synchronisation are exacerbated if both parents work within the blurring boundaries described above. Depending on the degree of overlap of parents' time schedules and their flexibility, negotiating tasks on a more or less daily basis is the result, an endeavour in which many other people belonging to the family network are included. Care arrangements have to be fine-tuned with grandparents, neighbours and friends (Alt and Blanke 2005) and coordinated into complex care mixes.

Empirical studies on the everyday life of parents with non-standard and flexible working times show that it is mostly mothers who suffer from time pressure and often feel rushed (Jurczyk and Rerrich 1993). Finishing times, leisure times, holidays and times for children have to be defended against the interests of the employer, and this is even more the case when boundaries between work and the family begin to blur. A recent study in the UK (La Valle et al. 2002) focuses strongly on the negative impact of all variants of atypical working times on the routines of the family and the relations between parents and children. In those English families there was less common reading, playing and eating; the parents also were unhappy about the amount of shared time they could offer their children. Furthermore, some specific family constellations emerged as very prone to being negatively impacted by atypical work schedules: families in which both partners work that way as well as families in which the (mostly male) partner works long hours and also travels away from home. Some single parents also expressed deep concerns about the possible effects of working hours on family life – possibly this is an effect of guilt feelings about working and not being able to care for their children as much as they think is necessary.

If it is possible to work at home, e.g. at the computer, the interference of work with the sphere of private life can still increase. It was in this context that we coined the term 'the work of everyday life' ('Arbeit des Alltags'), which is more like a precarious juggling act than a successful balancing act (Projektgruppe Alltägliche Lebensführung 1995). Furthermore we could show that working mothers were not only pressured for time, but that their everyday lives were much more fragmented than those of their working husbands. They also often tried to speed up the behaviour of their children to meet the obligations of kindergarten and school (Ludwig and Schlevogt 2002).

Nevertheless, there are possible positive results of more flexibility from the parents' perspective such as the opening up of options so they (and here again especially mothers) actually can respond to short term flexible requirements of their children so that they can combine their job and caring for a family and fathers get a chance to have time with their children so that more equal gender arrangements are possible. Christina Klenner et al. (2003) go into detail about the effects of sabbaticals and working time accounts and show that parents are very happy with the new possibilities of managing both work and the family and of co-parenting. They especially point to the positive effects of more flexible working time regimes for the changing requirements of children. This study shows that, especially in modern families, where every family member has his or her own rhythm, appointments are made to meet each other. Families establish some rituals like having dinner together on certain evenings or cooking together on the weekends. They create their own new little traditions that ease the organisation of everyday life.

However our conclusion is ambiguous. The effects of more flexibility on parents depend on many aspects, one important being the specific working time regime. To strengthen the potentially positive effects of more flexibility there is one clear crucial point. It is absolutely necessary that parents participate in the decision about the when, the where and the how of flexibility. Employers have to recognise care requirements as an undeniable social necessity. Given the current economic conditions of high pressure on workers it is realistic to assume that flexibility, that is not self-determined, will deepen the care crisis more than help solve it. It is an open question how the current generation of young adults will handle this conflict between their desire for children and the need for a job. Some scepticism is indicated by the fact that 60 per cent of women who work in very mobile jobs are currently childless (Schneider et al. 2002). The resources that can be mobilised for reconciling work and family obligations, for example financial resources for paying day-care fees, are also worth mentioning and these depend on the social class position of both parents. There is, on the one hand, evidence for long and partly atypical work schedules in the higher strata. But on the other hand it is obvious that parents from the lower strata have specifically adverse, split couple working schedules that do not overlap. The asynchronism of family time is particularly acute when members of a couple work at different times of the day or night, and the lack of time as a family unit that can result when such split schedules are worked, is linked to class.

Looking to the future, the 'Time Bind' study by Arlie Hochschild (1997) describes blurring boundaries in a different, even more frightening way. According to this study, the workplace is beginning to feel more and more like home, providing recognition and satisfaction. In this context, family life is taking on the character of being the area where work and stress are situated. This finding is even more noteworthy because the changing values of professional and family life were examined in organisations offering explicitly family friendly policies such as flexible working times. The varying coping strategies of fathers and mothers show that there is not only one answer to working conditions (Hochschild 2005). As far as blurring boundaries are concerned it is worth mentioning that both – the intrusion of employment into the private sphere and the privatisation of employment – result in the tendency of wearing away structural limits between spheres, but without (and this is the main problem) giving up the different styles of agency that come from distinctly different objectives. There is a tension between emotion-based care for dependent people on the one hand and employment-related activities that have to follow the rules of economy, efficiency and speed on the other, but both sets of tasks have to be combined in the same time unit and in the same place. All these complexities of new working conditions are exacerbated by the fact that family structures and forms are becoming more complex as well. One can easily imagine that the everyday life of a family with two earners and two children in West Germany with only partly overlapping work schedules is different from the work-life balance of an East German single mother working flexibly in a full-time job.

Switching from the impact of increasing flexibility on care time in families and on parents as carers to children themselves, we will argue in the following section that children are more than the 'objects' of care. They are active agents and co-negotiators in the 'doing time' of families, although we have to state a lack of empirical research on the specifics of this negotiating process.

Children's status as active agents is reinforced by the fact that culturally families have evolved from an authoritarian system to a negotiating system. Children's wishes are being heard concerning leisure activities, the use of media etc. (Alt et al. 2005) and they have their own complex time schedules that have become more demanding, especially in the middle classes.

Therefore we will now add the perspective of children to the perspective of parents instead of describing the process of co-production of family time. We will follow the argument (Fölling-Albers 1995; Grunert 2005) that the schedules of children and their parents interact with one another. As Wilhelm Kleine (2003) has shown with time budget data in Germany, as one result of this we have a sort of concentration of family life on the weekends. The following section discusses some consequences of these intermingling trends for children.

Children's Perspectives on their Parents' Work

From a subject-oriented perspective the question arises what the changing sphere of labour means for children's lives, their development and their socialisation as elements of their welfare and well-being. How do children themselves think about this topic and how do they handle these changes in their families?

The latter question stems from the result of the sociology of childhood's stress on children's agency: on its foundations and on its obstruction by certain circumstances (Jensen and McKee 2003: 6). But it is also a consequence of the development of a new paradigm in family life, namely the 'negotiating family' of today.

There are only a few and mostly exploratory studies about the impact of working conditions on the perspectives, the everyday life constellations and the active conduct of everyday life of children themselves, and there are still less on those whose parents have flexible work schedules as the outcomes of blurring boundaries. Therefore we have to use material from related fields of study such as the sociology of work and the sociology of the family and to look at studies that have been carried out in other countries and draw from their findings. In the following, we will concentrate on research from the perspective of children – qualitative and quantitative approaches that have asked children about working conditions and work schedules from their own point of view, a perspective that addresses children as experts on their own life.

Ellen Galinsky (1999) from the United States was the first researcher to ask: What do children think about the working times of their parents? What do they wish to change concerning their parents' work? How do they perceive their parents' jobs? What is their perspective on positive or negative spillovers from jobs to parenting and family life? Her survey shows some surprising results:

- She found that there are astonishing differences in the perception of time scarcity between children and their parents. More than the half of parents assumed that the children would want more time together and for them to spend less time at work. Asking the children themselves, they differentiate between wanting some more time with their fathers, but mainly more money, made by both, mothers and fathers.
- Children with employed mothers and those with mothers at home did not differ on whether they feel they have too little time with their mothers.
- The quantity of time together with mothers and parents does matter. Children who spend more time with their mothers grade their parents better and feel that their parents are more successful at managing work and family responsibilities.

Recent qualitative studies (cf. Christensen 2002; Klenner et al. 2003; Polatnick 2002; Zeiher 2005) give additional and, in some respects, more sophisticated answers. Rivka Polatnick, who examined 22 sixth and seventh graders in the USA, showed that general statements as formulated in quantitative surveys are not sufficient to record the ideas and feelings of children concerning this important topic in an appropriate manner. She presents five patterns of answers that show that the use of simple item-based questions do not cover this subject adequately:

- children's feelings about more time with parents were complex and contradictory,
- children seemed reluctant to express – or even let themselves feel – negative emotions about their parents' long work hours,
- some children who liked having more time with parents nonetheless put other considerations first – especially financial needs/desires and parents' well-being,
- children were influenced by social messages that they should not press for more time with parents,
- children tended to accept and not question their parents' work/family schedules; later, looking back, they might be more critical.

These findings mark important starting points for a thorough discussion of this topic. In their ambivalence and hesitation, children mirror the contradictory nature of their parents' work for themselves. On the one hand, they know very well that their parents have to work for their living as well as that the fulfilment of their specific material wishes, for example for toys, depends on their parents working. On the other hand, children's ambivalent and emotional reactions can be read as indicating their need for a social quality of life including being together with their parents.

Summing up the research about children's perspectives on the family and parents' times in Germany (Roppelt 2003; Klenner et al. 2003) and from other countries such as Norway, Sweden and the UK (Christensen 2002; Mc Kee et al. 2003; Näsman 2003) the first result is: Children from the age of six are able to think about the working conditions of their parents, but there are great differences in the details and specifics children report. Elisabeth Näsman (2003: 49) has shown that for children the temporal connotations of their parents' work are an important frame of reference:

> »They conceptualise the distribution, number and regularity of working hours when they say 'long time', 'sometimes', 'every day', 'late', 'overtime' and 'day or night'. Children comment upon where, when and with whom they stay during the day, night and week due to the temporal structure.«

The second result is that children articulate different needs in connection with care and time. The main thing they want from their parents is reliability, which turns up as an important dimension of their own understanding of well being. This means that children want to know who is responsible for them, when their parents are coming back from work and that they can rely on the agreed time arrangements (Roppelt 2003). As to flexible and irregular work schedules of their parents, children say they suffer from feeling dependent by not knowing when their parents will be at home. Their problem is not only that they are alone but also that they are restricted by having to wait, by not being able to plan and do something different on their own. Framed in the language of childhood research this result shows that children are eager to have and to develop their agency (Morrow 2003), which means, for example, to be able to pursue their own projects.

The third result is that they perceive, very subtly, the effects of work on their parents: Mc Kee et al. (2003: 37) report from their study on children's perspectives on middle class work-family arrangements:

> »Children were able to see and appreciate the contradictions of their parents' work and care experiences, and were also able to assess the pros and cons of their particular work-family arrangements. The children's pragmatism and adaptability were evident in many of the accounts with children appearing to understand and accept external

constraints on their parents' lives. They could also identify the contradictory effects of work on their parents, for example the children could describe their parents as feeling simultaneously happy and stressed or angry and excited in relation to work.«

These perceptions can be starting points for the agency of children in terms of caring for their parents – caring as it is done also in cases of divorce, as Carol Smart et al. (2001) have shown. But one has to concede that in the domain of their parents' working conditions, the agency of children is limited. Although children have more or less clearly stated interests and notions on family time patterns, they have restricted power to influence the specific arrangements of the family-work interface of their parents:

> »Parental work vulnerabilities and the advantages and drawbacks of traditional gender roles were appraised, although children could not directly influence how work and care were distributed between their parents.« (McKee et al. 2003: 43).

Irrespective of their limited power, children fourthly appreciate the combined care work of mothers and fathers, stressing that they are never alone in this constellation. Care work and time together with both parents is valued. Children experience both mothers and fathers as available care persons. They recognise the presence of both parents in their everyday life as a sign of appreciation and of the fact that they themselves are important to their parents. Flexible working time conditions of both parents are mentioned as a basis for such care arrangements (Roppelt 2003: 235).

Fifthly, children need not only the regular and reliable everyday times of their parents, they also want them to be available at special times and for special rituals, such as important school events, sports and other leisure activities, birthdays – and not to forget in times of illness.

Sixthly, children in their middle childhood explicitly state they want a certain degree of autonomy in determining their times and places. As a result, they see the work commitments of their parents as a resource for their own autonomous conduct of life and complain about overprotective mothers who are at home all day to look after and care for them. One 11-year-old girl in a German study expressed this as follows:

> »I've told her she should look for a job and go to work for a few hours every day.« (Roppelt 2003).

This statement indicates the active role of children in 'doing family time' as a process done by children and their parents together.

Besides children's perspectives on parents' flexible work we think it necessary to follow another line of research that focuses on the effects of working conditions and times on children's cognitive, emotional and social development and well-being by using classical standardised instruments of social research. We argue that both lines of research are needed to give a comprehensive picture of children's lives and perspectives for the future in a 24 hours/7 days society. Children's welfare embraces their current everyday life as well as its implications for socialisation and development. Until now, there are very few findings that point to possibly more negative than positive effects on children's development.

One of these results comes from representative research on dual earner Canadian families and their two to eleven year old children. Lyndall Stradzins et al. (2004) compared families where both parents worked standard hours with families where one or both worked non-standard times, i.e. evenings, nights or weekends. In nearly three quarters of the families one or both of the parents worked non-standard times. The authors found connections between children's well-being and parents' work schedules, with greater difficulties for children on scales for hyperactivity, emotional disorders and separation anxiety when parents worked non-standard times. These associations persisted after adjusting for several moderator variables including socio-economic status, parents' part-time or full-time work and the use of day care and were evident whether mothers, fathers or both parents worked non-standard times.

Further results on the impact of maternal non-standard work schedules on the cognitive outcomes of preschool children are presented by Wen-Jui Han (2005) in the United States. She examined mothers' non-standard work schedules as to their timing and duration in connection with children's cognitive outcomes in the first three years of life. Although results varied across developmental stages and dimensions of cognitive performance, the effects of mothers working non-standard schedules tended to be negative, particularly if these schedules began in the first year of life, and particularly for measures of cognitive development at age 24 months and expressive language at age 36 months.

These results from research approaches that differ clearly from our own subject orientation, point to possible ramifications of post-Fordist working conditions that should be taken seriously. However, they also raise some critical questions on the constructions, interpretations and possible missing links that are predominant in this type of research. Firstly, they allege a direct connection between two isolated factors, not taking into account that their interaction is extremely context dependent. The context is both structural and cultural: by structural context we mean the embeddedness of working time arrangements in the specific historical Fordist period of traditional family structures and male-oriented institutions. The noted negative impacts of non-standard work-schedules could, for example, be buffered by supporting families through community services as well as by a social climate that is responsive to families' concerns. By cultural context we mean the embeddedness in traditional values and norms about the 'good mother' who stays at home and the private 'familialised' child.

Secondly, they do not look at who is 'in charge of time': is it the parents who prefer and create non-standard working schedules because they help to organise everyday life and support more equal gender roles, or is it the employer who pushes employees toward more flexibility in the interest of the company without any concern for the impact on families? This question of power and participation probably has decisive consequences for the specific meaning of working time arrangements from the perspective of family members – parents as well as children.

With this we want to emphasise that a responsible discourse on childhood today cannot rely solely on the perceptions of children and their parents. Our conclusion is that parental working time conditions as crucial dimensions of children's welfare and well-being should be monitored regularly and systematically in the future using social scientific tools with plural approaches.

Parents Flexible Working Times and Children's Time Welfare

To sum up our arguments, it could be shown that blurring working time boundaries are not simply a burden for children and it is not even clear whether they are exacerbating the care crisis. Although mothers' employment rates are rising, and working times are becoming more and more flexible and increasingly non-standard, studies show that parents are not spending less time with their children. Research shows that especially mothers compensate for the lack of time by reducing their own sleeping time. But even if parents spend the same amount of time with their children as twenty years ago, one has to ask how this amount of time affects the quality of being together. Here, the strategy of reducing sleep reinforces the phenomenon of hurried and overworked parents and points to the important difference between care as a dimension of children's welfare and the mere presence of parents. From the viewpoint of children themselves we can identify the following as qualitative elements of a desirable care situation: clearly structured arrangements, reliability, availability of parents, relaxed parents who are not always in a hurry, the lack of waiting periods, children's desire for more common time with their fathers and less with their mothers and their desire for a certain amount of time spent alone. There are systematic variations in these elements according to age and the developmental stage of children – as children get older they prefer more time on their own and more of their own private places for autonomous action and plans. But even teenagers want to spend time with their parents – they appreciate these times as occasions to share ideas and to communicate as well as to share certain activities like watching television and eating pizza (Marchena 2004).

Flexibility can thus be a source of options that can be used to fulfil children's wishes and meet their preferences. These results also have implications for the debate about 'quality time versus quantity time' (Christensen 2002; Polatnick 2002). Children's statements do not necessarily support the conclusion that their requirements would be satisfied by small but intensive periods of time that are defined by their parents, since their needs are much more complex and self-regulated. In this respect, it is quite reasonable to suggest that the idea of quality time is largely a myth if it does not take into account children's perspective on it. The construction of quality time seems to serve more as a parental time saver than as an indicator for children's time welfare. If we try to place these research findings in a systematic conceptual framework of welfare and well-being, we would argue that children as individual agents want reliable and flexible access to times with their parents including care time and (depending on their age) individual autonomous times on their own as well as additional flexible access to non-family institutions of care and education. These three time reservoirs are highlighted as one important element of their individual well-being in the present and as well as for their future opportunities in society. On the social structural level, the access to these three forms of time is one building block of the welfare of children. It is important to stress the ambivalent impacts of recent developments of working conditions on these three time reservoirs for children. Flexible and non-standard work times can be used for the synchronising of parents' and children's times, but they can also interfere with their demands.

On the one hand we cannot deny the negative impact that the pressure of the working conditions of their parents has in determining children. This can have at least two dimensions: they can suffer from the lack of common time as well as be more controlled by their parents working at home. On the other hand children may gain time and space of their own and experience this as individual welfare and as an increase in autonomy. This greater self-determination is not a voluntary option but an individualistic answer to structural changes. We have argued that children as well as their parents will therefore have to strive to separate and integrate times and spaces by themselves.

In this light, welfare policies must cope with these imbalances and contingencies and try to maximise the potential of the new working time landscape, strengthening the possibilities for participation and time sovereignty of families and taking into account the perspectives of children. To look at this from another perspective, families' and children's needs must become the yardstick for the design of working time policies – they are the ones who are »doing boundaries« under the condition of post-Fordism anyway. It should be emphasised that parents and children should not only have to conform and adapt to a modernised working society but that their demands must, in fact, be integrated into government, local and companies' policies. This could be a way to cushion exaggerated demands on individualised 'doing space' and 'doing time' resulting from blurring boundaries. But complementing these political approaches, families, children and adults must also be systematically supported in their time planning skills and learn to set limits in order to cope successfully with the new demands of blurring boundaries and the ambivalent processes we have discussed. The potential of the new flexible working times can be used optimally by combining macro political and individual measures, including a new awareness of their possibilities for families and children.

With regard to Germany this implies that neither clinging unthinkingly to family centred models nor adopting institutional care solutions from other countries without examination is indicated. We feel that it is time to start a debate about the quality of children's care that takes the child's viewpoint on the quality of life and work-life balance as its starting point. This would include a critical view of how much and what type of care and how much autonomy children need from infancy to adolescence and also which forms of social life in the family, the care setting and the peer group they prefer. We suggest that there is no choice but to debate and spell out the ideas of a 'good childhood' in a process of social discourse. In this discourse both stereotypes – the stereotype of the autonomous child and of the child in need of protection – must be re-examined critically. This debate could also contribute to the positive potential of flexibility in modernising societies by helping it have a positive impact on children and their families and opening up options for shaping everyday life according to their own interests.

References

Alt, C. and K. Blanke (2005): »Wege aus der Betreuungskrise? Institutionelle und familiale Betreuungsarrangements von 5- bis 6-jährigen Kindern«. Alt, C. (ed): *Kinderleben – Aufwachsen zwischen Familie, Freunden und Institutionen. Band 2: Aufwachsen zwischen Freunden und Institutionen.* Wiesbaden: VS Verlag: 123-155.

Alt, C., M. Teubner and U. Winklhofer (2005): »Partizipation in Familie und Schule – Übungsfeld der Demokratie«. *Aus Politik und Zeitgeschichte* 41: 24-31.

Arendell, T. (2001): »The New Care Work of Middle Class Mothers«. Daly, K. J (ed): *Managing Child-Rearing, Employment and Time. Minding the Time in Family Experience and Issues.* Amsterdam: Elsevier: 163-204.

Bauer, F. et al. (2004): *Arbeitszeit 2003. Arbeitszeitgestaltung, Arbeitsorganisation und Tätigkeitsprofile.* Köln: ISO.

Bauman, Z. (2000): *Liquid Modernity.* Cambridge: Cambridge University Press.

Beck, U., A. Giddens and S. Lash (1996) (eds): *Reflexive Modernisierung. Eine Kontroverse.* Frankfurt am Main: Suhrkamp.

Bertram, H. (2000): »Die verborgenen familiären Beziehungen in Deutschland«. Kohli, M. and

M. Szydlik (eds): *Die multilokale Mehrgenerationenfamilie. Generationen in Familie und Gesellschaft.* Opladen: Leske und Budrich: 97-121.

Bertram, H., W. Rösler and N. Ehlert (2005): *Nachhaltige Familienpolitik: Zukunftssicherung durch einen Dreiklang von Zeitpolitik, finanzieller Transferpolitik und Infrastrukturpolitik.* Berlin: Humboldt Universität. (Gutachten im Auftrag des Bundesministeriums für Familie, Senioren, Frauen und Jugend).

Bien, W. and B. Riedel (2006 forthcoming): »Mehr Angebote für die Jüngsten: für wen, wo und wie viel mehr«? Bien, W., T. Rauschenbach and B. Riedel (ed): Wer betreut Deutschlands Kinder? *Die DJI-Kinderbetreuungsstudie. Weinheim*: Beltz.

Blair-Loy, M. (2003): *Competing Devotions. Career and Family among Women Executives.* Cambridge: Harvard University Press.

Bonß, W. and S. Kesselring (1999): »Mobilität und Moderne. Zur gesellschaftstheoretischen Verortung des Mobilitätsbegriffs«. Tully, C. (ed): *Erziehung und Mobilität. Jugendliche in der automobilen Gesellschaft.* Frankfurt am Main: Campus: 39-66.

Bothfeld, S. et al. (2005): *WSI-FrauenDatenReport 2005. Handbuch zur wirtschaftlichen und sozialen Situation von Frauen.* Berlin: edition sigma.

Büchner, P. et al. (1998) (eds): *Teeniewelten.* Opladen: Leske + Budrich.

Bundesministerium für Familie, Senioren, Frauen und Jugend und Hans-Böckler-Stiftung (2004): *Erwartungen an einen familienfreundlichen Betrieb. Erste Auswertung einer repräsentativen Befragung von Arbeitnehmerinnen und Arbeitnehmern mit Kindern oder Pflegeaufgaben.* Berlin: BMFSFJ.

Bundesministerium für Familie, Senioren, Frauen und Jugend (2006): 7. *Familienbericht.* Familie zwischen Flexibilität und Verlässlichkeit. Plädoyer für eine lebenslaufbezogene Familienpolitk. Berlin: BMFSFJ.

Christensen, P. (2002): »Why More Quality Time is not on the Top of Children's Lists: the 'Qualities of Time' for Children«, *Children & Society, Vol.* 16: 77-88.

Cornelißen, W. (ed) (2005): *Gender-Datenreport. Kommentierter Datenreport zur Gleichstellung von Frauen und Männern in der Bundesrepublik Deutschland.* München: DJI.

Corsaro, W. A. (2005): »Collective action and agency in young children's peer cultures«. Qvortrup, J. (ed): *Studies in Modern Childhood. Society, Agency, Culture.* Houndsmills: Palgrave: 231-247.

Crouter, A.C. and S. McHale (2005): »Work, family, and children's time: implications for youth«. Bianchi, S., L.M. Casper and R.B. Berkowitz (eds): *Work, Family, Health and Well-Being.* Mahwah, NJ: Lawrence Erlbaum: 49-66.

Döge, P. and R. Volz (2004): »Was machen Männer mit ihrer Zeit? Zeitverwendung deutscher Männer nach den Ergebnissen der Zeitbudgetstudie 2001/2003«. Statistisches Bundesamt (ed): *Alltag in Deutschland. Analysen zur Zeitverwendung.* Wiesbaden: Statistisches Bundesamt – Forum der Bundesstatistik: 194-215.

Dressel, C. (2005): »Erwerbstätigkeit – Arbeitsmarktintegration von Frauen und Männern«. Cornelißen, W. (ed): *Gender-Datenreport. Kommentierter Datenreport zur Gleichstellung von Frauen und Männern in der Bundesrepublik Deutschland.* München: DJI: 92-148.

Ehrenberg, A. (2004): *Das erschöpfte Selbst.* Frankfurt/Main: Campus.

Epstein, C. F. and A.L. Kalleberg (eds) (2004): *Fighting for Time. Shifting Boundaries of Work and Social Life.* New York: Russell Sage Foundation.

Fölling-Albers, M. and A. Hopf (1995): *Auf dem Weg vom Kleinkind zum Schulkind*. Opladen: Leske + Budrich.

Galinsky, E. A. (1999): *Ask the Children. What America's Children Really Think about Working Parents*. New York: William Morrow and Company.

Groß, H. and E. Munz (2000): *Arbeitszeit '99. Arbeitszeitformen und -wünsche der Beschäftigten – mit Spezialteil zu Arbeitszeitkonten*. Düsseldorf: Institut zur Erforschung sozialer Chancen.

Groß, H., U. Prekul and C. Thoben (1987): »Arbeitszeitstrukturen im Wandel«. Ministerium für Arbeit, Gesundheit und Soziales des Landes NRW (ed): *Arbeitszeit '87«*. Neuss: Ministerium für Arbeit, Gesundheit und Soziales.

Grunert, C. (2005): »Kompetenzerwerb von Kindern und Jugendlichen in außerunterrichtlichen Sozialisationsfeldern«. Sachverständigenkommission Zwölfter Kinder- und Jugendbericht (eds): *Kompetenzerwerb von Kindern und Jugendlichen im Schulalter*. München: DJI Verlag: 9-94.

Han, W. (2005): »Maternal nonstandard work schedules and child cognitive outcomes«. *Child Development* 76: 137-154.

Hausen, K. (2000): »Arbeit und Geschlecht«. Kocka, J. and K. Offe (eds): *Geschichte und Zukunft der Arbeit*. Frankfurt am Main: Campus: 343-361.

Hochschild, A. (1997): *The Time Bind: When Work Becomes Home and Home Becomes Work*. New York: Basic Books.

Hochschild, A. (2005): »On the edge of the time bind. Time and market culture«, *Social Research Vol*. 72: 339-355.

Hofäcker, D. (2004): »Typen europäischer Familienpolitik – Vehikel oder Hemmnis für das 'adult worker model'«? Leitner, S., I. Ostner and M. Schratzenstaller (eds): *Wohlfahrtsstaat und Geschlechterverhältnis im Umbruch. Was kommt nach dem Ernährermodell?* Wiesbaden: VS Verlag: 257-284.

Honig, M-S. (1999): *Entwurf einer Theorie der Kindheit*. Frankfurt am Main: Suhrkamp.

Jensen, A-M. and L. McKee (2003): »Introduction: theorizing childhood and family change«. Jensen, A-M. and L. McKee (eds): *Children and the Changing Family: Between Transformation and Negotiation*. New York: Routledge Falmer: 1-15.

Jensen, A-M., and J. Qvortrup (2004): »Summary – A Childhood Mosaic: What Did We Learn«? Jensen, A-M. et al. (eds): *Children's Welfare in Ageing Europe*. Trondheim: Norwegian Centre for Child Research: 815-832.

Jurczyk, K., T. Olk and H. Zeiher (2004): »German Children's Welfare Between Economy and Ideology«. Jensen, A-M., Ben Arieh, A., Conti, C., Kutsar, D., Nic Ghiolla Phadraig, M. and Warming Nielsen, H. (eds): *Children's Welfare in Ageing Europe. Vol. 2*. Trondheim: Norwegian Centre for Child Research: 703-770.

Jurczyk, K., and M. S. Rerrich (1993) (eds): *Die Arbeit des Alltags. Beiträge zu einer Soziologie der alltäglichen Lebensführung*. Freiburg: Lambertus.

Klaus, D., B. Nauck and T. Klein (2005): »Families and the Value of Children in Germany«. Trommsdorf, G. and B. Nauck (eds): *The Value of Children in Cross-Cultural Perspective. Case Studies From Eight Countries*. Lengerich: Pabst: 17-41.

Kleine, W. (2003): *Tausend gelebte Kindertage. Sport und Bewegung im Alltag der Kinder*. Weinheim: Juventa.

Klenner, C., S. Pfahl and S. Reuyß (2003): »Flexible Arbeitszeiten aus Sicht von Eltern und Kindern«. *Zeitschrift für Soziologie der Erziehung und Sozialisation*, Vol. 23: 268-285.

Krömmelbein, S. (2004): *Kommunikativer Stress in der Arbeitswelt*. Berlin: edition sigma.

Kübler, H-D. (2005): *Mythos Wissensgesellschaft. Gesellschaftlicher Wandel zwischen Information, Medien und Wissen*. Wiesbaden: VS Verlag.

Kuller, C. (2004): *Familienpolitik im föderalen Sozialstaat. Die Formierung eines Politikfeldes in der Bundesrepublik 1949-1997*. München: Oldenbourg.

La Valle, I. et al. (2002): *Happy Families? Atypical Work and its Influence on Family Life*. Bristol: The Policy Press.

Lareau, A. (2003): *Unequal Childhoods: Class, Race, and Family Life*. Berkeley: University of California Press.

Lohr, K. (2003): »Subjektivierung von Arbeit. Ausgangspunkt einer Neuorientierung der Industrie- und Arbeitssoziologie«? *Berliner Journal für Soziologie*, Vol. 12: 511-529.

Ludwig, I. and V. Schlevogt (2002): *Managerinnen des Alltags. Strategien erwerbstätiger Mütter in Ost- und Westdeutschland*. Berlin: edition sigma.

Mansel, J. and W. Heitmeyer (2005): »Spaltung der Gesellschaft. Die negativen Auswirkungen auf das Zusammenleben«. Heitmeyer, W. (ed). *Deutsche Zustände. Folge 3*. Frankfurt am Main: Suhrkamp: 39-72.

Marchena, E. (2004): *Silent Exchanges: Quality Time in Dual-Earner Families*. Atlanta: The Emory Center for Myth and Ritual in American Life. Working Paper No. 37.

Matzner, M. (2004): *Vaterschaft aus Sicht von Vätern*. Wiesbaden: VS Verlag.

Mc Kee, L., N. Mauthner and J. Gallilee (2003): »Children's perspectives on middle-class work-family arrangements«. Jensen, A-M. and L. McKee (eds): *Children and the Changing Family. Between Transformation and Negotiation*. London: Routledge Falmer: 27-45.

Melbin, M. (1987): *Night as Frontier. Colonizing the World after Dark*. New York: Free Press.

Milkie, M. A. et al. (2004): »The Time Squeeze: Parental Statuses and Feelings About Time With Children«. *Journal of Marriage and the Family*, Vol. 66: 739-761.

Morrow, V. (2003): »Perspectives on children's agency within families«. Kuczynski, L. (ed): *Handbook of Dynamics in Parent-Child Relations*. Thousand Oaks: Sage: 109-129.

Näsman, E. (2003): »Employed or Unemployed Parents. A Child Perspective«. Jensen, A-M., and L. McKee (eds): *Children and the Changing Family. Between Transformation and Negotiation*. London: Routledge Falmer: 46-60.

Ostner, I. (1978): *Beruf und Hausarbeit. Die Arbeit der Frau in unserer Gesellschaft*. Frankfurt am Main: Campus.

Pasquale, J. (1998): *Die Arbeit der Mütter*. Weinheim: Juventa.

Polatnick, R. (2002): *Quantity Time: Do children want more Time with their Full-Time Employed Parents?* Working paper 37. Berkeley: University of California, Center for Working Families.

Presser, H. (2003): *Working in a 24/7 Economy. Challenges for American Families*. New York: Russell Sage Foundation.

Projektgruppe »Alltägliche Lebensführung« (eds) (1995): *Alltägliche Lebensführung. Arrangements zwischen Traditionalität und Modernisierung*. Opladen: Leske und Budrich.

Roppelt, U. (2003): *Kinder – Experten ihres Alltags?* Frankfurt am Main: Peter Lang.

Schneider, N., R. Limmer and K. Ruckdeschel (2002): *Berufsmobilität und Lebensform. Sind berufliche*

Mobilitätserfordernisse in Zeiten der Globalisierung noch mit Familie vereinbar? Stuttgart: Kohlhammer.

Schütze, Y. (1986): *Die gute Mutter. Zur Geschichte des normativen Musters 'Mutterliebe'*. Hannover: Kleine.

Smart, C., B. Neale and A. Wade (2001): *The Changing Experience of Childhood. Families and Divorce*. Oxford: Polity Press.

Sommerkorn, I. N. (1988): »Die erwerbstätige Mutter in der Bundesrepublik: Einstellungs- und Problemveränderungen«. Nave-Herz, R. (ed): *Wandel und Kontinuität der Familie in der Bundesrepublik Deutschland*. Stuttgart: Ferdinand Enke: 115-144.

Statistisches Bundesamt (2004): *Wo bleibt die Zeit?* Wiesbaden: Statistisches Bundesamt.

Stehr, N. (2003): *Wissenspolitik. Die Überwachung des Wissens*. Frankfurt am Main: Suhrkamp.

Stöbe-Blossey, S. (2004): *Arbeitszeit und Kinderbetreuung*. Gelsenkirchen: Institut für Arbeit und Technik.

Stradzins, L. et al. (2004): »Around-the-clock: parent work schedules and children's well-being in a 24-h economy«. *Social Science & Medicine, Vol.* 59: 1517-1527.

Strehmel, P. (2005): »Weniger gefördert? Elterliche Arbeitslosigkeit als Entwicklungskontext der Kinder«. Alt, C. (ed): *Kinderleben – Aufwachsen zwischen Familie, Freunden und Institutionen. Band 1: Aufwachsen in Familien*. Wiesbaden: VS Verlag: 217-238.

Voß, G.G. and H. Pongratz (eds) (1997): *Subjektorientierte Soziologie*. Opladen: Leske & Budrich.

Voß, G.G. and H. Pongratz (1998): »Der Arbeitskraftunternehmer«, *Kölner Zeitschrift für Soziologie und Sozialpsychologie, Vol.* 50: 131-151.

Walter, H. (2002): »Deutschsprachige Väterforschung – Sondierungen in einem weiten Terrain«. Walter, H. (ed): *Männer als Väter. Sozialwissenschaftliche Theorie und Empirie*. Gießen: Psychosozial: 13-79.

Zeiher, H. (2005): »Neue Zeiten – neue Kindheiten? Wandel gesellschaftlicher Zeitbedingungen und die Folgen für Kinder«. Mischau, A. and M. Oechsle (eds): *Arbeitszeit – Familienzeit – Lebenszeit: Verlieren wir die Balance?* Wiesbaden: VS Verlag: 74-91.

Notes

1 I.e. full-time employment of 35-40 hours per week, distributed over five days from Monday to Friday, from morning to evening, at a single work place.